A CANOEIST'S GUIDE TO THE NORTH-EAST

The wrong way to shoot Stainforth Force
River Ribble

A CANOEIST'S GUIDE TO THE NORTH-EAST

SCOTTISH BORDERS, NORTHUMBERLAND, CO. DURHAM, YORKSHIRE DALES AND THE COAST.

by

Nick Doll

CICERONE PRESS
MILNTHORPE, CUMBRIA

This guide is dedicated to the
past, present and future members of
Newcastle University Canoe Club.

FOREWORD

A book of this sort can rarely be produced by any one person, but represents the contributions of many unsung heroes.

Nevertheless, special mention must be made of Graeme Gordon who talked me into writing this Guide in the first place, and who has been such a valued companion on the many trips which have formed the basis for this book.

Thanks also to all the valiant proof readers and in particular Steve Agar, who has helped convert my Geordie Canoe-speak into something like Queen's English.

Apologies for any remaining errors. I hope they don't prove too expensive or drastically reduce your life expectancy!

Please let me know of any major omissions or interesting rivers inadvertently excluded.

Having no previous knowledge of Sea Canoeing, I was particularly grateful to those contributing to this section. Geoff Burk (Coastline South of the River Tyne), Vic Brown (Amble Area), Martin Melling (Tidal Theory), Peter Hawkey (Natural History of the Farnes), Robert Egelstaff (Berwick Caves), and Geoff Wood (Newbiggin).

My thanks also to Richard Agar of North Shore Designs, for lending me their 'shoreline' sea kayak.

A B.C.U. Gold Star award should be given to Ann Bain for patiently deciphering my scrawl and translating it into beautiful typescript.

Finally, please let me wish you all happy, trouble free paddling in the North East.

Nick Doll
Newcastle upon Tyne
1991

CONTENTS

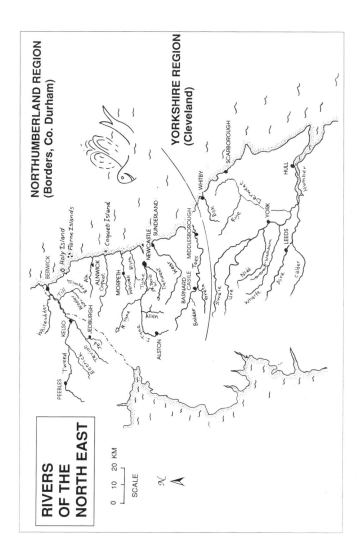

Seal launch on the North Tyne (between Bellingham and Wark)

INTRODUCTION

Canoeing, like other outdoor activities, is steadily increasing in popularity, due to a combination of increasing leisure time, and affluence (even in the North East!)

Established waterways are becoming more congested and many canoeists are looking for new areas to paddle. They are encouraged both by advances in canoe construction (in particular the introduction of plastic boats) and also improved paddling techniques. These mean that it is now within the ambition of any competent paddler to test himself on Grade 3, 4 or even 5 rivers.

An analogy with rock-climbing can be drawn. This too has developed in numbers and standards over the last decade. This, however, has been due in part to a constantly up-dated series of guidebooks to the crags, which means that knowledge of routes on a detailed grading system is spread within the climbing fraternity.

Canoeists have had no such core of knowledge. The B.C.U. *Guide to the Waterways* is seriously out of date, written as it was in the days of canvas canoes. Its use is now restricted to those who wish to paddle flat water, and it offers little for the white water canoeist.

By contrast, many of the new generation guidebooks have tended to cater almost exclusively for white water canoeists, usually at the expense of touring and novice paddlers, who do after all form a sizeable proportion of active paddlers.

This book attempts to tread a middle path by describing rivers on a geographical basis, as in the B.C.U. Guides, but with a slight bias towards white water. This allows both adequate description of potential hazards and invigorates the text.

It is hoped this guide will be of use to a wide variety of paddlers in the region, whatever their special interests and levels of skill. However, the text is angled towards the white water paddler of average competence who is either new to the area or seeking new water to paddle. It is not for use by lemmings wishing to stress test their canoes or cash in their life assurance policies.

Hopefully, the guide will tempt the more experienced paddlers away from their routine paddling to try many of the exciting but rarely canoed rivers in the North East.

Hours spent frantically driving up hill and down dale looking for some elusive stretch of white water, burning up precious fuel and wasting valuable canoeing time should become a thing of the past - at least in the North East.

Familiar rivers such as the Tyne, Tees and Tweed, will be found alongside such rare gems as the Greta, Devil's Water and Balder.

The countryside is interesting, wild and invariably beautiful. The observant canoeist will see everything from ruined abbeys, to an active Buddhist monastery; from dippers to herons and perhaps even the elusive otter.

9

USING THE GUIDE

This guide covers all the major easterly flowing rivers in the North East; from the Tweed running across the Scottish borders, down to the northern tributaries of the Ouse.

Northumberland and Yorkshire paddlers tend to confine themselves to their respective regions. The book has therefore been divided around the River Tees into these two areas, with the rivers being listed alphabetically for each region.

All the rivers covered in the guide have been paddled by the author, from as close to their source as practicable, down to their lower reaches. A few of the completely flat and featureless sections, mainly those around the Vale of York, have been omitted.

Whilst the majority of the guide is devoted to the description of rivers, in order to widen the book's appeal those parts of the north east coastline of interest to surfers and sea canoeists have been included, along with a few flat water areas, such as Kielder Reservoir, which are also extensively used by canoeists. In addition, any miscellaneous information of interest to the paddler on his travels, has been mentioned. The pubs and cafes in the Guide have agreed to accept canoeists in their 'natural state' but please shake yourself dry first! In addition, all the landlords have kindly agreed to offer limited credit to those paddlers who arrive cold or penniless with their hard earned cash stuck in the car at the other end of the river. This privilege accorded to canoeists may be dependent on providing suitable security such as a paddle until your pieces of eight can be retrieved.

Whilst every effort has been made to ensure the accuracy of the Guide, conditions will vary according to river level. As the river bed is in contact with a powerful dynamic force it is constantly changing, particularly after heavy rainfall. Old obstructions will be washed away and new ones will replace them.

Most experienced canoeists will have learnt by now to treat weirs with great respect, especially those with long towbacks and in spate conditions. An additional hazard, is fallen trees, which on some rivers, such as the Greta, represent the main threat to your well-being. The combination of lack of room to manoeuvre and 'Murphy's law', seem to dictate that the main flow of current directs you on to twigs, specifically aimed to pick your nose and eyes, whilst other branches suddenly reach out like the giant tentacles of some deep sea octopus wrenching the paddle from your arms and immobilising you. Upside down and with your oxygen supply cut off, it provides an excellent appreciation of the dying moments of a struggling bluebottle cocooned in a spider's web. Once experienced it is not quickly forgotten, so treat fallen trees with great respect!

The main aim of this book is to guide you to the right stretch of white water. It can not detail every hazard you will encounter, although it is hoped that all major falls, weirs and portages have been covered. This guide should not be used as a substitute for personal inspection. Whenever any doubts exist you must examine the river ahead and assess the situation in relation to both your canoeing abilities and your equipment. These factors should always take precedence over what you think we might have written!

River Descriptions
Most of the text follows a similar format with a brief introduction describing the river course in outline, followed by a more detailed description, with the river being arbitrarily divided into sections that either represent a convenient days' paddle or commonly used stretches. Occasionally several sections have been combined, especially on the duller stretches of the lengthier rivers such as on the Tweed. At the end of each river there is a summary with significant hazards in bold type. This provides a quick *aide memoire* before going down the river.

Because of the large distances covered, it has not been practical to provide maps of a meaningful scale for the entire river, except for important or complicated sections. Wherever possible photographs and diagrams have been used to illustrate hazards.

Most rivers have been paddled at average winter levels, unless otherwise stated, but obviously the younger rivers with small catchment areas have been canoed in spate conditions.

Only a few river level markers have been described for they are little used and of no practical help in planning trips. Once you've arrived commonsense will usually dictate whether or not the river is paddleable.

We have however described the weather conditions needed to make the rivers paddleable.

If you are uncertain of local conditions phone the weather centre or access officer.

Terminology and Grading
Landmarks, access and egress points are given in six figure grid reference numbers from 1:50,000 OS maps.

As paddlers are usually going down river the term left or right refers to river banks as the paddler faces downstream.

Waterfalls
Single drops over 2 metres in height have been measured to give an idea of what fate awaits you. Most plunge pools have been measured, but inspection on each occasion is essential, as not infrequently semi submerged objects lie in wait for the unwary paddler.

Portages
Unfortunately, some paddlers seem to regard portages as an instant challenge.

Rather than make absolute recommendations some portages have been subdivided into recommended or optional portages where hazards can be shot at certain levels and a few 'essential portages' where even the lunatic fringe freshly released from their padded cells will want to take at least a second look before shooting!

Portages which might be required because of transient hazards i.e. fallen trees are *not* classified a such although they may be mentioned in the text.

Grading

The conventional international grading system from I - VI has been used.

Each section has been given a Grade which represents the most difficult rapids on that stretch. Where there is a short but difficult rapid on otherwise easy water, the lower Grade is used, with the higher Grade in brackets.

Intermediate grades are expressed on an average of two grades, i.e. a difficult Grade III or easy IV being expressed as Grade III/IV.

Where grades alter significantly according to water level, they are hyphenated i.e. the Strid, on the River Wharfe which varies from Grade III to V will be expressed as III - V, it is *not* an average grading.

For those unfamiliar with the grading system this has been set out below in lyrical style translated from an Alpine canoeing guide.

Grades

I. Easy

Here are rivers with beautiful united waters, flowing in peaceful meanders down laughing valleys. The canoe may float any way which it pleases down the channel.

II. Moderate

The river is already quicker. At moments there is a disturbance which the canoe sails over with disdain. An overhanging tree forces the canoeist into some adroit steering. A rock in the main channel must be avoided. But always the channel is clear and obvious.

III. Fairly Difficult

Now things are more complicated. The current is swift. Sometimes the river becomes narrow with big waves. The canoeist may have to manoeuvre between rocks, stop in eddies, and cross currents. Nevertheless the best channel is easily recognized and remembered.

IV. Difficult

This is challenging water. Rapids follow each other in quick succession, or are continuous and difficult to read. Cushion waves build on obstacles and stoppers form below constrictions. The route is not obvious from the water, so inspection from the bank will be necessary to remember the way.

V. Very Difficult

Even after inspection from the bank, it is often difficult to recognise a route through Grade V water. There are pressure waves, whirlpools, boils, water-falls and holding stoppers. The water is always fast, often heavy, and the eddies are very sharp. A steep gradient, tight bends, and large boulders will hide the river from the canoeist on the water.

VI. Extremely Difficult

All previously mentioned difficulties are increased to the (present) limit of possibility, Grade VI water is a playing field of descents and foaming chaos. To all but the most experienced, and inexperienced canoeist, the river will appear impossible. It is runnable only at particular water levels. The paddler can expect at times to disappear completely, and at others to be hurled skywards by a prodigious force. The water sucks and surges unpredictably, often making route choice academic. Reaction skills must be of the highest order.

LEARNING TO CANOE

Once you've realised how much fun canoeing can be, the next question is, how do I start?

Fortunately canoeing is both a safe and easy sport to take up provided a few simple pitfalls are avoided.

Standing on the bank admiring a skilled slalomist in perfect control on the most impossible looking white water makes it all appear so easy, but once afloat the novice will soon discover that the canoe seems to develop a mind of its own, with a particular willingness to go round and round in circles! And when you finally do venture onto moving water it won't take long to find out just how easy it is to capsize, especially when you lean upstream. Coming up spluttering for air, you'll then be impressed at how quickly the river washes away your precious equipment to new and more careful owners.

So, for these and obvious reasons of safety those wishing to take up the sport are strongly advised NOT to go out by themselves and NOT to purchase any expensive new canoeing kit.

For most people this means that the best option is to join one of the many canoe clubs in the area. These are listed in the appendix along with their special interests.

It is far safer to make your mistakes when there are plenty of experienced people to help you out, and if you have to lose equipment it works out much cheaper to lose someone else's! Most clubs will not only provide free loan of equipment but early tuition will enable you to progress much more quickly than if you try to struggle along on your own.

Being a club member will also allow you to meet kindred spirits, learn from their experiences, and introduce you to a wide variety of canoe gear, so that when the time does come for you to buy an informed decision can be made.

Whilst most clubs in the area are able to provide a good range of basic canoe equipment (such as helmet, spraydeck, buoyancy aid, paddle and canoe) they don't usually supply specialist clothing so that those with funds to invest are often best advised to buy sensible canoe clothing. This will greatly add to your comfort and hence enjoyment of the sport.

Correct clothing is particularly important for those early trips on white water when a capsize is more of a probability than a possibility.

After all canoeing is really all about staying warm and dry in the cold and wet.

If you want to put someone off canoeing for life, just send them out for a paddle on a cold winter's day dressed only in a damp tee shirt and jeans.

A wet suit, long johns and canoeing cagoule with neoprene cuffs is a sensible combination favoured by many paddlers as it provides warmth and protection from the elements without unduly interfering with upper limb mobility.

Wet suit tops are best avoided especially on longer trips as they are too heavy, hot and restrictive for most canoeists.

A thin woollen jumper is often a good undergarment to wear next to your skin and beneath your cagoule as it retains its warmth even when damp. Helly Hansen's or similar garments make good alternatives but avoid cotton tee shirts which when wet simply act as personalised body refrigerators. They should not be worn even under a dry suit.

Paddle mittens are invaluable for the winter months and good quality wet suit boots with thick soles will be much appreciated by your feet for those unexpected portages or rescues.

Those wishing to paddle in complete warmth and comfort might consider enrolling for a course of basic instruction at a swimming pool. This is an excellent way to learn especially during the winter months. Swimming pools are also an ideal place to practice more advanced techniques such as rolling.

Most of the larger clubs organise at least one pool session per week in addition to the council recreation departments who also run regular courses.

Another alternative for those wishing to get away from it all (or lose their children for a few days) is to attend one of the short residential courses run by outdoor education centres (see appendix for details).

If you like doing your own thing, complete novices can have a wonderful day out by taking a picnic and exploring the shoreline of Kielder Reservoir in Canadian canoes. All the equipment including wet suits can be hired from the marina (see text for details).

Open Canadians are the most user friendly of canoes and a few minutes basic instruction will be sufficient for you to get around on placid water (rather more skill is needed for moving water).

Finally to those paddlers starting out who wear glasses, don't forget to tie them on! Most bespectacled canoeists seem to have to lose several pairs before they realise that glasses don't float!

ACCESS

Access and the Law
N.B. This section relates to English Law and does not apply to Scotland i.e. the Tweed, Jed, Whiteadder, Teviot, and Ettrick in this guide.

Rivers in Private Ownership (Non-tidal)
It is important for canoeists to have a good working knowledge of the law on access for several reasons. Firstly, to enable paddlers to keep within the law and respect the rights of landowners. Secondly, and perhaps more importantly to provide a legal framework which can justify the moral right which many paddlers feel to have the freedom of access to wild water rivers as many of our friends do on the continent (and throughout most of the world).

Except in special circumstances water cannot be 'owned' in the legal sense of the word but instead the law recognises certain rights of use that go with ownership of the bank of a watercourse. In legal jargon they are referred to as 'Riparian rights' which as you might expect are derived from the Latin word *ripa* meaning river bank.

In most situations where both banks of a river belong to a person this also carries with it the right of ownership to the river bed, where a single bank is involved, ownership of the river bed occurs up to the centre line of the river.

So what are Riparian rights? These were loosely defined by Lord Justice Denman back in 1853 who stated in perhaps rather flowery and legalistic language,

> 'the possessor of land through which a natural stream runs, has a right to the advantage of that stream flowing in its natural course, and to use it as he pleases for any purpose of his own not inconsistent with the similar rights of the proprietors of the land above and below'.

This last proviso is of great significance because it prevents landowners from being able to permanently remove water in the significant quantities, that might enable landowners to claim property rights over the water.

Landowners do however have the right to abstract water from a river for domestic and agricultural use. When a riparian owner who has abstracted water and stored it chooses to return it to a stream his right of ownership ceases and the water is returned to public ownership. Since riparian owners have only a limited capacity to take water into their possession it follows that riparian ownership is primarily concerned with the uses of the water rather than any right of property.

Riparian rights are also concerned with both fishing and navigation rights.

Yet another complication surrounding the law on access has been what many people consider to be an inappropriate prosecution of a canoeist under the Specialised Fisheries & Salmon Act 1975 for disturbing salmon beds. Quite how this could be proved in a court of law is not clear and remains open to question.

Of particular interest to canoeists is the judgement of the famous Lord Justice Park who stated in the case of Embrey v Owen (1851) that

'water in a watercourse is in public and common ownership in that *all may reasonably use it who have right of access to it, and that none can have any property in the water itself'*

In other words if you have right of access to a river via a road, footpath or other public right of way you should have a right of use to that water. Where there is no right of access you run the risk of falling foul of the law of trespass. However this is not a criminal offence unless the water is owned by a public body e.g. Water Boards.

Trespass is dealt with in the civil courts (just as motor accidents or contract disputes) and the Crown Prosecution Service can not prosecute canoeists for their infringement. This means that the Police will not become involved if a private landowner complains that canoeists are trespassing on his land, and canoeists will not end up in the magistrates court. The landowner could however, in theory, sue the canoeist for damage to his land, arising from the trespass. This is of little practical concern unless the canoeist tramples down a newly sown crop before launching his canoe. A moments reflection will indicate that no damage can be proved to the ever changing water down which the canoeist floats.

In one case it was held by Lord Denning that fishermen could sue for interruption of their fishing rights. This has not been followed and seems at variance with the basic principle of English Law, that only quantifiable damage can be recovered. More recently canoeists and fishermen have successfully obtained injunctions against each other to prevent use of rivers, but there have been no final decisions.

Arising from the law of trespass is the landowners right to ask the canoeist to leave his land by the quickest route. This request must be obeyed, but the reader will work out that if he is carrying a canoe, the most direct route will often be by water downstream in any event!

Waters in Public Ownership

Examples of these are reservoirs owned by the Water Boards, or lakes owned by local authorities. Trespass over these will be an infringement of the local bye-laws, and as such will bring the canoeist into conflict with the criminal law. Readers will realise that it is far more serious in practice to be caught canoeing without permission on these waters than over privately owned ones, as they could be fined, not merely sued for damages.

Rights of Navigation

Tidal Rivers

These are navigable without the owners permission from the sea up to the high water mark. Theoretically clearance to exercise these rights should be made with the harbour authorities.

The river banks remain private and permission from the landowner is required to launch and land.

Common Law Navigation

Certain rights of navigation may ensue where a river or waterway has been continually used without objection for at least 20 years, although these rights may be subject to local bye-laws.

Access and the Canoeist

Whilst the author does not share the rather parochial view that local rivers are only for local paddlers, the sad fact is that the access situation on many of our best rivers is rather like an angry looking boil which will not take much more pressure to burst.

One of the criticisms of guidebooks is that they allow more people to use the rivers particularly from outside the region, so destabilising the situation for everybody.

Readers of this guide, therefore, have a particular responsibility to all paddlers to ensure they are courteous to all anglers they meet, and make sure they are *au fait* with local access arrangements.

Wherever you go, almost without exception, the paddler has to cross private land, so that the goodwill of riparian owners has to be maintained.

You might get away with something on one or two occasions, but remember that paddlers will be coming after you and it will be them that have to answer for your actions.

As a general rule, the further north you go the easier access becomes. However, even where access is good it still remains an important issue, as canoeists in these areas are naturally keen to maintain their good relations with the community, and perhaps be seen as an example to other less fortunate areas.

Paradoxically such rivers often have no formal access agreements, as none are needed, but sometimes there are informal arrangements between local anglers and canoeists. For example, on Scottish rivers such as the Tweed, where fishing is banned on Sundays canoeists usually restrict themselves to Sunday paddling during the fishing season. It is reassuring that if such an exclusive salmon river such as the Tweed is able to keep a harmonious relationship between anglers and canoeists there is hope for the hot spots in Yorkshire and Co. Durham.

Here a number of usually rather fragile agreements have been introduced. Paddlers, especially from outside the region are strongly advised to contact their Local or Regional Access Officers before making a trip. This applies particularly to large groups and those paddling in the fishing season. The Local Access Officers are listed with their designated river and where none has been appointed the Regional Access Officer should be consulted. Their addresses are listed in the Appendix.

The Ashgill Beck - tributary of the South Tyne (See p106)

The second boulder garden on the Allen, (See p21)

The Rivers

Northumberland Region
(Borders to Co. Durham)

River Allen

Access	Cupola Bridge (OS Ref 800592)
Egress	Plankey Mill (OS Ref 795622)
Grade	III/IV
Length	5km
Portage	Optional - Hag Fall (OS Ref 798614)
OS Map	Hexham & Haltwhistle Sheet 87 1:50000
Local Access Officer	Jerry Tracey, Haefen House,
	Middle Hay Leazes, Allendale,
	Northumberland. NE47 9NP
	Tel: Allendale (0434) 683 409

Introduction

This is one of the finest stretches of white water in the area for few rivers in the North East have such a continuous stretch of virtually unbroken fast water. At full spate it requires the paddler to maintain constant vigilance throughout it's entire length, as every bend seems to bring the canoeist face to face with a new set of exciting challenges.

In addition the surrounding countryside is particularly beautiful as the river cuts down through a deep, heavily wooded valley to the South Tyne.

Although well known to local canoeists it is rarely paddled by people from outside the region partly because of its relatively short length but mostly due to difficulty in predicting the height of the water when expeditions are planned.

Unfortunately because of its small size and limited catchment area it cannot be paddled at ordinary levels but requires spate conditions which usually occur within six hours after the onset of heavy rainfall and lasts 12-24 hours after rain has stopped. Light drizzle for however many weeks or even months (as we frequently get in the North East) does not produce suitable conditions. Snow melt water can also produce good levels but these are notoriously difficult to predict.

A rough guide to water levels may be had by looking further down the valley at the rivers into which the Allen flows such as the South Tyne and the Tyne itself, however this is not always a reliable guide as after sudden heavy rainfall there is always a considerable delay before a rise in water level affects the lower Tyne valley. We have been caught out several times by this when the Allen has been in full spate and the Tyne rock bottom.

A more reliable indication is to look at the stream which follows the A686 as you climb up the hill towards Langley Castle. If the stream is full and the water muddied you know your luck is in. However, probably the simplest and surest way of all is to telephone Jerry Tracey, the local access officer, a

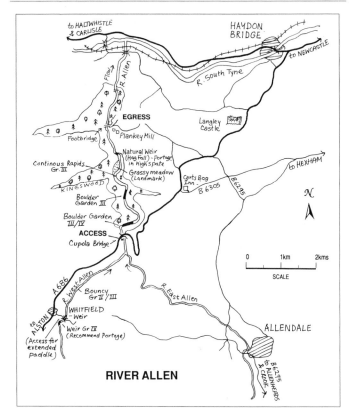

RIVER ALLEN

fanatical canoeist who runs an outdoor centre in Allendale itself. He is always happy to give advice on local conditions.

Access

This is fortunately not a problem as the river lies in a fairly remote area which has few anglers. Please respect the farmers privacy at Plankey Mill. They're usually very friendly towards canoeists.

River Course

The Allen is formed from two tributaries, the East and West Allen which drain a small area of the Northern Pennines just south-east of Alston. The usual

Playing in the stopper below Hag Fall on the Allen

access point is at Cupola Bridge just below where the two tributaries meet. Here the A686 crosses the Allen and provides easy access to the river. There is also a path forming a right of way from Cupola Bridge downstream. This more or less follows the right river bank down to Plankey Mill. Cars can easily be parked on either side of the bridge. Most people usually get on to the river 50 metres above the bridge on the left bank. Here a final assessment of water level needs to be made. If water is flowing only under the right hand arch, there is insufficient water. For a good paddle you need water flowing under all three arches.

For those wishing to extend their trip, a pleasant ride may be had on fast Grade II/III water by going 3km up the A686 road to Whitfield Village where there is a small bridge over the river on the Allendale road. If this point is selected be careful not to get in above the large weir (Grade III/IV), which is 100m upstream of the bridge and clearly not designed with the comfort of canoeists in mind with overhanging trees, an angled approach and steep descent sprinkled with iron spikes followed by a final vertical drop of 1.5m need we say more? The small weir immediately beneath the bridge is quite safe and easy to shoot. No major problems should be encountered down to Cupola Bridge, the usual access point, and you should be nicely primed to tackle the major rapids ahead by the time you arrive.

We regret to say that one of us didn't even make it this far on his first attempt, after hitting the main stanchion of Cupola Bridge, overturning and losing his helmet in the process which then disappeared into a large stopper only to be recovered 2 weeks later half way up a tree! Well the river was rather high - that's his excuse anyway.

What you should do after getting in, is to take the right hand arch beneath Cupola Bridge which leads into some turbulent fast water for about 300m before a sharp right hand bend leads into the first rapid (Grade III/IV). This consists of a boulder field about 100m in length. Just follow the main flow of the current from the left over to the right. Avoid staying left which simply leads into a series of boulder chokes. There follows a short stretch of slack water punctuated towards the end by two very small stoppers which are fun to play in. The river then turns left and a succession of minor rapids begin. At this point there is a shingle beach on your left and a high cliff on the right covered by moist lichen and ferns which combined with the dense coniferous woodland create the effect of a primeval forest.

After a further 300 metres a right bend leads you into the second boulder garden (Grade III). This rapid consists of several large boulders which although easily dodged form powerful eddies in high water.

Below this further rapids lead to two small steps in the bedrock which create two stoppers with strong undertows. However, they are usually safe to play in although it is not unknown to end up swimming out of them - in high spate they become washed out.

About 100m below this two rocky outcrops from either bank narrow the river to about 3m. In high water there are usually several good playwaves immediately above this constriction.

More rapids now whisk you steadily downstream before the trees suddenly thin on the left bank to reveal a grassy meadow. This should be carefully noted for in 250m a large natural weir occurs after a left hand bend. This is known locally as Hag Fall. In *high spate* the drop is often partially obscured by several stoppers which run across the *top* of the weir. The paddler is sometimes taken by surprise until it is practically too late for evasive action. If in doubt keep close to the left bank.

The weir itself is formed from a solid slab of rock with two large rips on the right and 3 smaller ones on the left which channel most of the water. The weir is a 7m band of rock with a drop of 2m and set at an angle of 15° to the bedrock. In high water the safest route is on the far left although a sharp right hand turn is necessary to avoid being swept onto the bank below. An alternative at lower levels is to take the most medial of the right hand chutes as the stopper slows you down and usually pushes you medially away from the large collection of fallen trees, rocks and debris which are present at the bottom of the right hand chute. Under most conditions this weir has a heart of gold and can be safely played in. For those who do get stuck in the stopper rescues may easily be affected by walking along the weir or simply wading in the plunge pool and pulling boats out. However this cannot be done in full spate when a thoroughly unpleasant stopper forms and the weir should be portaged by all but the most experienced.

After the excitement of the weir a small rapid follows round the next bend which usually has two stoppers across most of the river, but these are easily paddled through.

Sadly you're nearing the end of your paddle with 100m of fast water carrying you down to a small suspension bridge which shows that Plankey Mill (OS Ref 795622) has been reached.

Although the river is flowing quite fast at this point you should get out here even though it is tempting to continue. Failure to resist this temptation by paddling around the next bend will commit you to paddling some rather dull fast Grade II water down to the South Tyne, getting out at Haydon Bridge. This is a further 5km and the boredom is only punctuated by a small weir at Haydon Bridge itself. Far better to get out at Plankey Mill and go down again or pop over to the North Tyne and do Warden Gorge, although be warned it will seem dull in comparison to the Allen!

Summary

A fast exciting paddle with no serious problems for the competent canoeist. In high spate be aware of fallen trees and exercise caution at the natural weir. (Hag Fall.)

Kms		
0	**Access**	Cupola Bridge (OS Ref 800592) A686 crosses Allen. Upstream left bank.
0.5		**Rapid** Grade III/IV 100m in length. Start left then move over to right.
2		**Rapid** Grade III. 75m in length. Field large of large boulders.
3		A rocky outcrop narrows river to 3m.
3.25		Meadow left bank in forest clearing. (Landmark for weir which is 250m downstream)
3.5		**Natural weir** (Hag Fall) Shoot left, *dangerous* in high spate portage (L) bank (OS Ref 798614) 2m sloping drop.
5	**Egress**	Suspension Bridge. Plankey Mill (OS Ref 795622)
8		Joins river South Tyne.
11		Small weir. Haydon Bridge.

River Aln

Introduction

By contrast to the Allen the Aln is one of Northumberland's worst rivers to canoe! For not only is it narrow, shallow and for the most part flat, but much of it flows through the Duke of Northumberland's Estate so that one is likely to fall prey to the Duke's feudal army of bailiffs and estate managers, forever keen to repopulate the dungeons of Alnwick Castle!

However, the Aln does have some redeeming features as the river flows through some very beautiful parkland, providing excellent views of several historic buildings.

The Aln is some 40kms in length, rising on the eastern border of the Cheviots close to the village of Alnham. From here it flows almost due east passing through Hulne Park, before skirting around the town of Alnwick giving a magnificent view of the Castle.

Visitors to the area are strongly recommended to have a look around the castle, for even the most Philistine of wild water canoeists cannot fail to be impressed by the enormous armoury, fine paintings and wonderful furnishings that seem to outclass all other museums and castles in the North East.

Hulne Park through which much of the river flows can also be visited. Limited access is provided to pedestrians on Wednesdays and Sundays when passes may be obtained from the Castle ticket office. The Park was to a large extent designed by the famous local landscape architect, Lancelot Capability Brown. Lancelot is also well known for his work on Wallington Hall near his home village of Kirkharle in the Wansbeck valley. He also designed the gardens at Blenheim Palace in Oxfordshire. His main influence was to transform the rigid, geometric patterns of 17th Century gardens into the gentler more graceful mixed landscapes of the 120 parks and gardens he helped to design. In particular he used ponds and lakes to help create this effect. Still water was thus an integral part of many of his gardens. Sadly he tried to do the same here and was responsible for building a number of perilous weirs in the park, thus ruining the true character of the river. However perhaps he can be forgiven, for over two centuries had to lapse before the occasional canoeist was to grace the waters of the Aln.

Beyond Alnwick the river slowly winds its way down to Lesbury where it becomes tidal before meeting the sea at Alnmouth.

Access

Permission to canoe the upper section through the Duke of Northumberland estate is unlikely to be given. The lower stretch from Alnwick down to the sea is occasionally canoed usually without problems.

Alnwick Castle, overlooking the River Aln

Local Access Officer   Peter Clark
                                Windy Gyle Outdoor Centre,
                                Belford,
                                Northumberland. Tel: (0668) 213 289

Bridge End to Alnwick
Length 15kms **Grade** I - II **Portage** 4 weirs

This upper section of the Aln requires some rainfall to provide flow as well as depth to the river as the gradient is minimal and the river shallow.

The lower part of this stretch passes through the Duke of Northumberland's Estate where paddlers are not usually welcomed, especially during the fishing season.

Another problem is that all the weirs need portaging as they have vertical or near vertical drops on to solid rock.

Access to this part of the Aln is probably easiest at Bridge End (OS Ref 108132) which is the first road bridge above Hulne Park. In high water it is possible to paddle from Whittingham the other side of the A697. Here the river is too flat and narrow to interest the average paddler of sound mind and body.

From Bridge End the river winds its way through green pastureland, passing the odd farmhouse and scattered copse. Here the river is only about

0.5m deep and 3m in width.

At 4.5km one suddenly comes across an enormous hinged wooden portcullis which appears to block one's path. It looks built to repel the Viking invaders, being about ten feet high and flanked on either side by the high stone walls that surround the Duke's Estate. As there is no vehicular access at this point one has little choice but to venture forth into this forbidden land.

The wily canoeist will find that he can gently prise the two doors apart to squeeze between them, but as they snap shut like the wardrobe door propelling Lucy into Narnia you've passed the point of no return!

One soon enters a thickly wooded deciduous forest with easy shingle rapids taking you downstream. In several places small islands of bushes and trees divide the river.

After several kilometres a rather insignificant drop that fails to draw the eye hides a row of short iron spikes.

The forest dense at first gradually gives way to a mixture of woodland and park. Just below one bridge is the first of a succession of difficult weirs. This has a 1.5m vertical drop on to a long rocky slide. This must be portaged on the right bank.

Just around the next bend Hulne Priory is seen on the left bank. This dates back to the 13th Century. It was the first of the Carmelite monasteries to be established in England. It is believed that Ralph Fresborn, a Northumbrian Knight who had taken monastic vows, was found by one of the crusading De Vescey's in a monastery on Mount Ararat. He was brought back to England on condition that a Carmelite monastery should be set up. Even by monastic standards life was hard. Each Friar kept a coffin in his cell and each morning dug a shovel full of earth for his grave! Rising at five o'clock in the winter time they would creep to prayers on their knees, eating vegetarian food, but twice a day, and worst of all, white water canoeing was strictly forbidden.

Several kilometres beyond the Priory a large imposing square battlemented tower rises from a meadow on the left. This is the Old Gate Tower from Alnwick Abbey. At one time this was a large and powerful monastery, but following the dissolution of monasteries in the 16th Century it fell into ruin with most of the remains being used as quarry stone for other buildings.

The Abbey Tower is a useful landmark for round the next bend is the most unpleasant of all the unsavoury weirs on the Aln. It is a 2.5m vertical plunge on to solid rock. Portage on the left bank by the disused Mill House. There is a small weir below the next bridge, which is easily paddled over.

Half a kilometre beyond lies the well known Lions Bridge with the famous Percy Lion with its erect tail constructed in 1773.

On your right a flat stretch of water allows you to appreciate the magnificent view of Alnwick Castle, with its well known stone figures silhouetted along the battlements to dissuade or confuse attacking soldiers.

This leads up to a weir which has a 1.5m stepped drop with no plunge pool, that some may wish to shoot, although a portage is less of a bone shaker.

In another kilometre there is a similar type of weir with a 1.75m drop which should also be portaged on the left bank. Here a footpath leads up to the road bridge which makes a convenient point to egress. (OS Ref 197139)

Alnwick to Lesbury (Alnmouth)
Length 8km (11km)   **Grade** I - II (Bilton rapids Grade II/III)   **No Portages**

An easy stretch of water with little of special interest.

Get in at the road bridge of the B1340 out of Alnwick, where a blind offshoot of the road 150 metres before the road bridge makes a good car park.

The small weir 100m below the bridge is a 1.25m stepped drop which can be bounced down, although there is no plunge pool. (There is little enough excitement on this river.)

Several roadbridges are passed before a row of closely set stepping stones in the form of truncated pillars bar your way. Those with a flexible pelvis will just be able to tip the boat enough to squeeze through but generally most will find it easier to portage.

A kilometre or so beyond lies a brief bouldery rapid in two sections which forms a Grade II/III rapid.

Another dull stretch follows, briefly interrupted by a broken weir, just beyond the viaduct. This flows onto a few scattered rocks.

Half a kilometre beyond is a large weir with a 2.20m sloping drop. This is the only decent weir on the entire river having a good plunge pool and can be safely shot except in high spate.

Interestingly seals come inland above the tidal limit as far as this weir, and can sometimes be seen perched on the rocks.

Most people will want to egress at Lesbury road bridge on the right bank of the bridge.

Below here the river becomes tidal and very sluggish with the river banks lined with estuary mud.

River Aln Summary

Bridge End to Alnwick
Length 15kms   Grade I - II   Portage 4 Weirs (All near vertical drops with no plunge pool.)

Kms		
0	**Access**	Bridge End. (OS Ref 108132)
1		Footbridge.
2		Ford and footbridge below.
4.5		Hinged Portcullis affair across River.
		Boats can just squeeze between.

Kms		
5.5		(Approx.) Very small drop (10cms) with row of **iron spikes** easily visible.
		Various road and footbridges cross river.
8		Road bridge.
		Weir just below. 1.5m vertical drop. No plunge pool.
		Portage right.
8.5		Hulne Priory visible left.
12		Tower visible left bank.
		200m Horse shoe **Weir**. 2.5m vertical drop. No plunge pool.
		Portage left bank.
		300m Road bridge. Small weir beneath. Easily shot.
12.5		Ornamental Bridge.
13		Lions road bridge.
		Castle visible right bank.
13.5		**Weir.** 1.5m near vertical stepped drop. No plunge pool.
		Usually portaged.
14.75		**Weir.** 1.75m vertical stepped drop. No plunge pool.
		Portage left and
	Egress	Egress just above road bridge.
		100m Road bridge. (OS Ref 197139)

Alnwick to Lesbury (Alnmouth)

Length 8kms (11kms)   Grade I - II (150m Grade II/III Rapids nr Bilton)
No Portages

Kms		
0	**Access**	Road bridge upstream left bank. (OS Ref 197139)
		100m **Weir**. 1.25m steeply stepped. No plunge pool.
		Plastic boatists can bounce down but some may wish to portage.
1		Sewerage works. Right.
1.25		A1 Road bridge.
2		Stepping stones. Truncated concrete pillars.
		A Dancer can just be squeezed between if tipped heavily.
3		Balustraded Road bridge.
5		**Bilton Rapids** Boulder Garden for 150m. Grade II/III
6.5		Viaduct. 100m Broken **weir.**
7.5		**Weir** 2.2m sloping drop. Good Plunge Pool!
8	**Egress**	Lesbury Road bridge. Egress point. (OS Ref 233115)
11		Alnmouth Road bridge.

River Balder

Access	Above/Below Hury Reservoir. (OS Ref 968196)
Egress	Cotherstone. (OS Ref 014201)
Length	5km
Grade	IV
No Portages	(Beware fallen trees which frequently block river.)
OS Map	Barnard Castle. No. 92
Local Access Officer	(Area covered by Tees LAO)
	Mr. Len Smith,
	Four Seasons,
	44, The Bank,
	Barnard Castle.
	Co. Durham.
	Tel: 0833 37829

Introduction

If it is raining hard and you're looking for adventure then this is an excellent river to choose. For as the Balder flows out of Hury reservoir, steep, bouldery rapids bounce the canoeist down through a twisting tree lined corridor to just above Cotherstone where the river briefly flattens out before joining the Tees.

Whilst this is only a distance of some 5km the river falls at over 70 feet per mile so that most paddlers are usually quite relieved when they reach the bottom.

Although there are no major falls or heavy rapids here there are numerous obstructions so that the paddler is required to have the agility of a mountain goat in order to weave a safe path beneath fallen trees and around rocks. It, therefore, goes without saying that this is plastic boat country and definitely not a trip for large groups or novices!

Access

This river is rarely paddled so few problems arise, but there has been occasional harassment from landowners near Cotherstone.

River Course

As this is a small dam controlled river it is very difficult to predict when the river will become canoeable even after heavy rainfall.

However, if you're canoeing the Tees, the level is easily inspected at its confluence or from the road bridge in Cotherstone.

If the water is muddied and obviously up then this is too good an opportunity to miss - however tired you are.

The Balder. A tunnel of trees

Follow the road out of Cotherstone signposted to Hury reservoir and travel about 4kms up the valley. Eventually the road crosses the Balder as it emerges from the reservoir. (For route see also Map of River Tees. Eggleston to Barnard Castle.)

Most canoeists will want to get on to the river below the road bridge as a cattle fence lies directly beneath.

A brief honeymoon ensues with easy paddling for a few hundred metres before the gradient gradually steepens, with rocks starting to sprout from the river bed. The trees along either bank become more prolific as the paddler becomes submerged in a tangled web of arboreal decay.

There is no time to relax as each bend brings a new set of hazards to dodge or duck. Whilst there is nothing particularly venomous or difficult, good boat control and constant attention are required. An occasional broken paddle lying discarded on the bank concentrates the mind wonderfully.

Here and there a fallen tree completely blocks the river so necessitating a portage.

Soon a footbridge and then a disused viaduct cross the river shortly before the Balder emerges from the wood to meander through some grassy meadows. Here the river is a little more placid but just as you begin to relax a left hand bend heralds several rocky ledges which create a small fall with a turbulent stopper that can be quite entertaining.

The road bridge soon comes into view with the village green a further 200 metres downstream on the right where cars can be parked.

River Balder - summary
Length 5kms   Grade IV   No Portages   (Beware of fallen trees)

Kms		
0	**Access**	Above/below
		Hury Reservoir Dam. (OS Ref 968196)
		Get in below road bridge right bank.
		(Note cattle fence beneath bridge.)
0.5 - 4		Virtually *continuous* **bouldery**
		Rapids. With occasional fallen trees. Grade IV.
3		Footbridge.
3.5		Disused railway viaduct.
4		Woodlands recede as countryside opens out. Balder Grange
		Manor House visible high on right bank.
4.5		Series of rocky ledges with turbulent chute.
		Large modern house on right bank.
4.75		Road bridge.
5	**Egress**	Car park right bank on local village green. (OS Ref 014201)
5.25		Confluence with River Tees.

River Breamish

Access	Linhope Bridge. (On Linhope Burn) OS Ref 964163
Egress	Hedgley Bridge. OS Ref 058172
Length	11.5km.
Grade	II. (Alnhammoor Rapid. Grade II/III)
Portage	Hedgley Weir. OS Ref 059172
OS Map	Alnwick and Rothbury. No. 81

Introduction
Better known to walkers than canoeists and with some justification, the Breamish arises along the southern flank of the Cheviot, flowing almost due east down the attractive Ingram Valley, so named after the village which lies about halfway down.

    Throughout most of its length the river consists of fast, shallow rapids with the grassy Cheviots rising up on either side.

Kielder Water at dawn. Photo: Rob Egelstaff

Makerston rapids on the Tweed. Photo: Rob Egelstaff

The river soon passes beneath the A697 near Powburn, where it starts to turn northwards and becomes more sluggish. After a short distance the river passes beneath Bewick Bridge, when it becomes known as the Till, one of the larger tributaries of the Tweed.

Most people will wish to canoe this small river for its scenic paddle, for although the river falls quite steeply in its first few kilometres there are no major rapids here, with nothing above Grade II/III. The difficult weir right at the end will provide the more adventurous with a last chance to moisten their spraydecks.

This river is primarily of interest to local paddlers and the more adventurous touring paddler.

Access

This river is rarely canoed so there is no local access officer. Although there are no recorded objections some care will be needed at the access points which cross private land.

River Course

The intermittent, shallow, shingle rapids make recent rainfall strongly desirable, especially to make the topmost section canoeable.

To find the Ingram Valley, pass through the outskirts of Powburn village on the A697 to Wooler and across the road bridge over the Breamish with its intimidating weir. This is the egress point. After 300 metres take the left turn signposted to Ingram.

Most paddlers will wish to go all the way up the valley, through Ingram village to Linhope, where the road ends abruptly.

At this point the road crosses the Linhope burn. A small fall lies directly beneath the bridge and a bouldery rapid will require some deft paddling to take you 200 metres down to the confluence with the Breamish, where you are greeted by a 1.0 metre rocky fall.

Several sheep fences span the river before Alnhammoor road bridge is reached. In low water and for those paddlers who feel the Linhope burn might aggravate their piles, a gentler start may be had from here. The road bridge is found by taking a left turn about 1.5km before Linhope is reached. It is marked as a private road, so the local farmer who is quite amenable should be consulted.

From here the river narrows slightly as it starts to fall more rapidly, forming a brief Grade II/III rapid overhung with small trees on either side.

In about 0.5km a large tree partially obstructs the river course necessitating a portage in low water.

From here there is nothing above Grade II, as a series of easy rapids take you down the valley until Powburn road bridge is reached. Egress just above the road bridge on the left bank.

Immediately below lies a difficult weir with a 2.5m stepped drop in three tiers. In low water some may wish to shoot this via the broad 2 stepped fish ladder, after scrutinising the plunge pools for debris.

Below this the river meanders slowly across the valley until Bewick Bridge is reached, when it becomes known as the Till.

River Breamish - summary

Linhope (On Linhope Burn) to Hedgeley Bridge
Length 13kms Grade II (Alnhammoor Rapid Grade II/III) Portage Hedgeley Weir

Kms

0	**Access**	Linhope Bridge. (On Linhope Burn) OS Ref 964163. Small **Fall** beneath Bridge followed by **bouldery rapid.**
		300m. Confluence with Breamish. **Rocky Fall** 1.0m drop.
0.5		**2 Sheep Fences.**
1.5	**Access**	Alnhammoor Road Bridge.
		Brief Grade II/III **Rapid.** 200m.
2.0		Tree partially obstructs river. Portage in low water.
6		Road bridge.
8.5		Road bridge. Ingram village. Right.
13	**Egress**	Hedgeley Road Bridge. (OS Ref 058172)
		Weir immediately below. Portage. 2.75m drop in 3 steps.
		Fish Ladder just left of Centre. Can be shot in low water, after careful inspection.
19		Road Bridge. Harehope Hall visible right.
22.5		Bewick Bridge. Sheep fence beneath.
		(River then becomes the Till.)

River Blyth

Access	Bellasis Bridge (OS Ref 190777) or Stannington Bridge.
Egress	Bedlington riverside park. (OS Ref 277820).
Length	16kms.
Grade	II
Optional Portage	Weir (OS Ref 263798)
OS Maps	Alnwick/Rothbury No. 81 & Tyneside No. 88.

Introduction

The Blyth provides some easy rough water paddling through an attractive wooded valley only a few miles from Newcastle upon Tyne.

Access
Few problems as the river is rarely paddled. No L.A.O.

River course
Being a relatively small river it is best paddled in spate conditions. In high water the river Blyth can be paddled from as far up as Thornford Bridge (OS Ref 156773) or Bellasis Bridge (OS Ref 190177). However, these upper sections cannot really be recommended as the river winds slowly through some rather dull pastureland where it has cut deeply through the topsoil creating high banks which obscure much of the surrounding countryside. An additional feature of this section is innumerable sheep fences spanning the river, which interrupt the journey every kilometre or so, making the trip more like a game of musical chairs than a days paddling.

Alternatively those canoeists who live around Ponteland may wish to take advantage of the River Pont which flows through the town centre but it is 7kms of rather arduous paddling before the confluence is reached.

The best starting point for most people will be at Stannington Bridge. The new road bridge has a lay-by on the southbound carriageway which provides convenient roadside parking.

The river now passes through a pretty wooded valley which continues all the way down to the point of egress. After about 4kms a road bridge is reached which is overlooked by Hartford Hall high up on the left bank. This impressive building is now used as a rehabilitation centre by the NHS. 100m downstream a small weir with a 1m sloping drop should present no problems.

The river now begins to gather pace with a succession of Grade II rapids. After about 3-4kms a longer stretch of slack water warns of an approaching weir. In high water the 2m steeply sloping drop forms a vicious stopper which has the potential of sending many to meet their maker. Fortunately by keeping close to the right bank you can take a narrow channel which by-passes the main weir but still ends in a rather tricky 1.5m vertical drop. Those unfamiliar with this weir are advised to inspect it from the bank as some may wish to portage it. The rather smelly water present at this stage of the journey provides an additional incentive to avoid a swim.

Further minor rapids continue for two-three kilometres before a high road bridge is reached, some may wish to use this as an egress point as there is a convenient riverside park with a public footpath down to the river. This is followed by a second lower road bridge 2km downstream (OS Ref 277820) which is a suitable point to finish.

This spot may be reached by going over the River Blyth on the A189 from Newcastle and taking the first left, the B1331, and following road signs to Bedlington. After 2kms a public house called the 'Bank Top' is reached where another left turn takes you down to a small road bridge and riverside park. Although it is possible to continue paddling further downstream, the river soon flattens out and becomes tidal. An additional problem is that the river banks have a generous veneer of foul-smelling estuary mud which has to be negotiated before the safety of dry land is reached.

Summary of River Blyth (and River Pont)

Kms		
0	**Access**	Bellasis Bridge (OS Ref 190777)
5		or Stannington Bridge (OS Ref 216784) best starting point,
		or via River Pont - Ponteland Road Bridge (OS Ref 166728)
9		Hartford Bridge, Hartford Hall high on left bank, 100m downstream - **weir** 1m sloping drop - easily shot.
12		**Weir** - optional portage - dangerous central stopper. 2m steep slope. Inspection advised in high water. Shoot far right. Sloping channel by-passes main weir to angled vertical drop of 1.5m. (OS Ref 263798).
14.5		A193 Road bridge.
16	**Egress**	Road bridge. Egress upstream left bank. (OS Ref 277820)
16.5		Iron railway bridge.
17		Road bridge A189.
		Estuary.

River Coquet

Introduction

This river start in the Cheviots, running almost due east via Rothbury across the coastal plain to meet the sea at Amble.

The main areas of interest to white water paddlers will be the Upper Coquet just above Alwinton. Here there is fast water with a succession of small but interesting falls and a short stretch of rapids just below Rothbury at Thrum Mill.

The middle section from Alwinton to Rothbury contains little of interest to canoeists and is, therefore, best avoided. Touring paddlers will enjoy the rest of the trip from Rothbury down to the sea, which passes several interesting historic buildings, whilst threading its way through some pleasant countryside.

Access

Few problems on the topmost section down to Alwinton. Some harassment around Felton.

Local Access Officer   Tony Hall,
4 Wellfield,
Warkworth,
Northumberland. Tel: 0665 711314

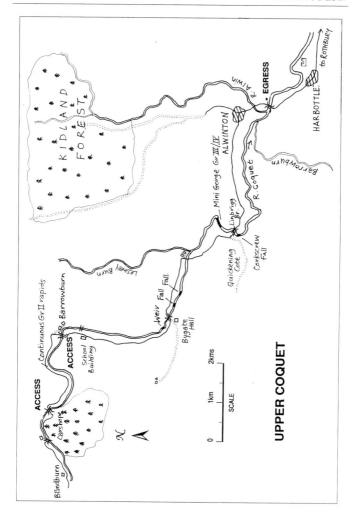

UPPER COQUET

The Coquet. Thrum Mill weir and rapids

Carshope Bridge to Alwinton
Length 15kms **Grade** III/IV **No Portages**

To paddle these upper reaches the river needs to be in spate conditions when the river can be canoed as high up as Fulhope or Blind Burn.

At this point the only major obstruction to impede one's progress down river is a series of sheep fences. A better starting point is several kilometres downstream at Carshope Bridge (OS Ref 846113) where fast water will swiftly take you down the steeply sided valley with the grassy Cheviot Hills rising up on all sides.

At 3.5km the Coquet passes beneath the road bridge at Barrow Burn which may be an alternative starting point for those wishing a shorter paddle.

One soon passes a small school building on your right and then underneath an iron footbridge.

At 6km Bygate Hall road bridge comes into view, with a small V shaped weir just above it. This has 0.5m vertical drop.

Beneath the road bridge another small weir is present, which although easily shot, does have a significant towback. The river now becomes a little more interesting, with a succession of quite technical falls.

The first lies 200m below the bridge, consisting of a two metre drop in two

38

steps. The first fall is quite straightforward, but the small bend that follows channels water over the second fall, directing the current against the right bank. This has a tendency to capsize you if swept against the right hand bank. The small stopper below is good fun to play in.

A few hundred metres beyond, a further 1.5m fall will probably require inspection. In high water the easiest route is down the far right-hand side, otherwise take the centre chute.

At 8kms Shillmoor Road bridge becomes visible, with a row of cottages on the left bank. The Usway burn adds a significant quantity of water from the left. The river now leaves the road and after a while enters a mini gorgelet about 50 metres long, known locally as Linbrigg gorge.

This forms a foaming torrent of water as it rushes down a narrow gully, creating a succession of small stoppers and turbulent eddies.

There is usually little choice of route as one is propelled at considerable velocity through the swirling flow down to the bottom where a calmer stretch provides a suitable place for swimmers to rendezvous with their equipment.

Just below this the river passes beneath Linbrigg road bridge, to deliver you to Corkscrew fall, a 1.25m drop in which water is funnelled and rotated over a large rock, which is exactly what happens to you and your canoe! Anybody who can roll should attempt this fall, but don't expect to get down it without capsizing as a roll is almost inevitable when the river is in medium spate. At very high or low levels the fall is much less interesting.

Some paddlers might wish to get out here and make their way up to Linbrigg road bridge, as the next 4kms to Low Alwinton road bridge OS Ref 923056 contains no further falls, although there are fast bouncy Grade II rapids for most of the way.

Alwinton to Rothbury
Length 22kms   **Grade** II   **No portages**

After the Coquet's rapid descent through the military ranges the river now seems to take a rest. Although it begins promisingly enough with a series of Grade I/II rapids, the valley gradually opens out with the river meandering slowly from side to side offering nothing more than the occasional shingle rapid to speed you on your way.

This part of the river cannot be recommended as having any particular merit for canoeists especially in low water when wide shingle rapids frequently ground the boat. However, you are able to give your trip an exciting finish by going just beyond Rothbury to incorporate Thrum Mill rapids into the paddle. (Grade III)

Rothbury to Felton
Length 20kms   **Grade** II   (Thrum Mill rapids Grade III)   **One Portage** Felton Weir OS Ref 173999

This middle section of the Coquet is probably most suited to touring paddlers although it does have one short but interesting rapid just below Rothbury at Thrum Mill. After this little burst of activity the river resumes its sedentary pace, gently winding down the pretty Coquet Valley with occasional shingle rapids and a few small falls created by steps in the bedrock.

Access is obtained by going over the road bridge in Rothbury and taking a right turn which brings you to a large car park just upstream of the bridge (OS Ref 058016).

After getting in, a few short rapids bring you down to a series of closely set stepping stones which usually require portaging although in high water one can paddle over them.

At 1km a short stretch of flat water indicates that Thrum Mill weir and rapids have been reached (Grade III). The initial one metre drop over a sloping concrete weir can usually be taken anywhere but in high water if you don't like the look of the stopper there is often a chute on the far right.

This is soon followed by a 1m rocky fall best taken on the left. A quick turning stroke or reverse ferry glide is then required to stop you being washed onto a small rocky ledge immediately below the falls. Although less of a threat to plastic boats in low water these rocks have sunk as many boats as would have cheered the heart of any U-Boat commander!

After this two large rocks briefly squeeze the river through an hour glass constriction which is easily paddled through although the rocks are deeply undercut.

At 6km the river passes beneath a stone road bridge before going over a small weir with an 0.25m vertical drop.

There is little else of note until at about 9km when a large wood joins the left bank and a footbridge spans the river. Then a stone walled embankment rises up on the left bank and a most impressive castellated mansion becomes apparent as the river sweeps around a left hand bend. As the river loops around the buildings two steps in the bedrock create several small rocky falls.

The deep silence of the woods, the ruined outhouses, the well-preserved yet completely deserted house with all its turrets and battlements combine to give Brinkburn Priory a deeply mysterious and melancholy air which cannot fail to impress any paddler passing through these grounds.

At 12km there is a wide sloping weir with a 1.5m drop which may be shot in most places despite a few small rocks along the bottom.

Although quite easy, memories of this weir are emblazoned on our brains after one of our team managed to capsize in sub-zero temperatures on a beautiful day in mid-January. The unfortunate individual wouldn't accept offers of warm clothing. (Not unusual in people developing hypothermia.) It is always worthwhile remembering that refusing help and failing to see that a problem exists is a cardinal symptom of early hypothermia. It is therefore sometimes necessary when the condition is suspected to force individuals to accept appropriate measures even when they consider it unnecessary at the time. But back to our friend whose brain cells were cooling by the minute.

Unfortunately not having a guidebook handy we weren't to know that the warmth and safety of the Anglers Arms was only 0.5km further on, which despite its unpromising name is very hospitable and provides good bar meals. Opposite the Inn lies Weldon Bridge which is a picturesque stone bridge which now carries minimal traffic as the A697 crosses the Coquet on a new concrete road bridge 100m downstream. This may well be a suitable point for many groups to finish as it is still quite a long haul to Felton and there is little in the way of exciting paddling.

At 17kms there is a low road bridge with 1m high arches. Under normal conditions these are easy to squeeze under but in spate may require a portage. As the paddle draws to a close the river enters an attractive wooded vale which temporarily removes your desire to reach Felton.

At 20kms you pass underneath the A1 Felton bypass. Soon afterwards the river slackens and you come upon a large horseshoe shaped weir with a 2m vertical drop with a wall to wall stopper. Portaging it is strongly recommended if you wish to be certain of reaching Felton which is only a further .5km downstream.

Egress right bank just above Felton Bridge (OS Ref 185003).

Felton to Warkworth
Length 18kms   **Grade** I/II   **One portage** Brainshaugh Weir (OS Ref 203029)

The river continues at a fairly gentle pace through a mixture of open countryside and woodland. The character of this lower section has been largely determined by a series of weirs which represent the main hazard to canoeists.

Access is achieved by getting in immediately above Felton Bridge where there is a small car park on the right bank (OS Ref 185003).

The first few kilometres contain little of note as one is gently swished through pastures green, occasionally exchanging glances with the odd inquisitive sheep or sending a moorhen scuttling for cover.

At 6kms there is a large horseshoe shaped weir with a 3 metre vertical drop onto *solid rock* which will provide an excellent opportunity to practice your back-paddling! Portage this on the right bank around by the fish ladder (In exceptional conditions when the river is in full spate it may be possible to shoot the weir on the extreme left where a small rocky prominence will direct you past the main stopper into a plunge pool.)

Further downstream a road bridge crosses the river followed by another weir 1km further on. Fortunately this presents fewer problems with a 1m sloping drop which can be shot in most places.

At 10kms a high viaduct carries the main London-Edinburgh railway line overhead. Several kilometres beyond, the broken weir at Morwick Mill has an irregular 1m sloping drop providing some easy stoppers to play in. One kilometre beyond this there is yet another weir, this has a vertical drop of only 0.5m but there is a deceptively strong undertow which novice paddlers might consider portaging.

As the coastal plain is reached the pace of the river eases. The final obstacle on this trip is, surprise, surprise, yet another weir! At 16kms it consists of a steeply sloping drop of 2m with a long flat chute at the bottom. Most paddlers should enjoy tackling this on the left to avoid the large rock easily seen below the weir in midstream and the small stoppers which tend to form on the right hand side.

After another few kilometres Warkworth Castle comes into view. This was the original home of the Percys before they moved to Alnwick Castle in 1750. Although the castle is largely in ruins a few rooms around the keep are still maintained for their use.

Egress right bank just upstream of WarkworthBridge. By turning left at the monument in the town centre a small lane leads past St Lawrence's church down to the river bank where there is ample car parking space.

For anybody waiting to pick paddlers up it is worth popping into St Lawrence's church, for although the exterior is unremarkable, it is one of the few complete Norman churches surviving in Northumberland, the nave and chancel being built as far back as the 12th century. In 1174 the churchyard was the scene of a massacre when the Scots slaughtered almost the entire village population.

Another few kilometres will take you down to the estuary where the Coquet meets the sea at Amble. If continuing downstream some caution is required at the tidal weir 1.0km below Warksworth Bridge. This can have a strong undertow at low tide when the Coquet is in spate.

River Coquet - summary
Carshope Bridge to Alwintom
Length 15kms   Grade III/IV   No Portages

Kms		
0	**Access**	Carshope Bridge. (OS Ref 846113)
3.5		Barrow Bridge. Alternatively access point.
		300m below school building on right bank with footbridge.
6		**V shaped weir.** O.5m vertical drop. Easy.
		100m below Road bridge with small weir directly beneath.
		Easily shot but significant undertow.
6.5		2m **rocky fall** in two drops.
		Tendency to be swept to right banks so take bottom step just left of centre.
6.75		1.5m **rocky fall.** Awkward drop. Best inspected.
8		Road bridge.
		Cottages left bank. Usway burn joins left.

Kms		
10		Small fall below.
		Linbrigg gorge Keep good speed in midstream.
		Water is channelled through 50 metres of narrow gorge.
10.25		Linbrigg Road bridge.
		Immediately below **Corkscrew Fall** 1.25m drop.
		Water is funnelled and rotated over a large rock. (In medium spate)
15	**Egress**	Low Alwinton Bridge. Left bank. (OS Ref 923056)

Alwinton to Rothbury
Length 22kms   Grade I/II   No Portages

Kms		
0	**Access**	Low Alwinton Bridge (OS Ref 923060)
4.5		Lattice girder road bridge.
6		Footbridge and Holystone Village on right.
7		River divides filtering through a series of bushy islands.
		Can be tricky - best channel usually left.
11		Road Bridge.
14		Quarry with low road bridge, may need portaging.
22	**Egress**	Rothbury. Egress 100m right bank above road bridge.
22.5		Stepping stones.
23		**Thrum Mill weir and rapids.** Grade III Weir 1m slope.
		Shoot anywhere but in high water right channel to by-pass stopper.
		Rocky fall 1m, shoot left then turn immediately to avoid rocks at bottom.
	Egress	Left bank 100m below rapids (OS Ref 070016).

Summary - Rothbury to Felton
Length 20kms   Grade II (Thrum Mill rapids Grade III)   Portage - Felton weir (OS Ref 173999)

Kms		
0	**Access**	Rothbury. Cross over road bridge, turn right. Car park 100m upstream of bridge (OS Ref 058016).
0.5		Stepping stones. Portage in low water.
1		**Thrum Mill weir and rapids** Grade III. Weir 1m sloping drop. Shoot anywhere, in high water take right channel by-passing stopper. Rocky fall 1m shoot left then avoid rocks immediately below fall.
6		Stone road bridge. Small weir immediately below 0.25m vertical drop.

43

9	Brinkburn Priory. Two small rocky falls as river loops round priory.
12	**Weir.** 1.5m sloping drop.
12.5	Weldon Bridge and Anglers Arms left 100m below new road bridge for A697.
17	Low road bridge.
18	Wooded Vale begins.
20	**Felton Weir 2m** vertical drop. Side to side stopper-**portage.**
20.5 **Egress**	Felton village upstream of bridge right bank. (OS Ref 185003)

Felton to Warkworth

Length 18kms   Grade II   Portage Brainshaugh weir   OS Ref 203029

Kms

0 **Access**	Just above Felton Road bridge. Right bank (OS Ref 185003)
6	Brainshaugh **Weir** 3m vertical drop (OS Ref 203029)
	Portage right bank.
6.25	Stone Road bridge.
7	**Weir.** 1m sloping drop.
10	Viaduct.
12	Broken weir at Morwick Mill. Irregular 1m sloping drop.
13	**Weir.** 0.5m drop. Strong undertow.
16	**Weir.** At Coquet Lodge 2m sloping drop. Shoot far left. Tidal limit.
17	Warkworth Castle. Right bank.
17.5 **Egress**	Right bank. (OS Ref 247063)
18	Warkworth Bridge.
19	**Tidal Weir.** Exposed at low tide, caution in spate conditions.

River Derwent (Co. Durham)

Introduction

This river arises near Blanchland, Co. Durham and provides water to Derwent Reservoir, which is much used by the sailing fraternity.

The narrow top section of the river is most suited to canoeists as it is cleaner and has a more consistent gradient, but tree lined banks create quite a technical paddle.

From Derwent Reservoir the river flows initially south east, but gradually turns northwards flowing through Shotley Bridge, Rowlands Gill, finally meeting the Tyne at Blaydon.

As the river flows northwards it becomes progressively more polluted, - a gas mask may be a life saver. However, the countryside remains remarkably unspoilt until one comes within spitting distance of the Tyne.

Access
Few problems as the river is rarely canoed. No local access officer.

Derwent Reservoir to Shotley Bridge
Length 14.5kms **Grade** II/III **No Portages**

The placid outflow from Derwent Reservoir doesn't seem to hold out much prospect of an exciting paddle. However, the river soon enters a pretty, wooded valley, which offers several kilometres of consistent Grade II/III water, with several small falls at the end to provide a memorable finale.

There is nothing really epic here to draw paddlers from afar, it is most suited to the curious, and experienced paddlers living in the locality.

Novices, and large groups are advised not to attempt this section of the river due to the filtering effect of the large numbers of trees encountered during the first few kilometres.

The river needs a good outflow from the reservoir. It is therefore best paddled after recent rainfall.

Access is obtained at Derwent Bridge. (OS Ref 032512)

Roadside parking either side of the bridge is probably most expedient, as use of the private road and car park close to the reservoir usually raises an objection. There is a sheep fence directly below the bridge, so put your boats in on the left bank below the bridge.

An alternative access point is Eddy's Bridge, just 1km downstream on the road to Muggleswick.

At 1.5km a straight-forward gauging with a 1 metre sloping drop is easily shot.

Initially, the first few kilometres are rather dull, but after the river enters a pretty, wooded valley, the gradient gradually steepens providing a succession of pleasant, bouldery rapids.

At 10km the river passes beneath a road bridge. Sadly, from here the character of the river is largely determined by a series of weirs.

The first three, each about 1m in height, are easily shot.

The fourth at 13km is a little more tricky, having a steeply sloping drop of 1.5m with an irregular bouldery surface.

At 14km the river enters a gorgelet where there are a succession of small, rocky sills, which create a series of angled stoppers for about 50m. These are easily tackled by following the main flow of the current.

From here a short stretch of flat water leads to a 1.5m U shaped rocky fall in which water is channelled down onto a rather inconveniently placed

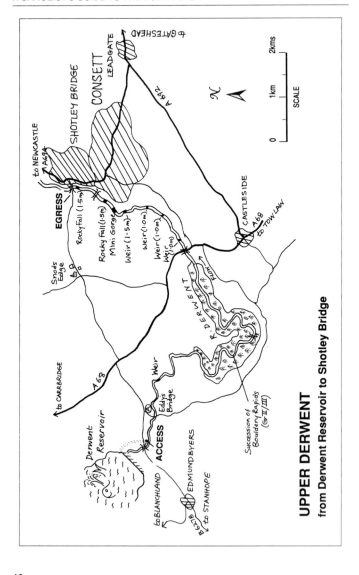

UPPER DERWENT
from Derwent Reservoir to Shotley Bridge

boulder in midstream. The slack water around the fall usually allows adequate inspection of the problem without getting out of your boat. The fall is probably best taken from the centre then (with luck) going to the left of the obstructing rock.

In another two hundred metres one comes to the final fall which lies just above the road bridge.

This modest little 1.5m vertical drop will remain in the authors' memories for some time to come. Being at the end of our paddle we were naturally rather tired, and in a hurry to finish. We felt that our cursory inspection from the bridge had provided all the requisite information, so taking the fall with less than our usual gusto (just in case there happened to be something unpleasant lurking beneath) the author found himself an unwilling guest of a small stopper.

Several rolls later he finally managed to extricate himself to egress below the road bridge on the left bank. This is not a difficult fall, so do have a go, but remember our experience that an inadequate inspection providing a false sense of security may sometimes be worse than no inspection at all.

Shotley Bridge to Rowlands Gill
Length 14.75kms   **Grade** I/II   **No Portages**

A relatively straight forward stretch of river with little to excite the experienced canoeist, although there are several weirs which add a little spice to the trip. The river flows at a gentle pace at first, through open countryside, and then a wooded riverside park. The volume of water has increased slightly, widening the river, so that overhanging branches and trees are easily avoided. Unfortunately much of this new water is courtesy of the Consett sewerage system, producing a characteristic odour that accompanies you for the rest of your journey.

Access is from the road bridge which takes the B6278 out of Shotley Bridge to Stanhope. The more adventurous will want to get in above the bridge to shoot the small falls. (see previous section) Otherwise get in below the bridge on the left bank. After a few hundred metres 2 large water pipes span the river at a height of 2 - 3 metres, which might prove a hazard in very high water.

From here the river proceeds at a fairly sedate pace, with the occasional shingle rapid. At 3kms there is a sewerage works on your right.

At 4km there is a two metre weir with a steep irregular bouldery slope, which might cause some trepidation. However, most plastic boatists should be able to bounce down without too much trouble, although fibre glass paddlers will probably find a portage less costly.

Below this the river passes beneath several roadbridges in quick succession.

At 11.5km another weir is encountered which has a 1.75m sloping drop which is most easily shot on the far left. After passing beneath a road bridge the river then loops around a disused mill on the right, before entering a wooded gorge which takes you down to Rowlands Gill.

After several kilometres the end of your journey is marked by an old disused railway viaduct which crosses the river where a footpath leads up to a riverside park on the left bank. (OS Ref 167581)

Rowlands Gill to Confluence with the River Tyne
Length 9kms   **Grade** I/II   **Recommended Portage** Weir   OS Ref 204627

There can be few reasons for anybody wishing to contemplate paddling this lower section of the river, the last few kilometres of which make grim paddling as you journey through an industrial wasteland on a tide of slowly moving effluent. However, the area is rapidly being transformed as it is close to the site of the Newcastle in Bloom Exhibition opened in 1990.

The first part of the journey starts off promisingly enough, in fact after passing through Rowland Gill you don't see another house for several kilometres, which is quite remarkable considering how close you are to the heart of industrial Tyneside.

The river itself has little to interest the average paddler, being mostly Grade I/II water with several rather unsatisfactory weirs.

Access is achieved by taking the Burnopfield road out of Rowlands Gill, the B6314, turning right just before the road bridge, (Stanley Road). There is a riverside park, just 100m further up on the left hand side. (OS Ref 167581)

After getting in below the disused viaduct the river passes beneath a road bridge with a small weir directly below it.

In several kilometres the ruins of Gibside are seen on the right bank.

The river now slows through an unspoilt woodland park for 2 to 3kms, before civilisation catches up with you at 3km with the appearance of a large coal tip on your right which is shortly followed by a small weir with a 0.5m drop.

This has quite a strong towback so it is most easily shot at the extremities where there is less current.

Several lattice girder bridges are now passed before Winlaton village is seen on the left.

A short stretch of flat water indicates an approaching weir. This is a large affair with a 2.25 drop which has a very long, gentle slope culminating in a 0.75m vertical drop.

Inspection is advised as the great width of the weir means there is little flow at any one particular point so that one usually gets grounded just before the final vertical drop, producing a less than controlled plunge into the small stopper of circulating effluent below.

A few more roadbridges later the river widens out into a small basin, the exit of which is guarded by a rather unpleasant weir, with a 1.75m vertical drop, producing a powerful holding stopper. This should be portaged by most people, although the fish ladder on the far right may offer a suitable route for enthusiasts at low water levels.

Below the weir the river is tidal with the banks becoming covered in a greyish sticky estuary slime. The air now becomes filled with the briny smell of rotting seaweed and fish.

Surrounded by this urban and industrial decay the paddler will soon feel this is no place for the white water canoeist who belongs amongst the sparkling waters of the upper river valleys with its clean air and nothing but rolling pastureland to please the eye. So quickly paddle down the remaining 0.5km to egress on the left bank just before the river goes beneath several railway bridges to meet the Tyne.

River Derwent - summary
Derwent Reservoir to Shotley Bridge
Length 4.5kms   Grade II/III   No Portages

Kms		
0	**Access**	Derwent Bridge. (Outflow Derwent Reservoir) OS Ref 032512
		Downstream left bank. NB. Sheep fence beneath bridge.
1		Stone Road bridge.
1.5		**Gauging Weir.** 1m sloping drop, take centre shoot.
5		Footbridge.
10		Road bridge.
11		**3 Weirs** over next km. Each 1m. Sloping drop.
		Easily shot.
13		**Weir** 1.5m steeply sloping drop.
		Irregular surface of stones set in concrete.
13.25		Footbridge.
14		**Small gorge.** Series of rocky sills for 50m.
		200m. **Rocky Fall.** 1.5m drop. Obstructed in centre by rock.
		Inspection advised. Shoot centre. Then left.
14.5		**Rocky Fall.** 1.5m vertical drop.
		Inspection advised. Shoot centre or left.
50m	**Egress**	Road bridge. Left bank downstream. (OS Ref 091528)

Shotley Bridge to Rowland Gill
Length 14.75kms   Grade I/II   Optional Portage Weir OS Ref 101555

Kms		
0	**Access**	Road bridge. OS Ref 091528
		Upstream right bank. If you wish to shoot falls.
		Otherwise downstream. Left.
.250m		2 water pipes span river.

		Might cause problem in high spate.
1		Water pipe but has 4m clearance.
3		Sewerage works. Right.
3.25		Water pipe and accompanying footbridge.
4		**Weir.** Optional Portage. 2m Steep irregular sloping drop. Inspect. Fibre glass boats may need to portage.
4.25		2 Roadbridges.
7		Footbridge.
7.75		Road bridge. Blackhall Mill Village. Left.
11		Road bridge. 100m below disused stone road bridge.
11.5		**Weir.** 1.75m. steeply sloping weir. Best shot on the left.
11.75		Road bridge and mill. Right.
14.5		Disused Railway viaduct.
14.75	**Egress**	Road bridge. Left Bank. Small weir immediately beneath bridge.

Rowlands Gill to Confluence with Tyne

Length 9kms   Grade I/II   Recommended Portage Weir 204627 (not on OS Map)

Kms		
0	**Access**	Railway viaduct. Downstream. Left bank.
0.25		Road bridge. **Small weir** beneath. 0.5m sloping drop.
3		Disused railway viaduct.
4		Coal Tip. Right. **Weir.** 0.75m. Vertical drop. Best shot either side.
4.5		Lattice Girder Bridge.
4.75		Lattice Girder Bridge - Footbridge.
6		Winlaton Village. Left. Dismantled Coke Works. **Weir.** 2.25m. Very long sloping drop leading to final vertical drop of 0.75m. Inspect.
7-7.5		Succession of roadbridges. River opens into small basin.
8		**Weir.** Recommended **Portage** (OS Ref 204628) 1.75 vertical drop. Strong Towback.
9	**Egress**	Railway bridge. Derwent Haugh. Joins River Tyne.

Devil's Water

Access	Road bridge. OS Ref 944581 or Peth Foot.
Egress	Dilston road bridge. A695. OS Ref 975636
Length	9.5km
Grade	III
No Portages	
OS Map	Hexham & Haltwhistle No 87

Introduction

This interesting little bywater is more often talked about than paddled, not so much because of any horrendous rapids or exciting paddling, but simply the combination of its intriguing name and the difficulty experienced in catching the river at a paddleable level.

This is because the peaty soil of Hexham Common acts as a giant sponge, soaking up water long after other spate rivers are overflowing their banks.

As a very rough guide, at least eight hours of heavy rainfall on wet soil are usually required to make the river navigable. Fortunately, the river level is easily inspected from the road bridge where the A695 crosses Devils Water midway between Corbridge and Hexham. This is en route to other rivers of the Tyne valley so that if Devil's Water is not canoeable it is often worth reinspecting the river on your way back from paddling further up the Tyne valley.

The river itself offers a pleasant and picturesque descent from Hexham Common down to where it meets the River Tyne just above Corbridge. Whilst the river has been canoed from as high up as Steel Crags Wood (OS Ref 915514) access is difficult and does not justify the awkward trek across Hexham Common. A better starting point lies about 5kms downstream 1km above Peth's Foot.

This section just above Peth Foot contains a few small falls and tight turns, but at this point Devil's Water is little more than a large stream and lacks the power to cause serious problems.

Below Peth Foot, most of the journey consists of being wafted down a leafy corridor with nothing but a short Grade III rapid, and a high weir to excite the competent paddler. As the floor of the Tyne valley is reached the river flattens out almost completely so that the last 2kms are hardly worth paddling.

Access

Rarely canoed. No recorded objections. No L.A.O.

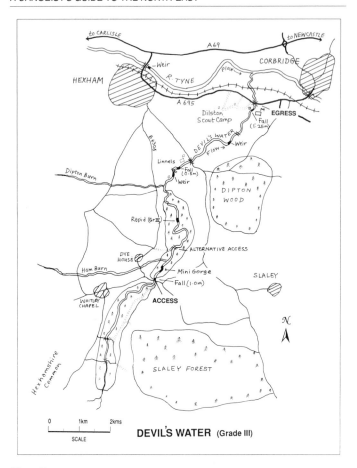

DEVIL'S WATER (Grade III)

River Course.

The traditional access point is at Peth Foot, where a small tarmac road winds down to within a few feet of the waters' edge. Here the river is crossed by a footbridge and the river is considerably swollen by the confluence with the Ham Burn. However, in high water it is worth going a further 1km upstream to where a small road bridge crosses Devil's Water. (OS Ref 944581) Before getting in it is advisable to look at the small fall immediately below the bridge.

A track provides access just upstream of the bridge on the right bank. The small one metre drop below the bridge is easily shot on the right.

After 200m the sides of the river begin to steepen and converge.

A small sloping drop just before a right hand bend introduces you to a gorgelet about 100m in length, which has several rocky steps before the river opens out again.

In 1km the confluence with the Ham Burn and an iron footbridge shows that Peth Foot has been reached.

From here a series of shingle rapids take you on a pleasant woodland journey for several kilometres before the river is suddenly seen to drop away.

Here the river loses about 2m in height over the next 40m in a long sloping drop, this is the only significant rapid of the trip. It is relatively rock free and so can be shot in most places. (Grade III)

In about 2km a house on the left is soon followed by a straightforward weir with a 1.25m drop, beyond this lies another footbridge and a sharp left hand bend which has several small rocky steps, usually taken just right of centre.

The large house on the left and road bridge shows the Linnels has been reached.

From here there is a fairly long stretch of easy paddling through open countryside, with the occasional patch of coniferous woodland until Dilston scout camp is seen on your left. This is heralded by a short stretch of flat water leading up to a large weir with a 2.2m near vertical drop in a series of small steps.

This little gem is worth inspecting for trees and other objects tend to collect in the otherwise deep plunge pool. However, it is best to avoid the extreme edges where the plunge pool is shallower. This weir should be portaged in full spate when a powerful stopper forms.

In the summer months you can usually be relied upon to get an audience of eager young scouts to provide spiritual encouragement, if the mind is willing but the flesh weak.

You are now nearing your journey's end, and after passing beneath a footbridge there is a small, rocky fall on a left hand bend, which is taken on the right. This fall is best given a brief inspection when doing the ferry before you start as it is easily seen from the road bridge which is 100m further on and marks the point of egress. This is where A695 crosses Devil's Water. OS Ref 975637. Below the road bridge the river flattens out as it crosses the Tyne valley to its confluence just above Corbridge.

Devil's Water - summary
Length 9.5km   Grade III   No Portages

Kms

0	**Access**	Bridge. Upstream right Bank. OS Ref 944581
		Small Fall immediately below 1m vertical drop.
		Shoot right

Kms

200m		**Sloping drop.** 1m. shoot centre. This leads to a narrow **twisting gulley** for 75m.
1		Confluence with Ham burn.
		Peth Foot alternative **Access** point. OS Ref 948589
		Footbridge.
3		**Rapid** Grade III Long sloping drop over 40m.
		Easily shot most places.
5		Confluence Dipton Burn.
5.5		**Weir** 1.25m sloping drop.
		Footbridge.
		50m below sharp left bend with small fall
		0.5m drop in two steps.
5.75		Road bridge.
8		**Weir** 2.2m vertical drop. Inspection advised.
		Low water. Shoot centre.
8.25		Footbridge. Dilston scout camp. Left.
9		Small **fall** on left bend. 1.25m drop. In two steps.
		Shoot centre right.
9.5	**Egress**	Road bridge A695. Egress upstream. Left bank. OS Ref 975636
10		Railway bridge.
10.5		Confluence with River Tyne.

Ettrick Water

Access	Road bridge to Ettrick Hawes Hotel. OS Ref 377233 (Off the B7009)
Egress	Ettrickbridge OS Ref 390243 (or Selkirk Road bridge)
Length	2kms (13kms)
Grade	III
No Portages	
OS Map	Peebles & Galashiels. Sheet 73

In spate conditions this small Border river offers an exciting but rather short paddle on the 2kms of water just above the village of Ettrickbridge.

Sadly, the rest of the river is rather a disappointment.

The topmost section above Ettrick Hawes Hotel is not worth attempting as the river is too small, with nothing more threatening than the occasional gravel bed.

54

Below Ettrickbridge the river is mostly Grade I - II with one straightforward weir.

Just above Selkirk the Jarrow adds a large volume of water before the Ettrick joins the Tweed the other side of town.

As this is only a short paddle this trip is best combined with other white water rivers in the area, such as the Border Esk.

An alternative in high water is to paddle the bottom few kilometres of the Jarrow which provides a fast, bouncy ride.

Access
Although the river is full of large, tasty Tweed salmon, the river is rarely canoed so that few problems arise. There is no L.A.O.

River Course
The access point is reached by following the B7009 out of Selkirk.

After about 12km the village of Ettrickbridge is reached which is the Egress point.

Two kilometres beyond the village there is a small road bridge off to the left which is sign posted to the Ettrick Hawes Hotel. This can be seen lying just across the river.

Get in just upstream of the bridge on the left bank.

Here easy water takes you round a loop in the river before the valley sides start to steepen and narrow in a rather ominous fashion.

A few hundred metres further on there is an obvious fall on a right hand bend. Most will wish to inspect this modest little 1.25m rocky fall.

A nice pool below tends to catch and recirculate canoeists and their debris.

An easier stretch now follows, before the rapids begin again. All straight forward stuff, with bouncy turbulent waves whisking you steadily downstream, with the occasional rock dodge to test your steering.

As Ettrickbridge is approached, take a right channel around a small island which will deliver you safely into a large frothing eddy.

Egress on the right bank below the bridge.

Some paddlers may wish to continue on to Selkirk, which lies about 11km downstream.

Ettrick Water - summary
Length 2kms   Grade III   No Portages

Kms		
0	**Access**	Road bridge (to Ettrick Hawes Hotel) off B7009. OS Ref 377233
0.5		**Rocky fall** 1.25m into loup pool. Intermittent turbulent **rapids** (Grade III) down to next road bridge.
2	**Egress**	Ettrickbridge. OS Ref 390243

Kms		
5.5		Road bridge.
8.5		Road bridge.
10.5		Yarrow Water joins left.
11		**Weir** 1.75m sloping drop.
13	**Egress**	Selkirk Road bridge. OS Ref 463286
19		Confluence with Tweed.

River Greta

Access	Bowes Road bridge on Gilmonby Road (OS Ref 995133)
Egress	Confluence with Tees (OS Ref 085144)
Length	15km
Grade	IV
No Portages	
OS Map	Barnard Castle & Richmond. No 92.
Local Access Officer	(For River Tees)
	Len Smith,
	44 The Bank,
	Barnard Castle,
	Co Durham. Tel: 0833 37829

(For Map see River Tees, Barnard Castle to Whorlton Page 75)

Introduction

This is one of the most interesting white water rivers in the North-East. It can be warmly recommended to any white water paddler of average competence. Why this river is so rarely paddled remains a complete mystery for there are few rivers in the area with such a sustained section of exciting white water going on for literally mile after mile. Anybody who still requires adventure after paddling this river deserves to be blindfolded and thrown off High Force backwards.

The river itself is very similar in character to the River Allan, although slightly smaller. It, therefore, needs to be paddled in spate conditions, the higher the better.

There are in fact, surprisingly few difficult sections, although there are two rather technical falls. The easier one lies just at the top of the gorge section, the other occurs right at the end just before the confluence with the Tees. (About 5km below Barnard Castle.)

Dodging rocks and trees on the Greta

Most problems on this river tend to be caused by fallen trees, of which there are always a considerable number. This is said with some feeling, having been swept into some particularly compromising positions by reclining trees lurking at the bottom of various rapids. Trees lying below white water are potentially much trickier than those at the top. Initially, they may command less attention as one's mind is naturally focused on the hazards immediately ahead, but by the time you reach the bottom it is usually too late to take evasive action, so that there is little else to do but give a desperate shriek as one becomes hopelessly enmeshed in the riverside vegetation.

Access
As the river is rarely paddled there are few access problems. Care should be taken at the point of egress although this is a public footpath. There is a convenient map on Mortham Towers Bridge showing the footpath's precise route. Please resist the temptation to park cars on the private road to the Rokeby estate. It's only a short walk up to the main road. Further advice may be had from the Tees L.A.O. Len Smith.

River Course
Access to the Greta is obtained by following the Gilmonby road out of the village of Bowes. After 0.5km there is a small road bridge over the river. (OS Ref 995133) Put in upstream of this bridge on the left bank.

A small fall with a 0.5m vertical drop immediately below the bridge will help

57

to remove the dust from the eyes, and set you on your way.

The river then winds down through pastureland at a gentle but sustained gradient, with shingle rapids and the occasional larger rock which creates a little interest.

At 5km a concrete gauging weir with a 1.5m sloping drop will help to concentrate the mind. Although it can probably be shot in most places, the easiest route is to the far left.

There is a small cluster of rocks obstructing part of the right channel, which is, therefore, best avoided. Immediately below the weir lie several small steps in the bedrock easily tackled by following the main flow of the current to the right.

In a few hundred metres a road bridge is reached, which provides a suitable access point for those who only wish to do the gorge section. (OS Ref 035123)

Below the bridge, the character of the river begins to change as the gradient steepens and larger rocks begin to obstruct the river course.

Bare faced rocks splashed with lichens and mosses begin to rise up on either side, as the gorge section begins. This is the point of no return. 7km of turbulent rapids, fallen trees and woodland lie between you and civilisation - what a luxury!

Just before the river narrows there is a small 1.0m rocky fall which really marks the start of the gorge. One hundred metres below this there is a rather awkward 1.5m drop, where the river is funnelled over a rocky chute onto an eccentrically placed rock. This is shot just left of centre.

From here a long series of turbulent rapids, none of which are above Grade III, take you steadily through a pleasant deciduous forest, free from human habitation except at 7km where there is a row of stone cottages just below an iron footbridge.

At 13kms Greta Bridge comes into view with the Morritt Arms Hotel high up on the right bank.

Just before the bridge a gentle slope in the bedrock produces several small but very affectionate stoppers which are easily bypassed on the left.

Shortly after this you pass beneath a rather less attractive concrete road bridge of the A66T. This marks the end of the main gorge; and the paddler has temporary respite from his adventures as the river takes a short rest, passing through flat pastureland.

As the river enters the Rokeby Estate it passes beneath a footbridge, where the gradient begins to steepen again. A stone walled embankment joins the left hand river bank as the river loops around Rokeby Hall, visible high on that side. After about 1km keep your eyes peeled for a stone road bridge and gatehouse, which marks the end of your journey and the most difficult fall on the Greta (Grade IV).

There is an easy break out on the right bank just above the fall, but the steep sided gorge makes viewing difficult. Despite this inspection is strongly recommended.

Water is channelled over a 1 metre rocky fall into a small pool, the exit of which is partially obstructed by a large rock.

In high water take the far left route when you can squeeze between the obstructing rock and the left bank. In very high spate these features are washed out.

Below this there is a small stopper beneath Mortham Towers Bridge, which leads on to a cluster of large rocks scattered across the river where it joins the Tees.

Egress right bank at the confluence where a public footpath takes you back up to the main road.

Unfortunately, Mortham Towers Bridge is on a private road so that vehicular access may be difficult.

An alternative is to continue down the Tees to Wharlton Falls.

River Greta - summary

Length 15km   Grade IV   No Portages

Kms		
0	**Access**	Bowes Bridge (OS Ref 995133) Upstream left bank
		50m Rocky fall. 0.5m vertical drop.
5		**Gauging Weir.** 1.5m sloping drop with final small vertical fall.
		Shoot left. Avoid right channel which has a small cluster of rocks at the bottom. Immediately below several small steps in the bedrock create a rocky fall. 0.75m drop. Follow main flow of current to right.
5.1	**Access**	Arched stone Road bridge. OS Ref 035123
		(Alternative access point)
5.5		**Rocky fall** 1.0m drop.
		River enters wooded gorge.
		Turbulent **rocky rapids for next 7km.**
		100m downstream water funnelled over **rocky chute.** 1.5m drop with eccentrically placed rock below. Shoot centre left.
7		Iron Footbridge. Stone Cottages. Left.
13		Arched Stone Road bridge. Morritt Arms Hotel. Right
		(Greta Bridge) Gorge Ends.
13.5		Concrete Bridge. A66T
13.75		Footbridge. Gorge Restarts. Rokeby Hall visible. Left.
14.5		Difficult **Rocky fall. Grade IV.** Best inspected. 1.5m drop onto centrally placed rock below. In high water shoot down far left.
		Stoppers below bridge lead to a large cluster of scattered rocks where Greta joins River Tees.
		25m. Mortham Towers Bridge.
15	**Egress**	Right bank of River Tees.
		Walk back up to Mortham Towers Bridge. OS Ref 085144

Jed Water

Access	Chesters Road bridge. OS Ref 628096 and Camptown OS Ref 679136
Egress	A698 Road bridge. OS Ref 661241
Length	23km (14km)
	Grade II. (Grade II/III rapid near Mossburnford)
No Portages	
OS Maps	Kelso Area. 74. and Cheviots. 80.

Introduction

This small border river flows almost due North from the Cheviots down through Jedburgh to join the Teviot as it makes its way to join the Tweed.

In high water the Jed offers a pleasant fast run, but there are a few surprises and no major rapids.

One of the most distinctive features of the paddle is that it has become little more than a graveyard for dead and dying trees, as the magnificent elm tree forest that once lined the river banks around Ferniehurst Castle has succumbed to the ubiquitous *Ceratocystis ulmi* with no tree escaping untouched! At several points along the river portages may have to be undertaken due to fallen trees.

Access

Rarely canoed. No recorded objections. No L.A.O.

River Course

Few people will wish to get in as high up as the Chesters Road bridge (OS Ref 628096) as the river is rather dull at this point although there is a small fall after 3.5km. The journey is also frequently punctuated by a series of exceptionally sensible cattle fences which consist of metal chains or wire thread suspended from a cross wire. These are easily brushed aside representing no hazard to canoeists. Other landowners please note! However, Brownie points have to be deducted for the hideous way old cars have been driven into the river along the major bends to prevent soil erosion. At times you feel as though the river has just taken a quick detour through a breakers' yard.

Below Camptown, easy rapids speed you uneventfully downstream accompanied on either side by the dead and decaying forest of elm trees.

Just below the caravan park at 13km a brief bouldery rapid offers some interest. Here the river is joined by a cliff of red shale, first on the right and then on the left, shadowing the river for a kilometre or so. Soon Ferniehurst Castle may just be seen peeping out from between the trees high on the right bank.

Once the home of the Kers, it is now used as a Youth Hostel. In the summer months it is open to the public.

Several roadbridges are then passed before the outskirts of Jedburgh are reached.

A brief stretch of flat water leads up to an easy weir with a 1.75m sloping drop.

The ruined Abbey is easily seen on the left. The original Priory was built in the 12th Century and was destroyed on a whim of Henry VIII, although it was subsequently rebuilt and was in use until 1873.

The river then winds its way through the town centre, passing beneath four roadbridges before another weir is encountered, again an easy 1.75m sloping drop.

As the houses thin an industrial estate and Jed Forest RFC grounds briefly make an appearance, before open country is reached again.

The finishing point is the A698 road bridge, which has convenient roadside parking in the form of a small spur of tarmac off the main road. Egress below the bridge on the right bank.

Jed Water - summary

Length 23km   Grade II (Grade II/III Rapid Nr Mossburnford)   No Portages

Kms		
0	**Access**	Chesters Road bridge OS Ref 628096
3.5		**Rocky Fall.** 0.5m
8		(approx.) Fallen Trees and debris
9.5		**Rocky Fall.** 0.75 vertical drop
	Access	100m Camptown Road bridge OS Ref 679136
13.5		Caravan Park. Left
		200m Bridge
14.5		**Grade II/III Rapid** for 50m
15.5		Bridge
16.5		Ferniehurst Castle just visible through woodland. Right bank.
17		Road bridge
18		Road bridge
18.75		Road bridge
		200m **Weir.** 1.75m sloping drop
19		Jedburgh Town centre. Abbey left.
		Roadbridges (2)
19.5		Roadbridges (2)
		100m **Weir.** 1.75m sloping drop.
20		Road bridge (2)
23	**Egress**	A698. Road bridge OS Ref 661240
23.5		Confluence with River Teviot

River Rede

Introduction

The Rede is the largest tributary of the North Tyne. Arising from the Cheviots near Carter's Bar on the Scottish border it soon flows into Catcleugh Reservoir which provides part of Newcastle's water supply.

It is canoeable from just below the reservoir all the way down to the confluence with the North Tyne, 41kms further on. The upper section is worth canoeing for the scenic paddle through Redesdale Forest, the lower section contains a few minor rapids which might be of interest to paddlers around the Kielder area. However, this river has few features that would make it worth travelling any distance for.

The middle section around Otterburn is rather flat and uninteresting so is best left alone.

Access

Most paddling is done on the lower section. No known access problems.

Local Access Officer:	Eddie Palmer,
	3 Middle Cowden,
	Birtley,
	Wark,
	Northumberland.
	NE48 3JB Tel: 0434 270318

Upper Redesdale   Catcleugh Reservoir to Otterburn
Length 23km   **Grade** I   **No Portages**

Access is provided by going along the A68/A696 from Otterburn until the entrance to Catcleugh Reservoir is reached, where there is a large layby. Although a public bridleway runs across the dam, access to the river is not permitted so that one has to scramble down a small embankment just below the layby. (OS Ref 753032)

The river is still quite small, so that it is best paddled after recent rainfall which is not difficult as this area is particularly wet even for the North East.

Soon some small trees partially obstruct the river course, but are easily brushed aside. A tiny weir is soon followed by a footbridge carrying a path from Byrness village seen on the left.

At 1.5km a ford is reached. This is probably a better access point for larger groups as there are car parking facilities on the waters' edge. This access point is found by taking a left turn immediately beyond the Esso Garage which lies on the A68 opposite the Byrness Hotel. A small track skirts around the village Chapel before going down to the river. (OS Ref 771022)

Get in just below the footbridge to avoid the cattle fence which lies beneath it. Another fence lies 300 metres downstream just above a small weir.

After a short while the river begins to enter Redesdale Forest with woodland first on one side then the other, finally reaching down to the waters edge on both sides, submerging the paddler in a sea of dense coniferous forest, the air rich with the muskiness of decaying pine and silence except for the faint babbling and gurgling of the river as it threads its way through the wood. Here at last one can forget the various pestilences that afflict mankind from the atomic bomb to Anglers and Income Tax Inspectors!

Every now and again the woodland canopy is broken by sunny glades richly carpeted with tall grass, begging the paddler to stop and savour the magic of Redesdale a while longer. Here and there the occasional fallen tree may necessitate a brief portage. Soon the trees begin to thin and are eventually left behind as Rochdale village becomes visible on the left bank. About 150 metres beyond, the river surges around a right hand bend forming a brief rapid. The river now begins to meander lazily down the valley, cutting deep into the pastureland creating high river banks edged with occasional trees. Long slow moving murky stretches of water are broken up by brief shingle rapids.

The main road accompanies the river all the way down to Otterburn on the left bank, with the A68 branching off just above the village to cross the river at 17kms.

At 21kms some slack water leads up to a weir with a double drop. The 1.25m sloping drop leads on to a brief rapid before the water resumes its sedentary pace.

A series of double bends in the river then seem determined to frustrate your attempts of ever reaching Otterburn Mill, but eventually this becomes visible on the left bank at 22kms and is soon followed by the humpbacked bridge carrying the B6320, which marks the point of egress.

Lower Redesdale   West Woodburn to Redesmouth
Length 11km   **Grade** II   **No Portages**

This part of the river offers a pleasant, if uninspiring trip, on Grade II water with little to test the skills of the experienced canoeist. It is best done after recent rainfall so that the gentle but fairly continuous gradient keeps you moving along at a respectable pace.

Unfortunately, the best rapids such as they are begin just above the most convenient point of access and below the usual point of egress.

To catch the top rapids just above West Woodburn, take the first right off the A68, at about 2km going north out of the village. It is a narrow tarmac road which leads down to a small humpbacked bridge. (OS Ref 901878)

There is a small 0.5m fall opposite a clump of Scots pine about 200 metres upstream of the bridge which some people might like to shoot. Below the bridge lies a straight-forward Grade II rapid. At 2kms West Woodburn village and road bridge is reached. The river winds peacefully along the valley with occasional shingle rapids to liven up the journey. At 9kms a small weir with a 0.75m vertical drop is reached just above a humpbacked bridge, most easily shot in the centre. A few kilometres further on Redesmouth Bridge is reached. Egress on the left bank just above the bridge. (OS Ref 864824) The village itself is hidden by trees high on the left bank, and is difficult to see from the river. Immediately below the bridge some minor rapids can be seen either side of an island, followed by a Grade II rapid down to the confluence with the North Tyne. Those enthusiasts who are tempted to paddle down beyond this point will probably have to get out at Wark a further 10kms down stream on the North Tyne, but nevertheless quite an interesting paddle. (See section on North Tyne.)

River Rede - summary

Upper Redesdale   Catcleugh to Otterburn
Length 23km   Grade I   No Portages

Kms		
0	**Access**	Layby on A68 just before Catcleugh Reservoir. (OS Ref 753032)
1		Footbridge. Byrness village seen left.
1.5	**Access**	Ford with footbridge beyond cattle fences beneath bridge at 300m.
2		Small **Weir.** 0.35m vertical drop.
3-6		River enters Redesdale Forest.
7		Rochester village left.
		150m Brief **Rapid** on right bend.
17		A68 Road bridge.
21		**Weir.** 1.25m sloping drop with minor Rapid below.
		Otterburn village left bank.
23	**Egress**	Road bridge. (OS Ref 888927)

Lower Redesdale   West Woodburn to Redesmouth
Length 12.5km   Grade II   No Portages

Kms		
0	**Access**	2kms above West Woodburn. (OS Ref 900877)
		Take A68 North out of Village. Take first right turn at 2kms. follow small tarmac road to river.
		Get in above/below.
		Rocky Fall. 0.5m drop.

Canadians on the upper South Tyne. Photo: Rob Egelstaff

Nick Doll shoots Rainby Force on the Swale

Shooting Wain Wath Force on the Swale

Kms

		200m Humpbacked road bridge.
		Grade II **Rapids** for 100 metres.
2		West Woodburn.
9		**Weir.** 0.75m Vertical drop.
		50m downstream road bridge shoot centre.
11	**Egress**	Just above Redesmouth Bridge. Left bank.
		(OS Ref 864824)
		200m downstream Grade II Rapid around island.
12		Shingle Rapid. Grade II.
12.5		Confluence North Tyne.

$River Tees$

Introduction

The river Tees arises in the Northern Pennines, draining an area on the eastern side of Crossfell before flowing into Cowgreen Reservoir.

From here the river spills over a dolerite outcrop forming a spectacular one hundred foot cataract known as Cauldron Snout. (see addendum p.136)

Whilst this is well worth a view this is not a viable canoeing proposition, although many may contemplate the possibility from the safety of their cars.

Five kilometres or so of easy Grade II water then brings you down to High Force.

This is another mass of dolerite which produces a waterfall of similar magnitude and beauty.

From High Force plunge pool down to Darlington, the Tees offers 50km of some of the best canoeing in the area.

Below Darlington the river loses its vigour as it changes course, flowing north eastwards. The river still offers pleasant if rather unexciting paddling down as far as Yarm. Below here the river flows through industrial Teeside meeting the North Sea at Middlesbrough.

The most popular stretches for white water canoeists are from Eggleston Bridge to Cotherstone and Barnard Castle down to Wharlton Falls. However in high water the sections from High Force plunge pool down to Wynch Bridge and from Wharlton Falls down to Winston can also be recommended, the latter is a short trip not worth doing in itself, but can be incorporated into an extended paddle down from Barnard Castle (which includes the Abbey Rapids.)

For those in the area one must also mention the River Balder which joins the Tees at Cotherstone and the River Greta which meets the Tees just below

65

Barnard Castle. The latter has a 7km gorge offering some of the most exciting paddling in the area, both rivers require heavy rainfall to become canoeable.

The character of the River Tees is to a large extent determined by the Millstone Grit which forms a series of steps and slopes in the bedrock, which produces a series of excellent stoppers for which the Tees is famed. This also means there is quick run off after heavy rainfall.

The culture bugs amongst you will enjoy the historic buildings in the area, particularly recommended are Raby Castle and the famous Bowes Museum at Barnard Castle.

For those requiring sustenance after their exertions, the Priors Cafe supplies wholesome food. It is just beyond the stone market place in the centre of Barnard Castle on the right, just as the main street known as the 'Bank' starts to descend steeply towards the river. They produce an excellent treacle tart, as well as the usual fare of soups and quiches. Canoeists are always welcome, however wet you are. Just across the road a little further down the bank is the Four Seasons Outdoor Activity shop, who sell canoe equipment. Unfortunately, they're not open on Sundays. The owners Russell and Len Smith have the right priorities, they're too busy canoeing!

Access

Because the Tees is heavily used by canoeists the access problem is particularly critical. The local access officer has put a lot of work into providing access agreements so that all paddlers should contact him before canoeing.

Due to problems of parking and access on Eggleston Bridge, paddlers wishing to canoe the 'racing stretch' down to Cotherstone are advised to start at Middleton.

Local Access Officer	Mr Len Smith,
	44, The Bank,
	Barnard Castle,
	Co. Durham.
	Tel. 0833 37829

High Force Plunge Pool to Wynch Bridge

Access	High Force Plunge Pool OS Ref 880284
Egress	Wynch Bridge OS Ref 904279
Length	3.5kms
Grade	I
No Portages	
OS Map	Barnard Castle and Richmond. Sheet 92

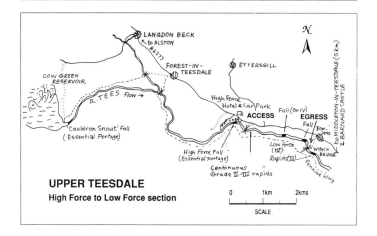

UPPER TEESDALE

High Force to Low Force section

This is a short, but exciting paddle, best suited to those with some white water experience. It must be paddled in high water conditions, otherwise the relatively wide river with numerous rocky reefs simply produces an obstacle course which is no fun at all. It is far better to save this stretch until the right conditions prevail, rather than be disappointed by doing it when it is too low. However, Low Force is often safer and easier in low water, so that it is often worthwhile just shooting this before going on to one of the gorge sections further down the Tees, which offer better paddling under average conditions.

No part of the Tees is good in low water!

For those who are not local, please do remember to get in below High Force and not above it! Whilst the drop of over one hundred feet does have a generous sized plunge pool, the fall drops in several steps, which probably accounts for the fatalities each year, when tourists inadvertently peer too far over the edge and then slip! The survival rate for going over High Force currently runs at about 30%, which are not favourable odds, even for the wildest of wild water paddlers.

To our knowledge High Force has not been canoed at the time of writing, although there are always plans and rumours to shoot it.

However, for us lesser mortals, after parking your car at High Force car park, make your way down the footpath to High Force, which actually takes you down to the plunge pool itself before winding uphill to overlook the falls.

Having got thoroughly wet from playing in the spray below High Force, minor rapids whisk you downstream underneath a small iron bridge which is an alternative access point, although roadside parking is somewhat limited.

At 1.75km a small rocky fall is encountered which can be taken in most places and provides a suitable warm up for what lies 200m ahead. This is a splendid rocky rapid, known locally as Salmon Leap Falls. It drops over three metres in several steps. (Grade IV)

There are a number of exciting alternatives. The easiest route is down the left channel where a foaming torrent of water with a succession of small stoppers rushes down a narrow cleft for about 30 metres into a plunge pool. You are advised to apply the Gofer technique of paddling by taking a deep breath and going for it.

In low water this narrow cleft has a 90° 'dog leg' turn at the bottom which makes it a definite portage. Under spate conditions this turn simply fills up with water forming a generous sized plunge pool.

After your triumphant descent of these rapids a succession of reefs and small falls will bring you to Low Force. (Grade IV)

This drops five metres in two steps. The top fall, although smaller in height (two metres) can cause more problems than the lower one. Most people take the first drop on the right, which is a near vertical chute with some small rocks at the bottom which tend to slow the boat down and turn it medially into the small but unfriendly stopper at the bottom. This has alas, caused the demise of several heroic boats that had survived the ravages of many an Alpine trip, but don't let this put you off as a confident paddle down the chute will (usually) get you through. On the left side is a simple two metre vertical drop into a deep plunge pool, which some may prefer to take.

The main drop is taken on the far right where there is an obvious chute where the three metre drop delivers you into a deep plunge pool. In low water it is quite safe, but it is always worth having a few rescue lines handy as the swirling eddy at the bottom does tend to bring you back under the fall for a second ducking. There is a lifebuoy with a long line of rope on the right bank next to Wynch Bridge 100m downstream, but please replace it - we often need to use it! To get over the fall successfully the most important thing is to get your line right, then sprint over it to clear yourself of the small turbulent area at the bottom.

In high water the more adventurous should consider the left hand channel which looks considerably more perilous, but in spate conditions is often safer as it takes you past the main stopper.

It consists of a steep rocky chute which propels you into an enormous boil at the bottom, giving you the sensation of a megasized cold water jacuzzi. If you don't fancy this, the centre chute will usually get you past the stoppers unless the water is very high.

One hundred metres of slack water will take you down over a one metre rocky fall, which by now you hardly notice. This is usually taken on the left except in spate conditions, when a very frothy stopper is found here. The easiest route is then to the right of the island.

The river now enters a short, flat, narrow gorge passing beneath Wynch Bridge before opening out again into an excellent 200m stretch of Grade III rapids. These culminate in a small fall which has a 0.75m vertical drop best taken left of centre.

From here to Middleton the river is no more than Grade II, so that most paddlers will want to get out here walking 200m upstream to Wynch Bridge. (OS Ref 904279)

A public footpath leads from the bridge up to the main road at the village of Bowlees.

Wynch Bridge to Eggleston Bridge

Access	Wynch Bridge. OS Ref 904279
Egress	Eggleston Bridge. OS Ref 996233
Length	14kms
Grade	II (Grade III Wynch Bridge Rapids)
No Portages	
OS Map	Barnard Castle and Richmond. Sheet 92.

This is a pleasant touring section of the Tees, but it is not suitable for white water paddlers as the only rapids of any significance occur right at the top with a long arduous paddle down to Eggleston Bridge, with little to entertain you apart from a couple of small weirs.

Access is achieved by driving up the Tees valley towards High Force, from Middleton in Teesdale to the village of Bowlees. On the far side of which is a clearly marked public footpath down to Wynch Bridge and Low Force. Go over the bridge, turning left where a footpath leads you to the top of Wynch Bridge rapids.

The more ambitious canoeists will not wish to miss an opportunity of shooting Low Force, (Grade IV see previous section) which lies 100m upstream.

It might be prudent for those getting onto the water below Wynch Bridge to inspect the bottom part of these otherwise straightforward Grade III rapids, which culminate in a small vertical drop of 0.75m after about 200 metres.

It is worth making the most of this part of the river as these are the only challenging rapids encountered above Eggleston Bridge.

After 2km a small broken weir, constructed of stone baskets, provides a welcome piece of white water.

The river winds down the valley at a gentle but steady gradient, with shallow shingle rapids occasionally broken by larger rocks.

The longer, slower moving sections provide you with an opportunity to appreciate one of the most attractive river valleys in the North. These upper sections are particularly tedious when the river is low, more energy being expended pushing off rocks than paddling.

In 4km a slightly larger concrete weir with a 0.75m drop is encountered. This leads to a gentle slope in the bedrock, producing a small play stopper at the bottom.

Several kilometres beyond is the bridge of Middleton in Teesdale. This may well be a suitable access/egress point for those wishing for a shorter paddle.

Two hundred metres below the bridge a tiny weir will not even cause our intrepid readers to blink.

About 1km below the bridge a left hand bend leads to a stretch of more pronounced broken water which flows on to some sloping bedrock which guides the flow around a sharp right bend with a small haystack cum stopper.

A large stopper can form here in high spate.

During the Slalom season competitions are also held here. Easy rapids now take you gently downstream until some high cliffs with receding ornate gardens lead up the hill to Eggleston Hall. The Hall can be seen high on the left bank and is the home of Lady Grey who is the major landowner here. This is soon followed by Eggleston Bridge at 14kms. Egress above the bridge on the right bank.

Eggleston Bridge to Barnard Castle

Access	Eggleston Bridge OS Ref 996233 (A recent access agreement recommends Middleton as a starting point for this stretch.)
Egress	Barnard Castle OS Ref 046167
Length	11kms
Grade	III
No Portages	
OS Map	Barnard Castle and Richmond. Sheet 92.

This is an excellent stretch of fast Grade III white water, which provides an interesting paddle suitable for all canoeists with some white water experience.

The top section from Eggleston Bridge down to Cotherstone is known colloquially as the 'racing stretch,' this being the usual venue for the white water races on the Tees.

Most of the rapids occur over the first four kilometres so that many people prefer to get out at Cotherston village to avoid the rather laborious paddle down to Barnard Castle. Since that makes it quite a short paddle (especially if you have come a long way) you can either do this stretch again or combine it with one of the other white water sections; - Low Force, Abbey Rapids, etc.

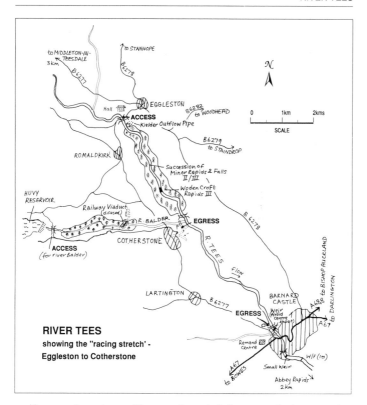

RIVER TEES
showing the "racing stretch" -
Eggleston to Cotherstone

However, in spate conditions one is carried along even the lower section fairly effortlessly, so that the bionic paddler can carry on through Barnard Castle to Abbey Rapids, then down to Whorlton and Winston, which are covered in the next section.

This part of the Tees valley is also extremely pretty as the river cuts down through a steep, heavily wooded valley towards Barnard Castle.

There are also the picturesque and unspoilt villages of Cotherstone and Romaldkirk each sporting several excellent pubs which might provide solace for those not on the river.

Access to the Tees is obtained by first parking your vehicle on the triangular patch of ground where the (B6281) road divides shortly after going over Eggleston Bridge. Descend to the river upstream of the bridge on the right bank.

Woden Croft on the Tees. Steve is seen cutting across the river to avoid the rock just visible on the left

A kilometre of fast Grade II water takes you to a large concrete structure on the left bank, where the outflow pipe from Kielder reservoir joins the River Tees.

Shortly after this the river narrows slightly with several small steps in the bedrock, producing a short turbulent rapid which usually terminates in a small stopper close to the right bank.

A brief stretch of slack water then leads to two small sloping steps in the bedrock each of which has a small stopper at the bottom, the second one being the larger. Under most conditions these are quite benign, being good fun to play in, but in high spate this spot becomes the home of two large holding stoppers. These are often quite difficult to see until it is too late to take evasive action. One moment the cheerful paddler is speeding on his merry way through large standing waves, blissfully unaware of his imminent obliteration from life on this planet; the next the unfortunate victim is suddenly confronted with a stopper across most of the river. There is usually a brief but unequal struggle as the canoeist is helplessly pulled back, back looped into the stopper and then ejected from his beloved canoe.

Large groups paddling in high water conditions should exercise caution at this point, as boats have been lost here although swimmers are usually ejected none the worse for their experience. This caveat does *only* apply at epic levels and should not put people off paddling this stretch in low to medium spate when it is possible to paddle straight through.

The river then sweeps around a left hand bend and down the first of the rocky falls which has a 0.75m sloping drop easily taken on the left.

A short stretch of slower water brings you to the top of 'Woden Croft.' This is a 75m long Grade III rapid, where the river narrows slightly, channelling water down a steep shingle rapid peppered with a few large rocks around a left hand bend.

Most problems arise at the bottom where two or three rocks obstruct the flow on the right side. Those new to the river should pre-inspect the rapid from the left bank.

In low water conditions, most paddlers go down these rapids starting just right of centre, then gradually across to the left to miss the rocks on the bottom right. (See photo)

Unfortunately, you can't start on the left side as the river is too shallow and rocky.

There is quite a strong current pushing you on to the outside of the bend towards the right (where you don't want to go!) so do make allowances for this drift.

In high water most of the rocks are covered so that any route is feasible.

Another 100m of slack water follows before the final fall, a one metre sloping drop best taken on the left.

The top and bottom falls on this stretch tend to be best in low water when the drop is most pronounced.

A succession of minor rapids take you down to a footbridge, at 4kms, which shows that Cotherstone has been reached.

For those getting out here, the egress point is 50 metres below the footbridge on the right bank, just where the River Balder joins the Tees. (This also becomes canoeable when in spate.)

A tarmac road leads up to join the main road, just opposite the Fox and Hounds Pub and next to a large monkey puzzle tree in the middle of Cotherstone. (OS Ref 014201)

These landmarks are worth noting as the road junction is rather unobtrusive, being flanked by two large stone houses.

After Cotherstone the river gradually loses its vigour, the fast shingle rapids giving way to longer stretches of deeper, slow moving water.

At about 8.5km a small step in the bedrock creates a 0.75m drop which should perk your spirits up a little, best taken on the right following the main flow of water.

There is some rotor as you go through the turbulence, water coming in from the left tending to rotate you anticlockwise, so that a support stroke is sometimes needed on the left.

A rather dull couple of kilometres follow which lead you past a ruined viaduct, before you turn a corner and Barnard Castle comes into view.

Egress right bank just beyond the footbridge and above the 2m weir.

(OS Ref 046167) This is immediately above the confluence of Deepdale Beck with Tees.

For those who are continuing downstream the weir can be shot on either side, but under **no** circumstances should the narrow centre section be attempted as there is always a very chewy stopper at the bottom.

In high water the extreme left usually provides a safe passage through the bottom stopper.

BARNARD CASTLE TO WHORLTON & WINSTON

Access	Barnard Castle	(OS Ref 048161)
Egress	Whorlton Falls	(OS Ref 106146)
	Winston Bridge	(OS Ref 143164)
Length	Whorlton 8kms	Winston 13kms
Grade	III (Abbey Rapids Grade III. High Water IV)	
No Portages		
OS Map	Barnard Castle and Richmond. Sheet 92.	

This is another fine stretch of the Tees which incorporates the famous 'Abbey Rapids' so that this part of the river is most suited to paddlers who know one end of their boat from the other. These rapids are now used extensively for slalom training. Contact Len Smith for details.

Although not as difficult as the top section of the Tees (High Force to Wynch Bridge) it is probably slightly trickier than the 'racing stretch' (Eggleston Bridge to Cotherstone) which lies just above Barnard Castle.

This difference is accentuated in high water when many of the rocky falls on the racing stretch become washed out (although some of the stoppers become quite impressive) whilst the Abbey Rapids tend to become progressively more difficult.

This is due to the funnelling effect created by a combination of the steepening gradient with a narrowing of the river as it thunders down into the gorge below. As you would no doubt imagine, in high spate this makes an ideal recipe for some impressive waterworks. An additional bonus is that whilst providing exciting paddling it is also reasonably safe as the descent into the gorge is clear of large rocks and ones terminal velocity at the bottom, whether swimming or paddling, is usually enough to speed you through any unfriendly eddies or stoppers. In fact, the experience of paddling the Abbey Rapids in high water is best likened to being flushed down a lavatory with a large cistern and small outflow pipe!

Whilst many people only paddle down to Whorlton Falls which is just 8km downstream, there is some excellent canoeing to be had, on the short stretch

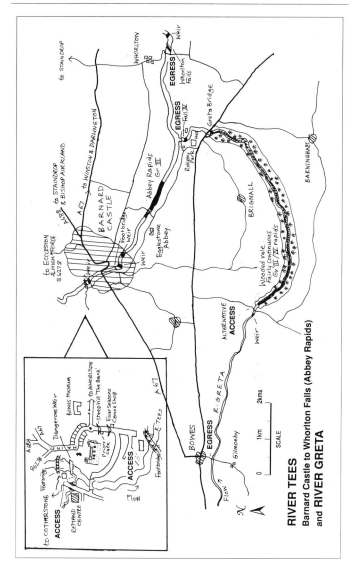

RIVER TEES

Barnard Castle to Whorlton Falls (Abbey Rapids)
and RIVER GRETA

from Whorlton Falls to Winston Bridge. Here the river descends in a series of sloping drops and rocky sills which whilst not worthwhile in low water, create a succession of large, exciting stoppers in high water.

Access to the river at Barnard Castle is obtained by going down the main high street past the stone market place and down the steep road known as 'The Bank'. Don't follow the main road around at the bottom, but continue straight on into a short cul de sac towards a green footbridge. One hundred metres before the end a right hand turning takes you into a small council estate. An offshoot of this road leads down to the river edge.

After getting in, 100m downstream you pass beneath a green footbridge which has a small broken weir immediately below.

A short stretch of flat water follows before a natural weir is reached at 0.5km.

There is a one metre vertical drop best taken just right of centre, where an obvious V shaped cut collects most of the current. There is a large rock immediately below the fall which sometimes causes problems. This is usually taken on the right. In very low water small volume boats sometimes become wedged beneath a rock on hitting the bottom as you go over the fall. If you do become stuck it's simplest just to get out and unwedge the boat; there's nothing particularly fearsome here.

After this a series of minor rapids lead down to a sluggish section of the river.

A rather foul smell at one kilometre indicates that Barnard Castle is adding its sewerage to the flow - a capsize here, especially in summer, usually involves sitting on the toilet for a couple of days!

Continuing on our merry way at two kilometres Eggleston Abbey becomes clearly visible on the right. The river can be seen to drop away in front of you and a bridge is just visible in the distance spanning the gorge. (This is not to be confused with Eggleston Bridge and village which is 12km upstream.)

One hundred metres upstream from the Abbey, Thorsgill Beck can be seen joining the Tees on the right after emerging from beneath a small stone bridge. This place is sometimes used as an alternative access point for those who just wish to paddle the Abbey Rapids.

Abbey Rapids are normally Grade III (but can be Grade IV in high water). Under 'average' conditions the technical grading is no higher than III because it is a straight run down with an easily recognisable course.

Even in spate when the water is fast and very turbulent, there are not usually holding stoppers, so that the worst you should expect is a prolonged swim. This is mentioned because in Geoff Woods' Yorkshire Guide, he grades these rapids as IV (although the old BCU Guide, which is usually over generous on the grading side gives them a III.)

The Abbey Rapids comprise of a 200m section of turbulent rapids which culminate in a rocky fall just upstream of the bridge. The water is channelled down two sloping drops approximately one metre in height into an area of

The standing waves at the bottom of Abbey Rapids, River Tees

relatively slack, deep water where swimmers and equipment can be rejoined.

The traditional route down the Abbey Rapids is to take the top section on the right, following the main flow of current over a series of rocky sills as the river progressively falls and becomes narrower.

Just above the first fall there are a number of suitable breakout points where inspection is advised to those unfamiliar with the river and in spate conditions.

In high water there is usually an impressive rolling stopper on the right (not holding) whilst the main flow of current on the left hand side sucks any flotsam (i.e. canoeists) into an enormous exploding haystack at the bottom, which is guaranteed to send you sky rocketing into orbit.

The river then becomes much deeper, entering a gorge below the road bridge. This lasts for about one kilometre.

About 200m into the gorge there is a brief rocky rapid followed in 100m by a final drop of one metre. This is easily negotiated just right of centre. It forms an excellent play stopper in low water, which is worth making the most of as the river calms down after emerging from the gorge. The fall easily becomes washed out in high water, becoming replaced by a series of standing waves.

At five kilometres the River Greta joins from the right. (Just in case you've missed it, an excellent Grade IV river well worth paddling.) Upstream from the mouth of the River Greta you can just see a small private road bridge going over the Greta, which has a public footpath leading up to the main road, which may make this a suitable egress point for those wishing to finish here, but most will want to continue further downstream.

A kilometre or so of flatter water follows, leading to a small island dividing up a shingle rapid. 0.5km beyond this two small sloping drops produce a splendid play stopper in spate conditions, but unfortunately they are not present in low water. If the stopper is a reasonable height, i.e. 0.5m high, don't be intimidated by it stretching most of the way across the river. It is quite easy to ferry glide from one side to the other. A good play here will help you to cope with the rather dull paddle for one or two kilometres until Whorlton road bridge is reached. In low water this is the best point to finish. But remember, if you get out here in spate conditions you'll be missing out on some excellent paddling. One hundred metres below the bridge lie Whorlton Falls, which are steeply angled across the flow of the river, having a 1.25m vertical drop. On the far right hand side there is also a rather unpleasant looking chute, cut in the bedrock, which can provide an alternative way down. In low water most people go over the falls on the right hand side where the drop is highest. In spate a powerful stopper forms here so that in these conditions the falls are most easily taken on the far left where the vertical drop is much smaller.

A short stretch of slack water follows before a 1.5m sloping drop in the bedrock forms a natural weir, with a succession of small stoppers immediately below it, leading to some faster turbulent water. Wycliffe village and Manor House can be seen on the right bank.

The river then splits around an island with a fairly innocuous looking stretch of fast water, but where the island ends several large stoppers form which can span most of the river breadth, and whilst these can be safely played in at low levels in spate conditions they have the capacity to backloop you into them.

Below this, further minor Grade II/III rapids lead down to several more stoppers which usually form on the left side.

From here the river calms down as it enters a wooded valley.

After about one kilometre a flat stretch of water leads up to another natural weir, with a 1.5m sloping drop which is easily shot in most places. Below this a short patch of confused water takes you to another longer stretch of flat water, which brings you to within sight of Winston Bridge.

From here the river can be seen to drop away in a series of rocky sills and turbulent rapids. Grade II/III. (IV in high spate.)

There are two main drops, each less than 0.5m in height, both easily taken by following the main flow of current. In high spate some of these sills generate strong undertows.

Egress right bank *150m upstream* of Winston road bridge. It is best to avoid being carried all the way down to the bridge as the bank is very steep on both sides.

From here the Tees has no more rapids of any interest, although several weirs near Darlington provide some sport. The river is regularly canoed as far as Yarm. Below this the river becomes too polluted and industrialised.

River Tees - summary
High Force Plunge Pool to Wynch Bridge
Length 3km   Grade IV   No Portages

Kms		
0	**Access**	High Force Plunge Pool. (OS Ref 880284)
1		Bridge. (alternative Access via farm track)
1.75		Small **Fall.** 1m Sloping drop.
2		**Salmon Leap Falls.** (2m) Take left channel (Grade IV)
2.75		**Low Force**. Grade IV
		Top Fall. 2m drop. Most routes feasible, but deceptive stopper. inspect
		Main Fall. 3m. Vertical drop. Shoot far right. (very high water, can go far left) Dangerous in flood.
		150m. **Small Fall.** Shoot left. 1m stepped drop.
		Very high water. Far right to avoid stopper.
3		Wynch Bridge. (OS Ref 904279) Egress point public footpath back to road at Bowlees.
3.25		**Grade III rapids** for 200m.
		Series of small ledges in bedrock.
		Culminate in small fall 0.75m. Shoot left.
3.5	**Egress**	Walk back upstream to Wynch Bridge.

Wynch Bridge to Eggleston Bridge
Length 14km   Grade II (Wynch Bridge Rapids Grade III)   No Portages

Kms		
0	**Access**	Wynch Bridge. (OS Ref 904279)
		250m. Grade III **rapids.** (Mentioned above) for 200m.
2		**Broken Weir.** Shoot centre.
4		**Weir.** 0.75m sloping drop.
6.5		Middleton Town and road bridge.
8		Minor Rapids. Slalom site.
14	**Egress**	Eggleston Bridge. Egress upstream. Right bank. (OS Ref 996233)

Eggleston Road Bridge to Barnard Castle
Length 11km   Grade III   No Portages

Kms		
0	**Access**	Eggleston Road bridge. (OS Ref 996233) upstream right bank.
0.5		Kielder outflow pipe left.
		Minor Rapids below.

0.75		Two **sloping drops** in Bedrock.
		Large stoppers form here in high water.
		150m. Shingle rapid on left bend leads down to;
1		**Rocky Fall.** 0.75m drop. Shoot left.
3		**Woden Croft.** Grade III. Steep shingle rapid on left bend. Inspect.
		(Caution rocks bottom right.)
		Shoot centre then *left* at bottom.
3.25		**Rocky Fall.** 1m. Sloping drop. Shoot left.
4		Footbridge.
		100m. River Balder joins right.
	Egress	Right Bank just beyond confluence.
		Tarmac road leads up to Cotherstone Village.
8.5		Small **Fall.** 0.75m. Shoot right.
9.5		Ruined Viaduct.
11		Footbridge above Weir.
	Egress	50m. Egress right Bank. (OS Ref 046167)
		100m. Deepdale Beck joins right.
		125m. **Weir.** 2m. Sloping drop.
		Dangerous central chute with chewy stopper.
		Shoot far left.

Barnard Castle to Whorlton and Winston

Length Wharlton 8km   Grade III (Abbey Rapids III. High Water IV)
No Portages   Winston 13km

Kms		
0	**Access**	Follow Main Street down hill into cul de sac. (OS Ref 048161)
		Turn right 100m before end.
		100m. Green Footbridge.
		Broken Weir immediately below.
0.5		1m vertical **Fall.**
		Shoot right following V shaped cut in Bedrock.
		Avoid rock immediately below chute.
2		Ruined Abbey seen on right.
		Thorsgill beck joins right.
		Abbey Rapids commence. Grade III. Inspection advised especially
		in high water.
		Series of rocky ledges. River narrows and falls for 150m.
		culminating in 2 stepped drop just above bridge. Shoot following
		main flow.
2.5		High Road Bridge.
		River passes into a **gorge**.
2.75		Rocky **fall.** 1m. Shoot centre right.

Kms		
3		Gorge ends.
5		River Greta joins right.
8	**Egress**	Road bridge. Whorlton Lido.
		75m. **Falls** below bridge. 1.25m. Vertical drop.
		Shoot right except in high water, when powerful stopper forms here.
8.25		**Natural Weir.** 1.5m. sloping drop.
		Wycliffe Village on right.
8.5		River splits around Island.
		Caution. Large stoppers form here in full spate.
9.5		**Natural Weir.** 1.5m sloping drop.
11.5		Series of **Rocky Sills** lead down to road bridge. *Caution* high spate.
12	**Egress**	Winston Road bridge. Egress 100m upstream right bank.
		Follow footpath up to bridge. (OS Ref 143164)

River Teviot

Introduction

At over 60km in length the Teviot is the Tweed's longest tributary, running just inside the Scottish border along the Northern flank of the Cheviots.

Arising at Branxholme just above Teviothead, it flows north eastwards through Hawick to join the Tweed at Kelso.

This river is probably best suited to touring paddlers as there are no major rapids. However, it is a respectable size and whilst the upper reaches are very disappointing, the river does pick up a little speed around Hawick where there are several broken weirs and a brief Grade II/III rapid at Trowknowes Mill.

As for the rest of the river, this is all very similar in character, with gentle broken water taking you through undulating pastureland with no major obstructions or falls to test your paddling skills. Touring paddlers will enjoy the lower sections which take you on a leisurely ride down to Kelso where it joins the Tweed.

Access

No known problems. The upper sections are rarely paddled. The minor rapids at the confluence near Kelso are used as a slalom site.

Branxholm Road bridge to Denholm

Length 13km   **Grade** II (Trowknowes Mill Rapid Grade II/III)   **No Portages**

Although this stretch is the best the Teviot has to offer, even the ark with all its animals aboard would face few problems here. Access is from Branxholm Bridge, which carries a side road off the A7 just outside Hawick. From here easy rapids take you down towards the town, first through a riverside park then beneath a footbridge which leads up to an area of flatwater above a rather curious weir with a 1.5m long sloping drop, the surface of which has a series of concrete blebs which can give you quite a bumpy ride on your way down.

A number of roadbridges are passed as the river goes through the town.

The large gasometer on your left lies close to a small broken weir which has small standing waves or a stopper. One hundred metres downstream a small weir creates a little entertainment.

The town soon recedes as cattle and sheep replace factories and houses.

At about two kilometres a small rocky fall comprises a brief Grade II/III rapid at Trowknowes Mill. Here the river narrows slightly as a road bridge passes overhead.

A long uneventful stretch then follows for about five kilometres before a small broken weir just above Denholm village is reached. This has a significant towback on the right, which can provide a last chance to get wet before egressing at Denholm road bridge. (OS Ref 568187)

River Teviot - summary

Kms		
0		Blackcleuch Bridge.
6		Road bridge.
17	**Access**	Branxholm Road bridge. (OS Ref 474127)
17.5		Borthwick Water joins. Left.
18		Road bridge.
20		Footbridge.
20.5		**Weir.** 1.5m. long sloping drop. Central Fish Ladder.
		3 Steps. Avoid far right. Rocks below Weir.
21		Road bridge. Hawick Town Centre. Slitring Water joins right.
21.5		**Broken Weir.** Gasometer seen left.
		100m small Weir below.
24.5		Trowknowes Mill. **Rocky Fall.** Grade II/III.
		River narrows.
24.75		Road bridge.
30		**Broken Weir.**
30.5	**Egress**	Road bridge. Denholm Village. Right. OS Ref 568187
38		(Old) Ancrum Road bridge. OS Ref 639238
39		**Weir.** 1m sloping drop.
		Monteviot House. Left.
39.5		Footbridge.
39.75		**Weir.** 1.5m sloping drop. Easiest far right.

Kms		
44		Jed water joins right.
46		Road bridge. Lattice Girder. Nisbet Village. Left.
51.5		Kalemouth. Wooden suspension road bridge.
		River Kale adds water. Right.
		200m Broken Weir. 0.5m drop.
55		Small **Weir.** Sun Laws Mill. Right.
56		Disused Railway Viaduct with footbridge crossing on the bulbous bases of the bridge stanchions.
		Roxburgh Village. Left.
57		Minor Rapid. (Grade II) Heiton Mill. Right.
60		Ruined Castle. Left.
61	**Egress**	Road bridge. Egress right bank. (Slalom Site) OS Ref 720336
61.25		Small **broken Weir.**
61.75		River joins Tweed in Kelso.

River Till

Introduction

The first part of this river has all the dynamism of a sea cucumber as it painfully snakes its way across North Northumberland, before eventually joining the Tweed just upstream of Norham only a few miles from Berwick-upon-Tweed.

The Breamish forms the first 30km or so of the river until Bewick Bridge is reached, when it becomes known as the Till. From here down to Etal the river is quite flat and lifeless. Narcolepsy is a real risk. Strong coffee and your Sony Walkman could be lifesavers.

However, below Etal the river shows some signs of life, with a series of rocky ledges and broken weirs to entertain you. This stretch provides a worthwhile and popular paddle for local canoeists seeking some easy rough water.

Access

Some friction at Heatherslaw Mill which is best avoided as an access point. Recent leasing of the fishing rights below Etal might produce objections if paddled during the fishing season. Avoid a conspicuous presence at Twizel Bridge which is a favourite spot for the landowner to confront paddlers.

Local Access Officer: Peter Clark,
Windy Gyle Outdoor Centre,
Belford,
Northumberland.
Tel: Belford 0668 213 289

Bewick Bridge to Etal
Length 47.5km   **Grade** 0 - I   **No Portages**

There can be few, if any, reasons for wanting to paddle this stretch of water unless you are writing a guide book, have a screw loose or have committed an unpardonable crime for which no punishment is too severe.

Heatherslaw Mill close to the end of the paddle is worth a visit, having a restored water driven corn mill which is open to the public during the summer months. There is also a broken weir which provides a short stretch of white water.

Etal to Twizel Bridge (Tilmouth)
Length 10km   Grade II (Twizel Mill Weirs Grade II/III)   **No Portages**

A more interesting section with easy paddling through pleasant countryside, and several weirs at the end to provide a little flourish. This is quite a popular paddle with local canoeists.

Convenient access is found by following the road through Etal village past the ruined castle to the ford. Get in just below the weir which has been blasted away in the centre and now provides a jet of fast water to practise your ferry gliding (and capsizing).

The old mill house by the ford is now used by local carpenters who produce some pine furniture made to order.

In a short while several rocky sills are encountered, otherwise the river proceeds at a gentle pace through quiet deciduous woodland.

In 10km there is a rather awkward weir with a 1.5m drop. This has a vertical plunge on the left, whilst a rocky scree forms a rather irregular sloping drop on the right. The smoothest descent is usually just right of centre.

A little way further downstream a broken weir with a central chute forms a good play stopper.

High on the left bank the imposing Tillmouth Park Hotel dominates the valley.

Soon a road bridge is encountered, with its disused forbear marking the point of egress. Most paddlers will want to continue 200 metres below the bridge to shoot another broken weir before climbing up the left bank.

Whilst Twizel Bridge might look a tranquil and peaceful spot, especially with its roadside parking at one end of the disused bridge, unfortunately the local landowner has a keen eye for suspicious looking vehicles with trailers. There is no easy alternative egress point, as continuing downstream past the railway viaduct, Tillmouth is reached where the Till joins the Tweed opposite a large island.

The next point of public access is six kilometres downstream at Norham, although a small, private road does lead close to the water edge near Twizel Castle.

River Till - summary
Bewick Bridge to Etal
Length 47.5km   Grade 0 - I   No Portages

Kms		
0	**Access**	Bewick Bridge. Downstream left bank. Cattle fence beneath bridge. (OS Ref 056225)
6		Newtown road bridge.
10.5		Lattice Girder road bridge.
11.5		Stone road bridge.
		Chatton village seen left.
14		Purple lattice girder road bridge!
		River becomes extremely sluggish.
18.5		Road bridge.
23		Stone road bridge.
26		Wooler Water joins left.
27		Doddington Bridge. Cracked left arch with supporting brace.
29		Small stone bridge.
32		River Glen joins left.
36.5		Lattice Girder Bridge.
42.5		Ford road bridge.
44		Heatherslaw Mill. Left. (a restored water driven corn mill)
		Broken Weir with minor rapid.
44.2		Road bridge.
47.5		Etal Castle visible right bank.
		Broken Weir with Ford below.
	Egress	Right bank. (OS Ref 926395)

Etal to Twizel Bridge (Tillmouth)
Length 10km   Grade II (Twizel Mill Weirs Grade II/III)   No Portages

Kms		
0	**Access**	Etal Ford. (Broken weir immediately upstream) OS Ref 925395.
		100m Footbridge.
0.5		**Broken Weir.**
1.5		Several **Rocky Ledges.** Highest 0.75m vertical drop.
7.5		Twizel Mill. Disused. Right.
		Weir. 1.75m. Vertical Drop. Inspect.
		Easiest sliding down rocky aggregates just right of centre.
		100m **Broken Weir.** Good play stopper below.
		Tillmouth Park Hotel visible high on left bank.
8.5		A695 Road bridge.
		100m Twizel Bridge. Disused.

Kms		
		200m **Broken Weir.**
	Egress	Below weir on left. (OS Ref 884434)
10		Viaduct. (disused)
10.5		Tillmouth. Confluence with River Tweed.

River Tweed

Introduction

Since the time when the Tweedsmuir Hills were first thrust upwards by volcanic activity, the effects of glaciation and weathering have been to erode the mountains to a fraction of their former size and to smooth out a path for the Tweed, leaving only the occasional hiccup from a minor rapid or man made weir.

The river is therefore, remarkably uniform in character, with a gentle but fairly continuous gradient and a relatively unobstructed shingle river bed making it ideal for touring paddlers, but rather a disappointment for white water canoeists.

Much of the Tweed is also well suited for use by open Canadians.

Arising at Tweedswell, just north of Moffat in the Tweedsmuir Hills, the river initially flows north eastwards to Peebles. Here it turns due east to flow through the border towns of Galashiels, Kelso and Coldstream, reaching the sea at Berwick-upon-Tweed.

It is about 160km in length and forms part of the border between England and Scotland from just below Kelso to near Berwick. Apart from the beautiful countryside and its famous salmon fishing, the river has much to offer the passing visitor in the form of its innumerable country houses dotted along the river valley, each sending a barrage of towers, turrets and chimneys into the heavens as testimony to the extravagance of its owners.

Sadly, most of the Tweed's tributaries are rather dull, but with two notable exceptions that are certainly worth trying. These are the Upper Whiteadder and the Ettrick Water, both of which have short, but exciting rapids associated with small falls. In addition the Till and Teviot offer scope for touring paddlers and provide some easy rough water paddling.

On the Tweed itself there are only two rapids of significance. The first of these is a small Grade III rocky fall lying close to the river's source at the village of Tweedsmuir. Unless the river is in spate there is usually insufficient water for it to be canoed. The second and rather better known rapids are those found at Makerstoun, between St Boswells and Kelso. These Grade III rapids probably offer white water canoeists the best chance of a decent paddle,

Lower Makerstoun Rapids on the Tweed

although there is a fairly arduous section on either side. There are also some Grade II/III rapids at Fairnilee which are suitable for introducing paddlers to easy white water.

Access
Despite its heavy use for salmon fishing there are good relations with local fishermen. This largely results from the use of informal access agreements, in particular trying to restrict paddling to Sundays when fishing in Scotland is banned.

Local Access Officer: Jim McPherson,
12 The Valley,
Selkirk.
Tel: 0750 20565

Fingland Bridge to Peebles
Length 37.5km   **Grade** I - II (Tweedsmuir Falls Grade III)   **No Portages**

This section is only canoeable after heavy rain!
   Whilst Fingland Bridge provides about the highest access point most people will find Tweedsmuir Bridge a better starting place. It also has a

convenient car park at the crossroads in the village centre.

First inspect the rapids which run beneath Tweedsmuir Bridge. They consist of a rocky fall in three steps, as the river progressively narrows to a strid beneath the bridge. The initial drop (1m) is usually taken by the centre chute, but watch out for the large boulder on the left with a slight overhang that does its best to push you in.

The only problem with such an exciting start is that the rest of the paddle will seem dull by comparison. After about 250 metres you soon pass a red sandstone church on the right where prayers can be offered for an exciting trip - but they're unlikely to be answered.

Most people will wish to egress around Drumelzier road bridge. In drier weather this road bridge makes a good starting point. For those continuing downstream, continuous gentle rapids take you on for about 10km before the valley sides narrow and steepen, with deciduous woodland rising up on either side. This is an attractive part of the river which should appeal to most touring paddlers.

The austere grey tower of Neidpath Castle stands out on the left bank, guarding the road through the valley.

A small weir is reached before the valley opens out again to reveal the border town of Peebles on the left.

Peebles to St Boswells
Length 57km   **Grade** I - II   **No Portages**

Easy water with no special features continue to take you downstream, but the surrounding hills are starting to mellow into undulating pastureland.

At 30km there are some minor rapids below Fairnilee road bridge where novice slalom competitions are sometimes held. This is also quite a popular starting point for less experienced groups.

Further downstream the river passes the impressive home of Sir Walter Scott, close to Galashiels. This beautiful building starkly contrasts with a housing development at Galashiels which is little more than a concrete staircase climbing the hillside. This unfortunate development does tend to be the one thing that sticks in your mind journeying down the Tweed, or through Galashiels on your way to Edinburgh.

Several straightforward weirs are passed before egressing at Mertoun Bridge.

St Boswells to Kelso
Length 18km   **Grade** I - II (Makerstoun Rapids Grade III)   **No Portages**

This is probably the most popular stretch of the River Tweed, as it contains the only rapids of significance on the river. But they do lie in the middle of a fairly arduous paddle, although those short on time can get on to the river from the A699, which runs close to the river just above the rapids.

After getting on to the Tweed at Mertoun Bridge, several easy weirs are encountered before Makerstoun House is reached at about eight kilometres. The dazzling white facade and large rectangular window give it the appearance of a doll's house plonked on the side of the hill. Two hundred and fifty metres beyond the house the river is split up by several islands which form the Upper Rapid which is quite straightforward. A little further on a small cauld washes through on the left. 0.5km downstream the lower rapid begins. Here the gradient steepens as water is forced between several rocky islands for about 75m.

Once described as 'dangerous rapids' in the old B.C.U. Guide, these Grade III rapids should cause few problems. In low spate, they are at their best. In high water they become washed out with only a few standing waves as witness to their existence.

After several kilometres the magnificent palatial outlines of Floors Castle can be seen set in attractive parklands that lead towards Kelso.

As the town is reached there is a weir with a 1.5m sloping drop, split by an island. This is most easily shot on the far right where it washes through. The left channel is best avoided as much debris collects there. This weir produces a dangerous stopper in spate conditions.

Just beyond the weir lies the confluence with the Teviot. Here the road comes to within 50 metres of the right bank, making it a convenient point to finish.

Kelso to Berwick-upon-Tweed
Length 50km   **Grade** I (Excluding Weirs)   **No Portages**

After parking your car in the layby opposite the racecourse on the A699, get on the Tweed just below the confluence with the Teviot.

At 5.5km there is an excellent weir which wins star prize for entertainment value. (OS Ref 760369) This oblique weir with a 1.25m sloping drop, should be taken on the far left where two smaller broken weirs have good play waves. Some caution is advised as a canoeist has drowned here in the past.

From just beyond Kelso downstream to below Norham, the Tweed forms the border between Scotland and England.

The bridge at Coldstream offers a convenient access/egress point. From here the river begins to be a little more sluggish.

At 50km the picturesque town of Berwick comes into view. It is probably easiest to egress somewhere along the southern bank to avoid the congested city centre of Berwick. Either just upstream of the medieval bridge or at the mouth of the river at Spittal beach.

RIVER TWEED

Tweedsmuir to Peebles
Length 37.5km   Grade II (Tweedsmuir Fall Grade III)   No Portages

Kms		
0	**Access**	Fingland Fm Bridge. (Off A701) (OS Ref 054195) (in high water only)
3.5		Small bridge.
4.5		Small road bridge.
6		Fruid Water joins. Right.
8	**Access**	Tweedsmuir road bridge. (OS Ref 098244) (high water only)
		Rocky Fall beneath bridge. Grade III. Inspect.
9		Small road bridge.
		(Plus 4 similar over next 5kms)
21.5	**Access/Egress**	Drumelzier road bridge.
26		Road bridge.
35.5		Road bridge. River enters pretty, wooded valley.
36		Disused railway bridge.
36.5		Neidpath Castle. Left.
37		Footbridge. Peebles town. Left.
		200m **Weir.**
37.5	**Egress**	Road bridge. B7062. (OS Ref 251403)

Peebles to St Boswells
Length 57km   Grade I - II   No Portages

Kms		
0	**Access**	Road bridge. B7062. (OS Ref 251403) Weir is 200m upstream.
6		Private road bridge. Site of disused Railway.
13		Inner Leithen road bridge.
13.5		Leithen Water joins left.
14		Old railway bridge.
15.5		**Weir.** 1.25m sloping drop. With good play wave.
17		Bridge. Walkerburn village. Left.
21		Arched stone road bridge.
30.5	**Egress/Access**	Fairnilee road bridge. Slalom site.
		Minor Rapids below.
34		Old stone road bridge. Disused.
		Ettrick joins. Right.
		100m Concrete road bridge. A717.

Kms		
38		Abbotsford Mansion House. Right.
		200m Concrete road bridge. A6091
38.5		River Gala joins left. Galashiels.
41		Red Sandstone road bridge.
43		**Weir.** 1.25m. Broken through in centre. Standing Waves.
52		Disused viaduct.
		Ornate red sandstone road bridge.
		Concrete road bridge.
57		1.25m. **Weir.** Washes through on the left.
57.5	**Egress**	Mertoun Bridge. St Boswells. (OS Ref 610321)

St Boswells to Kelso
Length 18km   Grade I - II **(Makerstoun Rapids** Grade III)   No Portages

Km		
0	**Access**	Mertoun Bridge. St Boswells. (OS Ref 610321)
0.5		Small cauld.
4		Suspension footbridge.
		Mertoun House. Left.
8		**Weir.** 1.25m Sloping drop. Washes through in several places.
		Rutherford Lodge. Right bank. Good play wave.
		Island below.
10		Large White House. Left bank. (Makerstoun House)
		200m. **Makerstoun Rapids.** (Upper) Grade II/III.
10.5		Small **Weir.** 0.5km drop.
11		**Lower Rapids.** Grade III. 150m. River surges around a number of small rocky islands.
16		Floors Castle. Seen Left.
17.5		**Weir.** 1.75m Sloping drop. Split across Island. Washes through on far right.
		Kelso Town. Left.
		100m River Teviot joins right.
	Egress	Below Confluence. Right Bank. (OS Ref 727337)
18		Kelso. Road bridge.

Kelso to Berwick-upon-Tweed
Length 50km   Grade I (Excluding Weirs)   No Portages

Kms		
0	**Access**	200m above Road bridge. Close to confluence with Teviot. On the A699 opposite the race course. (OS Ref 727337)

Kms		
0.5		Minor Rapid. (Cauld on OS Map)
5.5		Oblique **Weir.** 1.25m Sloping drop. (OS Ref 760369)
		Star prize for entertainment value. (Good play waves
		Keep to far left to incorporate 2 smaller broken Weirs.
11		Catham Church and Village visible right bank.
17		Small **Weir.** 0.5m drop.
20.5	**Egress/Access**	Coldstream. Left
		Road bridge. A698.
25		Island. River Till joins. Right.
31		Norham Bridge.
32		Norham Village and Castle seen Right.
39		Union Bridge.
44.5		Whiteadder joins left.
44.75		Concrete road bridge.
47.5		Railway viaduct.
48		Berwick-upon-Tweed.
		2 Roadbridges.
50		Tweedmouth Harbour.
	Egress	Sandstell Point. (OS Ref 005521)

River Tyne

(North Tyne, South Tyne & Tyne)

Introduction

This famous Northumbrian river is formed from two main tributaries, the South Tyne flowing down from the Northern Pennines and the North Tyne coming across from the Cheviots.

From their confluence just above Hexham, the Tyne flows due east through the city of Newcastle-upon-Tyne to meet the North Sea at Tynemouth.

It is a mature river with a fairly gently gradient throughout most of its length. However, it flows through some very picturesque countryside with many interesting historical buildings which make it ideal for touring paddlers.

As much of the river is heavily used by canoeists, we have described its entire course in outline but with particular emphasis on the two white water sections. These are the famous Warden Gorge found on the North Tyne between Chollerford and Hexham and the rather less well known but interesting triad of mini-gorges just above Garrigill on the South Tyne.

The 'chicken chute' in low spate, Tyne Gorge, North Tyne

Also some of the smaller tributaries of the Tyne river system offer excellent paddling, the best of these being the River Allen on the South Tyne.

The North Tyne

The North Tyne area is probably the prettiest part of the Tyne valley although much of the landscape has been dramatically altered in recent years by several man-made projects, initially with the afforestation of the Kielder area and then more recently with the formation of Kielder Reservoir.

The actual source of the river lies just north west of Kielder at Deadwater Farm, but at this point it is little more than a stream flowing into the top end of the reservoir and is therefore of no interest to paddlers.

The closest paddlers can get to the outlet of the reservoir is at Falstone Bridge one kilometre below the dam. (Avoid the temptation of taking the road to Yarrow, a small hamlet immediately below the dam where access is difficult due to a steep embankment.)

Details of water releases from Kielder may be obtained by ringing the Northumbria Water Authority on 0434 240 463. A talking timetable gives the dates for releases on a weekly basis.

For those paddling lower down the Tyne valley, remember that there will be a delay of about ten hours before the release will reach Chollerford.

The interpretation and analysis of Kielder releases is more fully discussed in the section on Kielder reservoir.

Access

The Tyne is now becoming one of England's premier salmon rivers but despite this relations with local anglers remain good. Please do your utmost to preserve this good relationship.

Try to avoid paddling the upper North Tyne above Chollerford during the fishing season and use your discretion on the over used Chollerford - Hexham stretch. Paddlers from outside the region should contact the L.A.O. before paddling. Particular care should be exercised at access and egress points especially with regard to parked vehicles. Avoid obstructing the Quarry road at Acomb as heavy lorries use this road at *weekends.* Please respect the privacy of the houses on the right bank in Warden Gorge. (i.e. keep the noise down!)

The 1990 Tyne access agreement applies to local paddlers only. It covers the whole of the River Tyne and all its tributaries. Canoeing is not allowed during the peak angling months of September and October unless the river is in spate. From November to March canoeing is permitted at any level. From April to August the water may be used except when it is low.

Local Access Officers: **North Tyne and Tyne.**

(Source to Chollerford)
> Phil Clegg
> Calvert Trust,
> Kielder,
> Kielder Water,
> Falstone,
> Hexham, Northumberland, NE 48 1BS
> Tel: (0434) 250 232

(Chollerford to Newcastle-upon-Tyne)
> George Thompson
> Dukeshouse Wood Centre,
> Hexham.
> Tel: (Work) (0434) 602 622
>   (Home) (0207) 570 652

Falstone Bridge to Bellingham
Length 15kms   **Grade** I/II   **No Portages**

Few canoeists favour this stretch of the North Tyne as the river has only just emerged from Kielder Reservoir and has not yet had time to be swollen by any tributaries.

The river is therefore rather shallow and rocky so that unless there has been a large release of water, most trips tend to be a bit of a bump and scrape. However, because of its proximity to Kielder, it is suitable for novice paddlers who are based there and wish to try something a little more exciting than flat water paddling.

Convenient access is provided at Falstone Bridge (OS Ref 723871). Cars can be parked opposite the cemetery gates on the right bank.

Once afloat paddling is relatively straightforward with frequent stretches of shallow broken water peppered with small rocks.

At 7kms there is a small suspension footbridge, followed by a small weir which has a drop of only 10cms and a tiny stopper which should not present problems to even the most timid paddler.

At 8kms the river passes underneath a concrete road bridge which might prove a suitable point of egress for those wishing a shorter paddle.

Soon after this several tributaries join the river, the Tarset Burn from the left and the Chirdon Burn from the right. Paddling now gets a little easier as the broken water is interspersed with more sluggish deeper stretches.

When canoed in autumn and early winter the most exciting part of this trip often comes from the salmon which are found in large numbers on this part of the river. Laden with eggs and exhausted after their journey from the sea, they are often too tired to move until the canoe actually touches them. Whilst it might be exaggeration to say they lift the boat out of the water there is often a resounding 'thud' as 20lbs of pure muscle hits the keel causing a sudden boil of water to erupt from beneath the boat before it streaks across the river like a torpedo, leaving a large wake and one rather frightened paddler.

At 15km Bellingham Bridge (OS Ref 834833) comes into view. Egress left bank just below the bridge.

Bellingham Bridge to Wark
Length 13km **Grade** II **No Portages**

This is one of the best stretches of river for the touring paddler as the river is now a respectable size and the countryside is showing a little more variety now that the harsh and bleak hills of North Tynedale are beginning to mellow into the softer rolling pastureland of the lower Tyne valley.

Access is provided by a footpath on the left bank which leads down from a small car park adjacent to the fire station. This is located by driving over the Bellingham Road Bridge on the B6320 from Wark and is 200m on the right just after a sharp right hand bend and before you reach the built up area of Bellingham itself. (OS Ref 834833)

Initially there is a rather unpromising stretch of flat water but the pace gradually quickens with short pieces of broken water alternating with deeper slow moving sections that enables you to just relax and appreciate the beauty of the surrounding countryside. At 3.5km the River Rede adds a considerable volume of water. Then the river enters a pretty wooded valley with a succession of Grade II rapids.

As the woods are left behind you gradually become aware of a towering cliff on the left bank as the river surges round a sharp right hand bend, this is a useful landmark for a small fall which is a 100m downstream. The 0.5m vertical drop should present no difficulty to experienced canoeists. It can be shot in most places but the centre is best avoided where there are small collections of rocks immediately below the fall.

About one kilometre downstream two islands are surrounded on both sides by a few scattered rocks which form a short Grade II/III rapid. Lee Hall island is the larger of the two being close to the right bank and populated by some impressive tall fir trees. Lee Hall House is easily seen on the right bank. The pace then slackens and several longer flat stretches lead down to the iron road bridge at Wark (OS Ref 863771) which is 13kms from Bellingham. Egress is probably best achieved by getting out on the left bank just above the bridge.

Wark to Chollerford Bridge
Length 14km   **Grade** II   (Barrasford rapids Grade II/III)   **No Portages**

This is another good stretch to paddle as it combines some pleasant countryside with views of two impressive castles, neither of which are open to the public and are therefore most easily appreciated from the river. There is also one set of Grade II/III rapids to add a little spice to the trip.

Access to the river is obtained by going over the road bridge from Wark (OS Ref 863771) and turning left into a small side road which provides some roadside parking on the left bank 20m upstream of the bridge. Immediately below Wark a small rapid leads to several large islands. There follows a rather slack stretch before a succession of minor rapids leads to Chipchase Castle set high on the left bank. Originally a Northumbrian peel tower built in the 14th century but extensively added to in 1641 which now makes it a most imposing building.

At about 7km the pace of the river quickens again and several easy rapids lead to Haughton Castle on the right bank. Just before the castle is reached a gently sloping natural weir concentrates the mind back on the river. It is a 1.5m drop with a small standing wave cum stopper which can be played in although one is easily washed out.

One hundred metres downstream lie Barrasford rapids Grade II/III. Here the river splits around a small island. On the right is a steep shingle rapid which is easily negotiated and is the route of choice for the less adventurous. On the left is a rather tricky rocky fall. This is not usually a problem in low water when the rocks are clearly visible but in spate this is a definite black spot for unwary canoeists as the water is funnelled at considerable velocity between the island and the river bank onto several sharp edged semi-submerged rocks.

Those paddlers who like an exciting finish might wish to get out here as the road comes to within 100m of the left bank and there are no further rapids till Chollerford.

One hundred metres below this a small weir channels water towards Barrasford Pumping Station, a large rectangular red brick building standing out from the left bank.

A little stretch of broken water leads into two kilometres of flat water which goes down to Chollerford Bridge and weir.

Egress is usually on the left bank immediately below Chollerford Bridge.

White Water Section

Chollerford to Hexham
Length 10km   **Grade** II/III   (Warden Gorge - Grade III)   **No Portages**

This is perhaps the most well known and frequently paddled part of the River Tyne as it is the closest stretch of white water for canoeists based in the Newcastle area. It also has a special place in the hearts of many North Eastern paddlers as the gorge is often their first confrontation with white water, so people often affectionately recall their first swim, roll or other canoe epic here. Some (such as the author) can even produce long lists of equipment and personal effects which have been condemned to a watery grave by these rapids.

The most usual point of access is just below Chollerford Bridge on the left bank (OS Ref 920706). Paddlers are advised to go over the bridge and park beyond the roundabout on the B6320 to Wark where a large lay-by functions as a splendid open air changing room.

For late risers requiring a little dutch courage a quick pint may be had at the George Hotel before crossing the bridge.

After getting in there is a small patch of slack water above the weir to give you a gentle start to the day. The weir itself is quite straight-forward with a long sloping drop of 1.5m. It is best shot just to the right of centre where a small cut in the top of the weir collects most of the current. The small stopper present under most conditions is easy to play in, but in spate becomes rather more possessive, however swimmers are usually quickly ejected. Occasionally in high spate the weir becomes completely washed out but this is a very rare occurrence.

There follows about 1km of slack water before a stretch of minor rapids runs past the Roman fort of Chesters, easily visible on the right bank.

At two kilometres a small but imposing manor house, Walwick Grange, comes into view high on the right bank. One hundred metres below this at the bottom of some easy rapids is a small 'Play' stopper which is worth taking advantage of as there are no further stoppers until the gorge is reached. Unfortunately this is only present at low to average levels and easily becomes washed out.

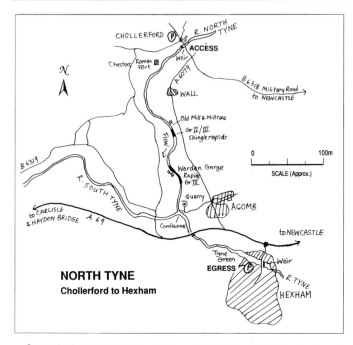

CHOLLERFORD
R. NORTH TYNE
ACCESS
Chesters Roman Fort
Weir
A 6079
WALL
B 6318 Military Road
to NEWCASTLE
Old Mill & Millrace
Gr II / III
Shingle rapids
Flow
Warden Gorge
Rapid
Gr III
Quarry
ACOMB
B 6319
R. SOUTH TYNE
to CARLISLE
& HAYDON BRIDGE
A 69
Confluence
to NEWCASTLE
0   100m
SCALE (Approx.)
Tyne Green
EGRESS
Weir
R. TYNE
HEXHAM

NORTH TYNE
Chollerford to Hexham

Several minor rapids follow before some slack water is reached and a millrace with a disused mill becomes visible on the left bank. This marks the start of 150m of (Grade II/III) 'Millrace' rapids best taken in the centre following the main flow of current, as it is channelled round a right hand bend. The river narrows slightly at the bottom producing some small standing waves which gives a pleasant bouncy ride. This then flows into a stretch of flat water with a sandy beach on the left where boats can be quickly emptied and composure regained before the gorge is tackled. This beach is private. It is not for picnicking or sunbathing.

There is now nearly one kilometre of completely slack water below the Millrace Rapids which lead up to the beginning of the gorge which is marked by a steep wooded embankment on the right hand side. At this point the flow of water increases slightly along with a perceptible quickening of the pulse.

Warden Gorge
Whilst most people get to the gorge by paddling down from Chollerford those who only wish to do this section may park two kilometres downstream on the

road leading to the confluence of the River Tyne and walk one-two kilometres up the old railway track to the top of the gorge.

Conversely those who don't feel ready to take on the challenge of these rapids may go a further 100m downstream before getting out at 'Private' Notice Rock and taking a much shorter but slightly more tricky lower path (see diagram) around the main rapids. Walkers in either direction should not be put off by innumerable signs saying 'Beware Adders'. To our knowledge no such creatures have ever been seen. Any that may have existed in the past will have long since been scared away by the considerable volume of human traffic through these woods.

For convenience, we have divided the gorge into three sections; top. middle and bottom. The main component of the top section is usually referred to as the 'chicken chute' and consists of an angled ridge of bedrock re-inforced on the right side by some concrete and timber to direct water down the old mill race which has now gone leaving just a sloping chute. (There is some disagreement about which side the chicken chute lies. The author believes it refers to the extreme right-hand chute.)

The traditional route for canoeists is to take this right hand chute which usually presents no difficulty. However, the water flows onto a cliff face round a sharp left hand bend, so that a good turning stroke is required. Whilst this is not a problem for experienced paddlers many novices tend to get swept up against the cliff and in panic lean upstream only to capsize!

Although it may sound like a description of a medieval torture chamber a few other features are worth mentioning; as you go down the chute, three small iron spikes protrude about six inches from the rock - nasty though they may look the current usually washes you away from them, however when paddling upstream into the small stopper at the head of the chute one occasionally get caught against them. Secondly, at low water a large metal grill becomes exposed onto which less experienced canoeists are frequently washed. If this happens to you, again don't lean upstream! just wait till you have come to rest then push yourself off.

To our knowledge no unpleasant incidents have been recorded from encounters with these artifacts. In spate conditions all these hazards can be bypassed by keeping to the extreme left but this makes it almost too easy!

Plastic boatists often go over the one metre rocky fall in midstream, which is now a favoured route. A small stopper is present below these falls where 'pop outs' can sometimes be done. Then follow the current down through some minor rocky rapids towards the left bank into some slack water lying immediately above the main gorge section. Those new to the gorge will want to get out here and have a look at the pleasures to come, this is best achieved by getting out at 'Private' Notice Rock, a large sloping rock which lies almost opposite the first of two houses over-looking the gorge. On this rock a misguided landowner (who has now gone) has concreted an iron notice with some allusive message to canoeists!

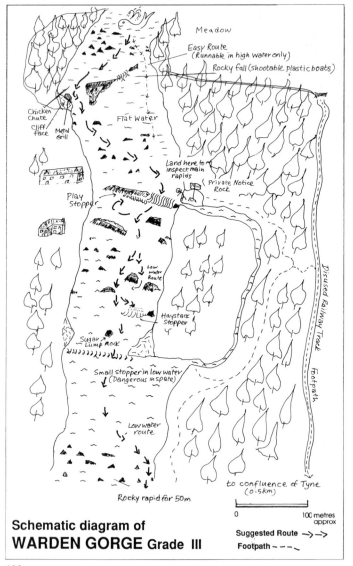

Meadow

Easy Route
(Runnable in high water only)

Rocky fall (shootable, plastic boats)

Chicken
Chute

Cliff
Face

Metal
Grill

Flat Water

Land here to
inspect main
rapids

Private Notice
Rock

Play
Stopper

Low
water
Route

Haystack
Stopper

Sugar
Lump Rock

Small stopper in low water
(Dangerous in spate)

Low water
route

Rocky rapid for 50m

Discused Railway Track

Footpath

to confluence of Tyne
(0.5km)

0   100 metres
approx

Suggested Route →→ →

Footpath – – –

Schematic diagram of
WARDEN GORGE Grade III

Falling prey to the playstopper, Tyne Gorge

The rock provides a good vantage point to view this middle section of the gorge although some may wish to get a better view by walking some 50m downstream but it is a bit of a scramble. In the unlikely event of an emergency help should always be sought from the bottom of the two houses on the gorge, as the family here is very friendly towards canoeists, but to maintain their goodwill please try to respect their privacy along the right bank.

The middle section of the gorge starts with a small sloping drop with a rather deceptive benign looking stopper on the right. For experienced paddlers it is worth breaking out here and playing in it. Although quite easy to paddle through both lengthways and sideways, once you let it pull you back there is often quite a struggle to get out again. In low water rolling here is a favourite place to break your paddle, so you've been warned! This stopper should *only* be played in at low water levels.

For those of you still in your boats, that should be most people, just keep roughly to the centre following the main flow of the current through more turbulent water.

In low water about halfway down this middle section, just below the bottom house you will find there is little choice of route, with most of the water being channelled between two rocks close to the left bank, creating a tight gap. Inexperienced paddlers often fail to get round quickly enough becoming broached across the two rocks. Fortunately, under most conditions one can usually go straight down the middle of these rapids through a succession of standing waves and small stoppers to the bottom.

More adventurous paddlers like to keep just left of centre towards this bottom end where there is a good sized standing wave cum stopper which is fun to play in. However, it lies just above a small rock known locally as the sugar lump. Easily seen in low water it forms an impressive haystack under most conditions, but this disappears in high water. The gorge is probably most exciting in low to medium spate, at higher levels it becomes washed out. When very high it flattens out almost completely apart from a large very powerful stopper across the bottom. Those foolish enough to take on the gorge at this level usually enjoy the ride as far as the stopper where they are often backlooped with the unfortunate paddler being rapidly ejected from his boat. The canoeist then goes for a long and painful underwater journey whilst the canoe remains a guest of the stopper for some considerable time to come.

To our knowledge no fatalities have occurred on this section of the river which is a true testimony to its safety considering the large number of relatively inexperienced paddlers who try their luck here. Every conceivable route has been attempted with varying degrees of success, both with the canoeist the right way up and the rather less fortunate who end up as involuntary submariners head bumping their way along the river bottom.

The final lower section which is really just beyond the actual gorge, consists of a final 50m of rocky rapid, most easily paddled down on the far left hand side where there is a relatively rock free channel close to the bank, but any route will do, provided you avoid the large number of rocks scattered across this rapid. There are quite a few capsizes on this section of river as people tend to relax after the main rapids and get caught unawares.

One kilometre downstream the confluence with the South Tyne is reached where there is a shingle beach on the left and a short footpath leads up to the road (OS Ref 919662). Those paddlers who park their cars in the small road that leads from Acomb to the confluence of the Tyne are urged to ensure that there is always space for heavy lorries to pass on their way to the quarry. (This includes nights and weekends.) If there is insufficient space available along the road the quarry owners have given permission to use the large quarry yard at the end of the road. A much better option than emerging from the water only to find your car has been towed away! For those who like a longer paddle, Hexham is a further three kilometres downstream, but it is a rather arduous paddle especially the bottom section which is completely flat. However large groups are probably better off paddling down to Tyne Green where there are better car parking facilities.

Those paddlers keen on real ale should visit the 'Miners Arms' at the top of 'main' street in Acomb. In one year they usually sell about 70 different draught beers so there is always plenty of choice. The best tea shop in the area is the Watling Coffee House in Corbridge. Amongst a wide range of irresistible cakes their home made scones with jam and cream are difficult to beat.

North Tyne - summary

Touring sections

1. **Falstone Bridge to Bellingham**
Length 15km   Grade I-II   No Portages

Kms		
-1		Kielder Dam
0	**Access**	Falstone Bridge. OS Ref 723871 - Right Bank
7		Suspension Footbridge 100m downstream small concrete weir with miniscule stopper.
8		Concrete road bridge 300m downstream River Tarset burn joins left.
15	**Egress**	Bellingham Bridge. OS Ref 834833. Footpath left bank below bridge up to the road.

2. **Bellingham Bridge to Wark**
Length 13km   Grade II   No Portages

Kms		
0	**Access**	Bellingham Bridge. OS Ref 834833. Left bank below bridge.
4		River Rede joins left.
7		High cliff left bank warns of approaching **small fall** 0.5m vertical drop. Shoot either side to avoid rocks below middle of fall.
8		Lee Hall Island and rapids.
		Two islands with Grade II/III rapids
		on either side. Usually shot on the left.
12		Gold Island.
13	**Egress**	Wark Bridge. OS Ref 863771. Left bank just above bridge.

3. **Wark to Chollerford**
Length 14km   Grade II (Barrasford rapids II/III)   No Portages

Kms		
0	**Access**	Wark Bridge. OS Ref 863771. Upstream left bank.
3		Chipchase Castle high on left bank.
7		Succession of Grade I/II rapids leading to
8		**natural weir** 1m gently sloping drop to stopper/standing wave.
8.5		Haughton Castle on right bank. **Barrasford rapids Grade II/III,** safest route right down shingle rapid. More fun left down rocky fall but inspect in high water.
9		Barrasford Pumping station on left bank.
14	**Egress**	Chollerford Bridge. OS Ref 920706. Below Bridge on left bank.

4. Chollerford Bridge to confluence (and Hexham)
Length 7km   Grade II/III (Warden Gorge Grade III)   No Portages

Kms		
0	**Access**	Chollerford Bridge. OS Ref 920706. Left bank below bridge and above weir. **Weir** 1.5m sloping drop. Shoot just right of centre where maximum flow. Two islands immediately below.
1		Minor rapids. Chesters Roman Fort right bank.
2		Walwick Grange manor house overlooks Grade I rapids with small stopper. Easy and safe to play in.
3		Mill Race left bank. 150m of bouncy **Grade II/III rapids** around right bank. Shingle beach left bank and 1km slack water leading to
4.5		**Warden Gorge begins. Grade III rapids.** See text and map.
5.5		Rocky rapids below gorge. Usually easiest close to left bank.
7	**Egress**	Confluence with South Tyne. OS Ref 918661 left bank.
8		Road bridge.
8.5		Derelict bridge. Few stanchions surviving.
10	**Egress**	Tyne Green and Hexham Bridge. OS Ref 941648.
		NB. Hexham **Weir** immediately below bridge

South Tyne

Many canoeists feel this river to be the poor relation of the North Tyne. This is because it is both smaller in size and lacks anything comparable to the heavy rapids found at Warden Gorge on the North Tyne. Even so there are several stretches that are worthy of consideration.

The topmost section from Tynehead to Garrigill has a triad of mini gorges which are in themselves fairly trouble free, but as they frequently become at least partially blocked by fallen trees, they usually provide a memorable paddle.

By contrast, the bottom section, from Haydon Bridge to the confluence just above Hexham with its easy rapids, picturesque countryside and good access points, makes it a suitable and popular place for introducing less experienced paddlers to the thrills of white water. This is also a good spot for open Canadians.

Between these sections the steady gradient from Garrigill through Alston down to Featherstone Castle, provides a swift, interesting run in spate conditions, although in low water it becomes a painful bump and scrape. Below Featherstone the gradient gradually eases, providing pleasant if uninspiring paddling through Haltwhistle and on to Haydon Bridge.

Access

No recorded problems on the upper stretches. Occasional problems below Haltwhistle down to the confluence. Generally good relations with anglers. Jerry has negotiated a number of agreements with riparian owners so paddlers are strongly advised to contact him before planning a trip. Th s applies particularly to large groups. Avoid paddling the river in low water. The river is covered by the Tyne access agreement. (See North Tyne Access.)

Local Access Officer: Jerry Tracey,
Haefen House,
Allendale, Northumberland.
Tel: Allendale 0434 683 409

Tynehead to Alston

Length	11kms
Grade	III/IV Tynehead to Garrigill
	II/III Garrigill to Alston
Portage	Strid at Crossgill
OS Map	Ref 709408

After arising on Alston moor at Tynehead, the young river is still very small and can only be paddled in spate conditions.

Most of the interest lies in the first three kilometres so that many paddlers may prefer to get out at Garrigill. This does make the trip rather short, but it can easily be combined with other spate rivers in the area such as the Allen or Upper Tees. In really high water it may be worthwhile continuing downstream to Alston or even Featherstone on a swirling tide of café au lait.

The relatively high technical grading given to this section of the river takes account of the potential hazard of fallen trees and other difficulties associated with paddling narrow channels rather than because of inherent difficulties in the stretch itself.

Access is achieved by following the Tynehead road out of Garrigill for about four kilometres until a cattle grid is reached where the car can be parked. A few hundred metres further on the road degenerates into a bridleway and a small track can be seen leading down towards the river to a farm at the other side.

No sooner have you got in your boats than at 200m you encounter a wooden footbridge which often has a sheep fence beneath. Just beyond lies a one metre rocky fall which leads on to some minor rapids.

In one kilometre a small rocky promontory on a right hand bend marks the start of the first and easiest of the gorgelets. They are all similar in character being some six metres wide, with sheer rocky walls four metres high. These are decorated with mosses and pendulant vegetation dripping with moisture.

As you go into the top gorge a number of fallen trees lie wedged overhead,

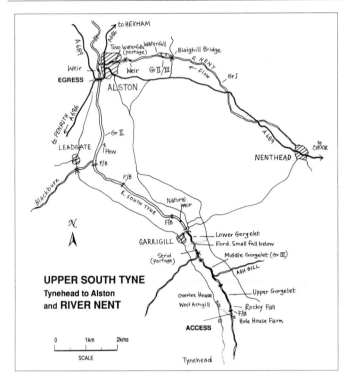

UPPER SOUTH TYNE
Tynehead to Alston
and RIVER NENT

forming a rather unsatisfactory and leaky roof. Despite their apparently unstable position, they seem to remain there from year to year. Although the river is flowing quite fast it is little more than Grade II at this point, for there are few rocks and little turbulence, but a watchful eye needs to be kept for obstructing trees which can easily block the whole width of the river.

After 0.5km a footbridge is reached as the channel opens out before it re-enters the slightly trickier middle gorge, which is a little more turbulent. There are usually a series of small stoppers about half way down where Ashgill Beck joins on the right.

About fifty metres below the confluence with the Ashgill Beck there is a small rocky fall with an 0.5 metre drop. Whilst in spate conditions this quickly becomes washed out, in low water the small cleft in centre of the fall is best avoided as boats can become wedged.

In another few hundred metres the gorge opens out a little, passing beneath a small bridge shortly followed by a large stream joining on the left,
106

Middle section South Tyne Gorge.
Tynehead to Garrigill

(Crossgill Beck) and an arched stone roadbridge partially hidden by trees becomes visible.

These landmarks are worth noting as a very tricky strid which usually has to be portaged lies directly beneath the bridge. It is advisable to carry your boat beneath the bridge on the left bank, and do an angled seal launch off the rocks. This avoids a very tedious 200 metre portage along the left bank.

The river now opens out and a wide ford is reached which has a bevelled edge with a 0.5m fall.

This soon leads into the short final gorge, which takes you down to Garrigill Bridge, where most will want to finish. Those continuing downstream will come across a small natural weir in 200 metres. This has a straightforward 2.0m sloping drop.

From here the river is now less exciting as a succession of minor rapids take you down to Alston Bridge. Egress upstream of the bridge on either bank.

Alston to Haydon Bridge

Length	41kms
Grade	Alston to Featherstone Castle II/III
	Featherstone Castle to Haydon Bridge II
Optional Portage	Featherstone weir OS Ref 672610

Whilst this section has no major rapids, the steady gradient from Alston to Featherstone Castle makes it a worthwhile paddle in high water. Below this the only excitement comes from shooting the small fall below the viaduct at Haltwhistle.

Access is from the road bridge at Alston where the A686 crosses the river on its way to Penrith.

In 250m a small weir is encountered with a 0.5m vertical drop. The River Nent adds a significant quantity of water from the right bank after 1km. From here a series of shingle rapids with the occasional larger drop, take you gradually down this pretty valley accompanied for some of the way by the South Tyne railway. After a few kilometres a small boulder garden forms a brief Grade II/III rapid, with a steep wooded embankment on the right.

At 16kms some shingle rapids lead down to an impressive viaduct which straddles the valley. A small footbridge runs across the bottom between the arches. High up on the left bank the village of Lambley can just be made out.

After 19kms Featherstone Castle is reached, which has a very large weir which must be carefully inspected and usually portaged. The weir is divided into two halves by a concrete pillar. On the left is a 2.0m sloping drop, whilst on the right there are two one metre steps.

It is rumoured that the local Laird put this here as a canoe trap for in high

Shooting Featherstone Weir, South Tyne

water a thoroughly unpleasant holding stopper forms here.

Even in low water the weir is difficult, although it can be shot on the right side.

Below this, Featherstone road bridge is reached which may be a suitable egress point, as from here the gradient eases further as shallow rapids give way to longer stretches of slow moving water.

Five kilometres beyond this lies Haltwhistle, easily visible on the left bank. Here the river is crossed by two roadbridges and a viaduct. It is advisable to get out above the viaduct to inspect the 1.5m vertical fall which lies just beyond. There is sufficient plunge pool along most of its length to allow a variety of routes to be taken, but in low water it is best shot in the centre which collects most of the flow.

From here the river meanders lazily down the valley, except for a brief burst of activity three kilometres downstream from Haltwhistle on a left hand bend forming a 50m stretch of easy Grade II/III water.

The next landmark is Bardon Mill, which has a footbridge and consists of a few houses seen on the left bank.

Shortly after this the river Allen joins from the right. There soon follows a larger collection of houses with two road bridges, which mark the arrival of Haydon Bridge.

A brief stretch of flat water lies immediately above the stone road bridge, caused by a small weir just beyond this which has a 0.5m sloping drop, shootable in most places.

Egress beyond the second road bridge on the left bank. (OS Ref 843644)

Haydon Bridge to Confluence (Tyne Green, Hexham)

Length	9.75kms (13km)
Grade	II
No Portages	

This is the most commonly canoed part of the South Tyne. The river has now become a respectable size and is easily paddled at average winter levels, although during the summer months there is usually insufficient water for a comfortable paddle. For expeditions who suddenly find themselves 'caught short' of paddleable water, one can usually splash about in the deep, murky waters of the Tyne Green. The reasonable proximity of this stretch to Newcastle, good parking and easy rapids, make this a favourite spot for introducing larger groups to white water.

Riverside parking is found by going over the A69 road bridge into Haydon Bridge and immediately turning right down a small track which leads to a picnic area along by the river. (OS Ref 844644)

At one kilometre a minuscule weir with a 0.25m drop is easily negotiated. Just below lies Haydon Spa on the right bank.

Around the next corner is a slight constriction in the river which produces some bouncy fast water for about 75 metres. This is a favourite spot for early swimmers, especially those who belong to the school of prophylactic capsizing, that is those who believe they might as well swim sooner rather than later, and so promptly keel over at their first sight of moving water. From here gentle rapids take you down for a further kilometre before the river enters a pretty wooded vale, where broad shingle rapids with the occasional larger rocks are the worst hazards Allerwash Gorge has to offer. The railway now joins on the left bank, with the River Allerwash emerging about half way along the stone walled embankment.

A slower stretch of water takes you up to Fourstones village, barely visible on the left bank but approximates to where the railway parts company with the river.

The scene of rural tranquillity is briefly interrupted at 8km with a large paper mill on the left bank as the river surges round to the right.

One kilometre further on the river is crossed by a stone road bridge leading to the village of Warden. This might be a suitable egress point, especially for those wishing for a bite at the Boatside Inn on the far side of the bridge. For those continuing, some shingle rapids take you beneath a railway bridge and down to the confluence with the North Tyne, forming the river Tyne proper. From here the Tyne then passes beneath the large concrete A69 road bridge, where the rapids gradually peter out as an area of flat water is reached above Hexham road bridge. A riverside park known as Tyne Green runs along the right bank. This large area of deep, still water is a favourite place for teaching

basic paddling skills and rescue techniques, especially on cold winter days!
    A weir lies just below the road bridge, so egress well above the bridge on the right bank. (OS Ref 941646)

South Tyne - summary

Tynehead to Alston
Length 11kms Grade Tynehead to Garrigill III/IV Portage Strid at Crossgill
    Grade Garrigill to Alston II/III   OS Ref 709408

Kms		
0	**Access**	Just downstream of Hole House Farm (OS Ref 759388)
		250 metres footbridge with sheep fence.
		1m **Fall** immediately below.
0.5		**Upper Gorge** starts. (Grade II/III)
1.0		Footbridge. River opens out.
1.25		**Middle Gorge** starts. Slightly more difficult.
1.5		Ashgill Beck joins right.
2.5		Small concrete bridge. (Note Portage 200m downstream)
2.75		Crossgill Beck joins left. River opens out.
		Arched stone bridge. **Strid** beneath (OS Ref 719408)
		Portage left bank.
3.5		Ford. 0.5m vertical drop.
3.75		Final **gorge** section begins.
5	**Egress**	Road bridge Garrigill. Gorge ends.
5.25		Natural **weir**. 1.5m sloping drop.
5.75		Iron footbridge.
9.5		Footbridge. Black Gill Beck joins left.
11	**Egress**	Road bridge. Alston. OS Ref 716462

Alston to Haydon Bridge
Length 41kms Grade II/III Alston to Featherstone Castle
        Grade II Featherstone Castle to Haydon Bridge
        Optional Portage Featherstone weir   OS Ref 672610

Kms		
0	**Access**	Alston road bridge (OS Ref 716462)
		250m. Small **weir**. 0.5m vertical drop.
		Disappears in spate.
		750m. River Nent joins right.
1.5		Railway bridge.
3		Steep wooded embankment. Right.

Kms

		Small **boulder garden**. Grade II/III rapid for 100m
5		New concrete road bridge on old stone stanchions.
9		Slaggyford road bridge.
		Caravan park. Left.
12		Eals road bridge
16		Viaduct.
17.5		Lambley road bridge.
19		**Featherstone weir** (and Castle) **Dangerous stopper** in high water.
		Inspection essential. **Portage** usually necessary.
19.25		**Egress** Featherstone road bridge.
24		Two road bridges. 200m apart. Haltwhistle left.
24.5		Viaduct with **weir** immediately below.
		Inspection advised. Get out above viaduct.
		Shoot centre in low water.
28		Easy Grade II/III **rapid** on left bend for 50m.
33		Bardon Mill. Left. Footbridge.
34.5		Railway bridge.
35		Road bridge.
35.5		River Allen. Joins right.
37.5		Railway bridge.
41		Stone road bridge at Haydon Bridge. **Weir** below with 0.5m drop.
		Shootable in most places.
		100m. Concrete road bridge. A69 crosses river.
	Egress	Left bank just beyond bridge. (OS Ref 843644)

Haydon Bridge to Confluence (Tyne Green, Hexham)
Length 11kms (13km)   Grade II   No Portages

Kms

0	**Access**	Turn right immediately after passing over A69 road bridge, into
		Haydon Bridge. OS Ref 844644
1		Small **weir**. 0.25m drop. Haydon Spa. Right bank.
8		Paper Mill. Left bank.
9	**Egress**	Road bridge. (To Warden)
9.25		Railway bridge.
9.75		Confluence with North Tyne.
10.5		A69 Road bridge.
13		Tyne Green Hexham. Road bridge. **Weir** below.
	Egress	Above road bridge. Right bank. OS Ref 941646

River Tyne

Hexham to Wylam

Length	21km
Grade	II
Portage	Riding Mill Weir
OS Map	Ref 027620

This is a pleasant touring stretch of river with a reasonable flow of water after the confluence of the North and South Tyne just above Hexham. It can, therefore, be paddled during the drier months when higher sections of the river are too rocky.

Although there is still much pretty countryside to be seen especially in the area around Hexham and Corbridge, one is beginning to say goodbye to rural Northumberland as the valley becomes more urbanised in the lower reaches. There is still good paddling down as far as Wylam. Below this the river becomes tidal and rather grimy.

The usual starting point is at Tyne Green just above Hexham Bridge on the right bank where there is ample parking space and even a small wooden jetty providing easy access. However, before getting in those unfamiliar with Hexham weir should inspect it, especially in high water.

The weir lies immediately below the bridge and has a 1.5m drop in two steps. The weir is best shot on either side avoiding the difficult box like central section which functions as a fish ladder. It is also important to avoid the area immediately adjacent to the centre box where two angled ridges direct flow to the centre, these are likely to drop paddlers sideways into the stopper at the bottom. If in doubt go on the far right hand side. Below the weir one can see the historic town of Hexham on your right whilst on the left a rather large pulping mill belches forth clouds of steam filling the air with the delightful aroma of pine oil. Just beyond the factory lies a tiny weir with a drop of 100-200cms which would hardly disconcert a flea rafting on a postage stamp.

There now follows a series of deep slow stretches occasionally interspersed with some Grade I rapids as the river winds it's way towards Corbridge. This is marked by a road bridge at 6.5km. The town being easily visible on the left bank. Some minor rapids immediately below the bridge lead into a tree-lined stretch of flat water really more suited to punting than canoeing but don't despair it only lasts 200m before the river gathers pace again. Riding Mill pumping station and weir are soon reached at 12.5kms.

This is part of the Kielder Water scheme and pumps water up to Airy Holm Reservoir which is then taken by gravity feed through underground tunnels to the outlet below Eggleston Bridge on the River Tees.

A small dam across the river channels water through a 10m concrete gap which has a small weir halfway down. Although the drop is small the large volume of water gives the weir a powerful wall to wall stopper and a swim here is likely to prove more than just an inconvenience! This weir should always be portaged.

A few kilometres further on Bywell Castle comes into view, although only a ruined keep remains it was once quite a grand castle with an outer wall. Richard III was believed to have hidden here during the Wars of the Roses.

This is quickly followed by Bywell road bridge. We advise you to savour these last moments of rural harmony as the river now becomes more urbanised, first with a steep concrete embankment supporting the railway line which then leads into the town of Prudhoe seen on the right bank.

A flimsy looking iron bridge spans the river with a small rapid immediately below - best taken on the left. This is the home ground of one of the North East's newer paddling clubs, Tyne Valley Canoe Club, who often practise on this stretch of water. The ruins of Prudhoe Castle are just visible on the right bank. Pleasant countryside and easy rapids take you gently downstream for another four-five kilometres before Wylam Bridge is reached at 21km, this is immediately followed by a small weir which can be shot in most places. Not a problem in low water but caution should be exercised in high water. There is some good fast water just below the weir which is the last rapid on the river.

Egress is probably best achieved by climbing the steep bank on the left side immediately below the bridge (OS Ref 118646). After this the river becomes tidal. The river now flattens out although the countryside remains pretty as far as Newburn where the power station marks the start of Industrial Tyneside.

For those who enjoy watching the industrial panorama of the dockland an interesting paddle may be had by going from the Tyne Bridge down to Tynemouth.

River Tyne - summary

Hexham Bridge to Wylam

Length 50km   Grade I - II   Portage   Hexham Weir OS Ref 941648
Riding Mill Weir OS Ref 027620

Kms		
0	**Access**	Hexham Bridge. OS Ref 941648. Tyne green car park.
		Upstream right bank.
		Weir 1.5m drop in two steps - see text for details.
		Easiest shoot right in high water. **Recommended portage.**
1		Small weir 200cm drop.
5		Devil's Water joins right bank.
6.5		Corbridge road bridge and town left.

Kms		
12.5		Riding Mill pumping station right and **weir. Essential Portage** - wall to wall stopper with strong undertow.
13		Concrete road bridge.
16		Bywell Castle left bank. Roadbridge.
21	**Egress**	Prudhoe road and footbridge. Ruined castle visible right hillside. **Minor rapids** below bridge - keep left. Good plays spot.
25		Wylam Bridge. **Weir** 10m downstream. 1m vertical drop. Shoot most places, *caution in high water*. Pre-inspect. Portage in spate.
	Egress	Left bank immediately below weir. OS Ref 118646. 100m Wylam Rapid. Grade II. River now becomes tidal.

$\mathcal{R}$iver $\mathcal{W}$ansbeck

The Wansbeck begins life on Chesterhope Common near Cambo. From here the river flows due east through the market town of Morpeth passing between Ashington and Guide Post to meet the sea at North Seaton.

This river is mainly of interest to touring paddlers based in the locality. The best section is probably from Mitford, where the river is swollen by the River Font, downstream to Bothal Castle and beyond. This provides an attractive journey through a wooded vale, with most of the excitement being provided by the weirs. In high water a bracing run may be had on the steady gradient from Meldon Park down to Mitford.

Novice groups sometimes use the riverside park just below Sheepwash, where a long stretch of flat water is suitable for basic instruction.

In Autumn this area is also a good place to pick sloes, especially around the railway viaduct.

Access

Upper section rarely canoed. Occasional problems below Morpeth which is quite heavily fished.

The flat section below Sheepwash is regularly used for boating so that objections are very unlikely.

Wallington Hall to Mitford

Length 20.5kms   **Grade** II/III   **No Portages**

Few people will wish to paddle the very topmost section of this part of the river which is very narrow and sometimes obstructed. It can only be paddled after heavy rainfall when other more interesting rivers become available.

It is possible to start from the balustraded stone road bridge close to Wallington Hall (OS Ref 034838). Non paddlers visiting the area should certainly pay a visit to this impressive countryside house, run by the National Trust. It is famed for its china, furniture and splendid walled gardens.

After getting in, a rather tortuous stretch follows with the narrow river twisting its way across rich pastureland, the banks frequently lined with trees, bushes and reeds, which further hinder your progress. Occasional sheep fences and fallen trees necessitate the odd portage.

At 8km the road bridge at Low Angerton is reached. This is a more practical starting point for most paddlers, as the best water such as it is lies between Meldon Park and Mitford.

Several kilometres below Low Angerton the river Hartburn swells the flow. Here there is a footbridge and just beyond lies a 1.0m rocky fall. A collection of rocks immediately below makes inspection advisable. High up on the left bank Meldon Hall is easily visible.

The river now enters some deciduous woodland, with several kilometres of easy rapids, but there is still nearly 10km before the village of Mitford is reached. This is heralded by a church seen just above the trees on the right bank.

A stone road bridge soon comes into view, with a small weir beneath, usually shot through the right arch, which collects most of the flow. Just below the bridge the ruins of Mitford Castle are seated on a grassy hillock. Two hundred metres beyond several rocky sills are most easily avoided by keeping to the left.

The river Font soon joins from the left. Below the confluence a gauging weir is reached where some steps lead up to the roadside providing a good point to egress.

The layby beneath the giant A1 road bridge arcing overhead makes a convenient shelter for those changing in wet weather.

Mitford to North Seaton

Length 18kms   **Grade** II/III (including weirs)   **No Portages**

By now the river is more a respectable size. This trip offers easy paddling through mostly wooded countryside, passing through the market town of Morpeth, before reaching the estuary near Ashington.

The main challenge to canoeists comes from the multiplicity of weirs, which although quite high, are rarely a problem unless the river is in spate.

Begin at the road bridge over the Wansbeck in Mitford, close to the ruined castle (not to be confused with the road bridge over the River Font at the other end of the village).

A footpath below the bridge leads down to the river on the right bank.

After several hundred metres two rocky sills are avoided by keeping to the left.

At 0.5km the River Font joins from the left. A flat stretch of water leads up to a small gauging weir with a 1.25m sloping drop with a central chute. Whoever designed this monstrosity should be sent to Neuremberg for crimes against humanity as jagged stones have been embedded in the concrete base of the weir either side of the central chute. Presumably to reduce scouring and to facilitate aeration of the water. Provided the central chute is used the weir is quite safe at all water levels. Some steps lead up from the weir to the road on the left, which makes this a good alternative starting point as there is also good roadside parking.

Soon the large A1 roadbridge arches overhead. A little way downstream several iron water pipes span the river. This heralds a large weir with a 2.75 sloping drop. The bottom section of the weir has a long plateau before a small vertical drop, but there is usually enough algal slime to enable you to slip down without difficulty.

A kilometre or so of woodland now follows, before a road bridge and a smattering of houses indicate the outskirts of Morpeth has been reached.

Here there are some stepping stones which can just be squeezed through by tipping your boat.

Several road bridges are then passed, before an area of flat water is reached. Innumerable warning signs for an approaching weir are found just below the footbridge. These seem to imply that Armageddon is just round the next bend but the signs are directed to those crewing hired rowing boats found here and shouldn't perturb the steely nerve of passing canoeists. In fact most white water paddlers will probably be disappointed by the fairly innocuous weir that follows with a two metre sloping drop, which can usually be slid down without difficulty.

Several road bridges are then passed before the houses begin to thin again.

Just beyond the green footbridge and ford, an unsavoury smell often greets the nostrils. This is due to Morpeth abattoir which lies along the left bank.

Another stretch of flat water leads up to East Mill Weir, built in the 1860's to serve the flour mill on the left. It worked for only 50 years before being closed down in 1914. The two metre horseshoe shaped weir develops a powerful stopper in high water, when it should be portaged. Otherwise shoot it on the far right.

Soon the river passes beneath another bridge before entering woodland again. Gentle rapids take you down to a large railway viaduct and then to Bothal Weir. This has an unusual construction with a fish ladder running down the middle. The two metre stepped drop is usually easiest on the left where most of the flow is collected. Small boats such as Rotobats may be able to bounce down the fish ladder, but as we discovered to our cost Dancers tend

117

to get stuck!

One hundred metres downstream lies Bothal road bridge and 0.5km further on the compact and well preserved 14th century Bothal Castle is seen on the left.

This is owned by Welbeck Estates and currently leased to Welwyn Electronics Ltd, for entertaining favoured clients.

A footpath leads up to the village on the left. Many paddlers might prefer to finish here because the best of the paddling is now over as the gradient eases further.

A series of concrete stepping stones with narrow channels necessitates a brief portage here.

Although the woodland vale continues the rapids gradually peter out. In several kilometres a small angled weir with a 1.0m sloping drop curves beneath Sheepwash road bridge.

From here the river is now completely flat as it passes through a riverside park which runs for about three kilometres before a tidal dam is reached at North Seaton.

Those finishing here can egress up the left bank just opposite the water ski jump.

The access road down to the riverside is found by turning off the A189 from Newcastle at the roundabout, following signs to Ashington. After 0.5km another left turn signposted North Seaton will take you down to the riverside.

River Wansbeck - summary

Wallington Hall to Mitford
Length 20.5kms   Grade II/III   No Portages

Kms		
0	**Access**	Wallington Hall road bridge. Access in high water. (OS Ref 034838)
1.5		Bridge at Scarlet Hall.
2.5		Road bridge.
6.5		Railway bridge. (Disused)
8		Low Angerton road bridge.
10.5		Confluence with Hartburn. Footbridge below.
11		**Rocky Fall.** 1m drop. Rocks below. Meldon Hall. Left.
12		Bridge.
12.5		Road bridge.
20		Mitford road bridge. Mitford Castle. Right.
		Weir below. 0.5m sloping drop.
		250m. Two **Rocky Sills.** Keep left.
20.5		Font joins left.
	Egress	Left bank. (OS Ref 174859)
		Above **gauging weir.** Steps lead up to road (use central chute only)

Mitford to North Seaton (Ashington)
Length 18kms   Grade II/III   No Portages

Kms

0	**Access**	Mitford road bridge. (OS Ref 171856)
		Small weir below.
		50m. Two **Rocky Sills.**
0.5		River Font joins left.
0.75		**Gauging Weir.** 1.25m drop use central chute *only.*
1		A1. Road bridge.
1.5		Iron water pipe spans river.
		25m. **Weir.** 2.75m sloping drop with a long plateau and final small vertical step.
1.75		Road bridge.
3		Road bridge.
		Houses appear. Outskirts of Morpeth.
3.5		Footbridge.
3.75		Stepping stones.
4		Road bridge.
4.25		Iron girder bridge.
		100m **weir** 2.0m sloping drop.
4.5		Footbridge.
		100m road bridge.
5.5		**East Mill weir.** Horse shoe shape 2m drop. Inspect.
		Powerful stopper in high water.
6.5		Lattice girder bridge.
7		Viaduct.
9		Bothal **weir.** 2m stepped sloping drop. Shoot left of Fish Ladder.
		100m road bridge.
10.5	**Egress**	Egress point. Bothal Castle. Left. (OS Ref 241865)
		Stepping stones. Path leads up to Bothal Village. Left.
13.5		Low road bridge with 1.0m **weir** beneath.
15.5		Road bridge.
16		Viaduct.
16.5		Left bank. Opposite ski jump. (OS Ref 288856)
16.75		**Weir.** Tidal dam.
17		A189 Road bridge.
18		North Seaton Estuary.

River Wear

Introduction

Few canoeists jump for joy at the mention of the river Wear, as most of the canoeing is restricted to the picturesque but relatively unexciting rapids between Durham and Finchdale Abbey. However, white water canoeists should not despair! Hiding away at the top end of the valley is an interesting white water section, conveniently placed just south east of Alston near the source of the South Tyne and Allen, which also offer good prospects in high water.

The river arises in the Northern Pennines from the union of Killhope Burn with the smaller Burnhope Burn at Wearhead. From here the river descends rapidly following an easterly course through Stanhope and Woolsingham. At Bishop Auckland the river turns northwards flowing through Durham, finally meandering slowly across the coastal plain through Chester-le-Street to meet the sea at Sunderland.

Access

The upper sections which are rarely paddled tend to be trouble free. Durham to Finchdale Abbey is an established canoeists' run. Below Finchdale canoeing is discouraged and there are many signs to that effect. There has been some harassment to canoeists from game keepers on Lord Lambton's estate although most of the river is a public navigation as the upper tidal limit extends almost to Chester-le-Street (Lambton bridge).

Local Access Officer: Dave Pope,
142 Raby Road,
Newton Hall,
Durham City,
Co. Durham.
Tel: 091 386 2866

Wearhead to Stanhope

Length 17kms   **Grade** III   **No Portages**

This is undoubtedly the best stretch on the Wear. Whilst not quite in the same class as the Allen or Upper Tees, white water canoeists should certainly give this section a try for most will not be disappointed. It consists of a sustained gradient through a series of small steps in the bedrock which create a regular series of small stoppers and turbulent rapids every few hundred metres for about 17kms.

For the sake of clarity only the more significant drops have been mentioned. Likewise most of the innumerable footbridges and waterpipes which span the river have been omitted. One of the lowest occurs shortly after you begin (at 0.5km) so if you get under that alright, waterpipes are unlikely to be a problem.

It goes without saying that this is a stretch for paddlers with some experience, for whilst there are no heavy rapids here the continuously fast water gives little time for manoeuvring around the unexpected hazards which invariably occur on this type of water.

The river is very small at the starting point so that it must be paddled in spate. After very heavy rainfall you can gain access higher up the valley on the Killhope Burn at Cowshill to incorporate Burrtree Falls into your trip. For those not in their boats Killhope lead mine is well worth a visit, lying four miles up the valley on the A689 to Alston.

The access point is found by continuing over the main road bridge at Wearhead, parking 150m further up the road towards Alston. Here a signpost to a footpath directs you over a stone bridge where you can get in 50m upstream just below two small falls.

After 250m you pass beneath the main road bridge with an easy rapid beneath. In half a kilometre you reach the footbridge with several flimsy waterpipes running across.

It is worth getting out of your canoe at 1.5km beneath the stone road bridge to inspect several falls below.

A small drop leads to a more substantial 1.25m vertical fall, which has a significant towback especially in the centre. Then walk a further 100m down the left bank to inspect a smaller drop (0.5m) which may also prove tricky. This usually has a clear channel just left of centre.

These drops are the most difficult and once negotiated you can look forward to a similar sequence of small drops, pleasant stoppers to play in and the Weardale countryside to entertain you for the next 17kms. The only exception being the Blue Circle cement works at 12km, which rudely interrupts this rural tranquillity with its noisy conveyer belts spanning the river and the large factory complex visible on the left bank.

At 16km the Stanhope gauging weir should be inspected, although there is usually a stopper free zone just left of centre.

Egress on the right bank when the ford is reached about 0.5km below the weir. (OS Ref 993392)

Stanhope to Durham

Length	63kms	
Grade	II/III	Stanhope to Woolsingham
Grade	II	Woolsingham to Durham
Grade	III	Durham Weir
Portage	Durham Weir	
OS Map	Ref 273425	

This is a pleasant but not outstanding touring section best paddled in high water.

After Woolsingham the gradient flattens out further. The paddle through Durham city is interesting and Durham Weir represents a challenge to those competent to do it.

Access Stanhope ford. (OS Ref 993392)

Apart from one small weir the only significant rapids occur as you come into Woolsingham. After passing beneath a railbridge the large steel rolling mills become visible on the left. A small drop heralds 75m of Grade II/III rapids.

Several small weirs are interposed between Woolsingham and Durham, then as the city is reached the water flattens out completely. The rural tranquillity becomes broken by the gentle hum of city traffic. Durham is probably one of the prettiest cities to paddle through as the skyline is graced by the magnificent Cathedral and Castle around which the river loops. An ever present hazard are the University sculling crews which whiz up and down this stretch of water, rowing as if to eternity, oblivious to all but the cox shouting the stroke.

After going around the main part of the loop you pass beneath a large stone footbridge (Pretends Bridge) a small weir with a 1.0m drop is just beyond, which has a convenient chute on the left.

Pull in just *before* the next bridge (Framwellgate Bridge) on to the left bank to inspect Durham Weir. This is a long, angled weir with a 2.75m drop. Initially vertical, then steeply sloping. This combination makes it difficult to see the stopper at the bottom. Hence, careful inspection is necessary. In addition there is a small weir 100m downstream which develops a very strong undertow in high water.

Once the main weir is shot you are virtually obliged to take this second more dangerous weir, as high walls link the two drops. (See diagram.)

In low water Durham Weir is best shot down the three steps, forming a fish ladder on the left.

The bottom weir can be shot in most places in low water but in spate your best chance of survival lies in taking a line on the far right close to the generator outflow from the ice-rink where the fish ladder may take you past the stopper. (But you shouldn't be trying to shoot it at this level.)

Those wishing to portage the weir to continue downstream should paddle along the top of the weir to the right bank beneath the large concrete road bridge which straddles the weir. You can then walk behind the ice-rink and get in at the car park. Otherwise egress 100m below the bottom weir where the embankment ends on the left bank. (OS Ref 274431)

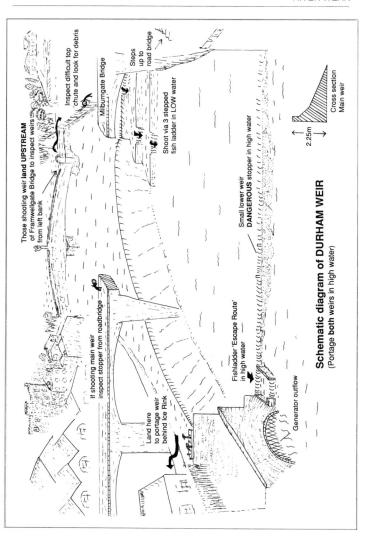

Those shooting weir **land UPSTREAM** of Framwellgate Bridge to inspect weirs from left bank

Inspect difficult top chute and look for debris

Milburngate Bridge

Steps up to road bridge

Shoot via 3 stepped fish ladder in LOW water

If shooting main weir inspect stopper from roadbridge

Land here to portage weir behind Ice Rink

Fishladder 'Escape Route' in high water

Generator outflow

Small lower weir **DANGEROUS** stopper in high water

← 2.25m →

Cross section Main weir

Schematic diagram of DURHAM WEIR
(Portage both weirs in high water)

Durham to (Finchdale Abbey) Chester-le-Street

Length 19kms   **Grade** II   **No Portages**

This is the most well known part of the River Wear as Finchdale Priory is extensively used as a venue for slalom competitions.

The paddle down to Finchdale is made worthwhile by the attractive wooded vale that accompanies the river for most of its journey from Durham.

The easy shingle rapids make this stretch particularly suitable for introducing novice paddlers to white water. Most canoeists will wish to egress at Finchdale Priory, as the woods soon disappear and the river begins to meander lazily across the flood plain.

There have also been some access problems below Finchdale Abbey, so that those venturing further downstream will often encounter some less than friendly notices directed towards canoeists on their way down to Chester-le-Street.

The best starting point is from Framwellgate waterside (OS Ref 993392) or from the ice-rink car park, which lie close to the city centre.

After a few hundred metres a strong smell comes from the sewage works which can be smelt but not seen.

In just over 2km attractive mixed woodland rises up on either bank.

A large viaduct at 5km shows that you are just over half way to the Priory.

At 8km caravans can be seen peeping out from between the trees, and then the Priory ruins are seen on the left bank as a brief shingle rapid takes you beneath a footbridge.

Those wishing to finish here egress at the left bank 50m below the bridge, when some rather crude footsteps take you up to the car park.

Those continuing downstream face an arduous paddle to Chester-le-Street. A road bridge is passed at 11.5km.

Although Lumley Castle soon comes into view, several broad meanders seem calculated to frustrate your journey. However, finally new Lumley road bridge comes into view. Egress left bank.

Chester-le-Street to Sunderland

Length 21kms   **Grade** I (Ex. weir)   **Portage** (opt.) Chester-le-Street Weir

There are no rapids below Chester-le-Street and one could easily be forgiven for thinking that you had inadvertently entered the canal system. In fact the water is so sluggish that at times it is difficult to tell which way the water is flowing.

There have been access problems with Lord Lambton's estate, although this presumably relates to the stretch above Lambton Bridge which marks the upper tidal limit. Below this the river is tidal and therefore a public navigation.

The river is now quite polluted and in a warmer country one might expect to see a yawning hippo, or the glinting eye of a crocodile emerging from the deep, dark, murky waters. However, there is usually plenty of wildlife as the magnificent Lambton Castle and its estate are festooned with pheasants and other game, which provide a pleasant distraction from the less savoury aspects of this paddle.

To find the starting point take the B1284 out of Chester-le-Street towards Lumley Castle. Two hundred metres before the road bridge is a car park on the right. Access is easiest on the left bank just upstream of the river. One hundred metres beyond the road bridge lies a small but unpleasant weir with a 1.0m vertical drop, which has a powerful towback in high water when it is best portaged, otherwise it is easily shot on the periphery.

Several road bridges are then passed before you enter the Castle grounds. The attractive arched Lambton Bridge in the middle of the estate marks the upper tidal limit. A few hundred metres beyond, Lambton Castle is easily visible on the left.

Once Fatfield village is passed small seagoing vessels may be seen.

Those going all the way to the sea will want to egress near the yacht club at the North Pier. (OS Ref 409585)

The tale of the Lambton Worm

Whilst passing through the deep grubby waters of Lambton Castle it is worth reflecting on the origins of the extraordinary legend of the Lambton Worm. For according to folklore it was on this estate that the young Earl of Durham caught a strange worm whilst fishing in the River Wear.

On his way home he threw the worm into a deep well at Lambton Castle. For many years it lay there undisturbed and forgotten by all. Slowly it grew and grew until it was able to crawl out of the well and began to terrorise the neighbourhood. All attempts to kill the monster failed, as when the worm was cut in two the halves simply rejoined.

The monster was so enormous that at night it slept coiled "Ten times around Penshaw Hill". This hill is easily recognised, being crowned with Penshaw Monument, erected in 1844 to the Earl of Durham. An alternative version of events states that it wrapped itself around Worm Hill a small hillock overlooking the banks of the Wear.

Many years later the young Lambton returned from the Crusades.

On hearing of the death and destruction wrought by the worm he felt responsible for having brought the beast to the estate, so he felt duty bound to try and kill it although many had tried and failed.

He decided to seek the help of a witch who advised him to cover his armour with sharp blades and fight the worm in the river. This advice was given on the condition that whosoever came first to congratulate him after slaying the worm should themselves be slain by Lambton.

The young Knight succeeded in luring the monster into the river where it coiled itself around him. The monster was cut to shreds by the razors, the pieces being carried away by the river and unable to rejoin.

In his excitement on slaying the beast he signalled to the Castle and his Father came out to meet him. Unable to kill his Father to fulfil the condition set by the witch, a curse was put on all the family that no male Lambton would die in his bed! Allegedly many young Lambtons of subsequent generations met untimely deaths in a series of mysterious accidents and battles.

River Wear - summary

Wearhead to Stanhope
Length 17kms   Grade III   No Portages

Kms		
0	**Access**	Wearhead. Go over main road bridge on A689 towards Alston. After 150m roadside parking and follow footpath signs to river. OS Ref 857397.
		250m. Road bridge. Minor rapid beneath.
0.5		Footbridge. Several water pipes traverse river.
1.5		Stone road bridge. West Blackdene hamlet. Left.
		Get out beneath bridge to inspect several **falls**.
		1.25m. **THEN** walk a further 100m to another drop. 0.5m. and which may have strong undertow.
2		Bridge.
2.5		Concrete road bridge.
3		Small **fall** on right bend. 0.5m drop.
		Footbridge below.
4.5		Large water pipe.
		Footbridge.
		Huntshield Ford. St John's Chapel. Right.
5.5		Daddry Shiel road bridge.
6		Footbridge with stepping stones beneath.
7		Road bridge. Westgate village. Left.
12		Blue Circle cement works.
		Conveyor and rail bridge.
13		Road bridge.
16		Rail bridge.
		50m **Gauging weir.** Inspect. 1.5m sloping drop.
		Shoot centre. Leads into wide gorge for 200m.
16.5		Road bridge.
16.75		Ford and stepping stones.
	Egress	Right bank. OS Ref 993392

Stanhope to Durham
Length 63kms

    Grade II/III - Stanhope to Woolsingham Portage Durham Weir
    Grade II   - Woolsingham to Durham
    Grade III   - Durham Weir

Kms		
0	**Access**	Stanhope ford. OS Ref 993392
		(Those wishing to shoot the Gauging Weir get in 250m upstream)
		250m Footbridge.
0.5		Rail bridge.
1		Rail bridge.
1.5		Road bridge.
3.5		Rail bridge.
5		Frosterley road bridge.
8		Road bridge.
		250m **Weir.** 1m sloping drop. Inspect high water.
11		Rail bridge. Woolsingham. Left. with Steel Mills.
		Grade II/III **rapids,** commencing with small 0.25m drop.
12		Rail bridge.
		After Woolsingham river flattens out.
24.5		Road bridge. Witton-le-Wear. A68.
24.7		Stone road bridge.
26		**Weir.** 1m vertical drop. Inspect. Portage high water.
28		Viaduct crossed beneath by road bridge.
		100m **weir** 0.5m drop. Shoot centre.
		50m **Broken weir.** 1.25m drop.
31		**Weir.** 0.5m drop.
		Escomb Village. Right. Council estate of white houses.
34.5		Bishop Auckland Road bridge.
		100m viaduct.
35		Auckland Castle right bank.
43.5		Willington road bridge.
47		Road bridge.
50		Viaduct.
50.5		Stone road bridge.
		Weir beneath. Inspect. 1.0m stepped drop.
		100m. Road bridge. A167.
51.5		River Browney joins left.
58.5		Shincliffe Bridge.
59.5		Concrete footbridge.
61		Footbridge.
61.5		Concrete road bridge.
		100m. Elvet Bridge.

62		Stone road bridge. (Pretend's Bridge)
		100m **Weir.** 1m drop. Shoot extreme left.
		Cathedral right bank.
62.5		Stone road bridge.
		Get out left bank to inspect both weirs.
		Durham Weir. Angled 2.75m sloping drop.
		Fish ladder left. 3 steps. Route in low water.
		Road bridge.
		150m **Weir.** 0.5m vertical drop.
		Dangerous towback. Shoot extreme right,
		in high water. (**Portage advised**)
63	**Egress**	Left bank. OS Ref 274431

Durham to (Finchdale Abbey) Chester-le-Street
Length 19kms   Grade II   No Portages

Kms		
0	**Access**	Framwellgate waterside. (OS Ref 993392)
2.5		River enters wooded vale.
5		Railway viaduct.
7.5		Footbridge carrying large water pipes.
8.5		Caravan and camping site left.
		Finchdale Priory left.
		Minor **Rapids.** Grade II 100m down to Footbridge.
	Egress	50m below footbridge. Left bank.
11.5		Road bridge.
19	**Egress**	Road bridge. Left bank OS Ref 284509.
		Lumley Castle. Right bank.

Chester-le-Street to Sunderland
Length 21kms   Grade I (Ex. weir)   Optional Portage Chester-le-Street Weir

Kms		
0	**Access**	Bridge at Lumley Castle. (OS Ref 284509)
		250m **Weir.** 1.0m vertical drop. **Inspection essential.**
		Portage in high water. Strong towback.
1.5		Concrete road bridge. A1(M)
2		Road bridge.
		100m Old stone road bridge. Small weir beneath.
4.5		Arched stone road bridge. Lambton Bridge. (Tidal limit)
4.75		Lambton Castle. Left.

Adventure on the River Swale. (Kisdon Force)

Offshore from Bamburgh Castle. Photo: Rob Egelstaff

A moment of magic - playing with a dolphin in the North Sea.
Photo: Nick Doll

Kms		
5.5		Iron road bridge.
7		Concrete road bridge. Fatfield village. Left.
7.5		Box girder. Road bridge.
8		Viaduct.
9.5		Footbridge. Cox green.
13.5		Concrete road bridge.
17.5		Road bridge.
20		Wearmouth Bridge.
21	**Egress**	North Pier near Yacht Club. (OS Ref 409585)

The Whiteadder
(Pronounced Wit - Adder)

Introduction
Although lying just outside the North East region, this northern tributary of the Tweed has been included as it contains several rapids and falls of interest to local paddlers.

Arising in the Lammermuir Hills of East Lothian and Berwickshire, the headwaters soon flow into Whiteadder reservoir, from which some five million gallons of drinking water are drawn off each day.

In the winter months there is a standard release of 0.5 million gallons per day, which is increased on the 1st May to 2.5 million gallons for the duration of the summer months.

Immediately below the reservoir there is usually too little water to canoe and the gradient is minimal, but after about five kilometres the river is swollen by the Dye Water.

The Whiteadder then forms a gigantic loop around the village of Abbey St Bathans, where the best of the paddling is to be found with a Grade III rapid, and several challenging falls.

Below this the river has little of interest except for several weirs (including one with a fearsome reputation known as the 'gobbler') before its confluence with the Tweed close to Berwick.

Access
No known problems. Most canoeing is done on the upper section around Abbey St Bathans. Objections unlikely if paddled in high water.

Ellemford Bridge to Preston Haugh

Length 14.5km   **Grade** III (One Fall Grade III/IV)   **No Portages**

129

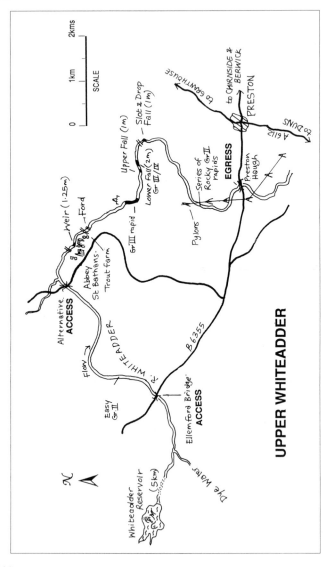

UPPER WHITEADDER

As some of the headwaters are removed by Whiteadder reservoir, it is worth paddling this river only after a generous amount of rainfall.

Most paddlers will wish to get in at Ellemford Bridge. Along with the egress point at Preston Haugh, this lies at the neck of a large loop so that ferry is surprisingly short and can easily be cycled or even walked. This is quite a lengthy paddle and as all the major rapids occur after Abbey St Bathans those wishing to shorten the journey can get in at the next road bridge or the ford, in the middle of the village.

Below Ellemford Bridge, easy Grade II rapids take you uneventfully down to Abbey St Bathans. Heralded first by a rusty lattice girder bridge, soon followed by a pristine wooden footbridge opposite a church and a few houses easily visible on the right bank.

Here some flat water leads up to a small weir where water is drawn off to a trout farm on the right, which is usually worth a visit.

The enormous number of peacocks found at the other end of the village come from a game farm just out of sight on the left.

Another footbridge is soon reached with a concrete ford. This sometimes requires a portage as water flows beneath the ford through several drainage pipes.

After another few kilometres an attractive house looking rather like a gigantic dovecote appears on the left, known as 'Retreat House'.

This marks a more interesting phase in the river course. Here there is a small 1.0m fall then as the river rounds a left hand bend, larger rocks begin

The falls just beyond Abbey St. Bathans

to obstruct the flow as the gradient steepens forming 150m of Grade III rapid.

No sooner has this ended than a small 1m rocky fall is easily shot on the left. Most people will wish to pre-inspect this, and the much larger fall 25 metres beyond. This second fall is most easily seen from the right bank. It is usually shot in two steps by the centre right chute. The left hand chute is blocked by a rather nasty looking jagged rock near the bottom so that this can only be used in high water. The fall is Grade III/IV at most levels, but usually presents few serious problems.

Below here some flattish water passes beneath a footbridge with a straightforward slot and drop fall about one metre in height.

There are still several kilometres of minor rapids to go before egressing at Preston Haugh Bridge. (A Dancer will slip between the drainage holes which take most of the flow beneath the ford.)

Preston Haugh to Allanton Bridge

Length 14km   **Grade** I   **No Portages**

Few people will wish to paddle the middle section of the Whiteadder as the most exciting event the river has to offer is watching the crystal clear waters of the Whiteadder being turned a green turbid colour, as Chirnside Paper Mill pollutes the water with industrial effluent.

Allanton road bridge to confluence - River Tweed

Length 17.5km   **Grade** I - II   **Optional Portage** Allanton weir

After getting in, easy rapids take you down to a series of small rocky ledges at about 1km.

Soon a ford and footbridge herald a small but nasty concrete weir affectionately known as 'the gobbler.' In high water the weir should be portaged and also in low water, when only the difficult central chute has water.

Several kilometres downstream a castle is seen high on the right bank as an easy weir with a 2m drop is approached. Edington Mill which produces porridge oats is seen on the left. Originally driven by water power, much of the old machinery is still intact.

Halfway up the side of the mill a metal plaque commemorates the level at which the Whiteadder reached on the 13th August 1948, following the worst floods in recorded history.

Another straightforward weir follows before egressing at the next road bridge (OS Ref 958527) carrying the B6461. The Whiteadder then meanders peacefully for another kilometre or so before joining the River Tweed.

Whiteadder - summary
Ellemford Bridge to Preston Haugh Bridge
Length 14.5km   Grade III (One Fall Grade III/IV)   No Portages

Kms		
0	**Access**	Ellemford Bridge. (OS Ref 728601)
4.5		Lattice girder road bridge.
5		New wooden footbridge. Village. Abbey St Bathans. Right.
		200m **weir.** 1.25m sloping drop.
5.5		Footbridge and ford. Trout farm. Right.
7.5		Retreat house. Left. Small fall.
8		Grade **III Rapids** for 150m.
8.5		Upper **fall.** 1m stepped drop. Shot on the left.
		25m Lower **fall.** (Grade III/IV) 2m rocky fall. In low to medium water centre right shoot most easily inspected on right bank. Left chute feasible in high water only.
9		Footbridge.
		25m Small **fall** below. 1m drop.
		Shoot right slot.
12.5		Pylons stride alongside river bank. Not far to go!
14.5	**Egress**	Preston Haugh. Elevated Ford on drainage pipes. (OS Ref 775578)

Preston Haugh to Allanton road bridge
Length 14km   Grade I   No Portages

Kms		
0	**Access**	Preston Haugh (OS Ref 775578)
6.75		Castle. Left.
7		Road bridge.
9		Chirnside **weir.** 3m sloping drop and small vertical drop.
		Central fish ladder may be shot if clear of debris.
9.5		Road bridges.
		Chirnside Paper Mill.
13.9		Blackadder joins right.
14	**Egress**	Allanton Bridge. (OS Ref 865545)

Allanton road bridge to confluence - River Tweed
Length 17.5km   Grade I - II   No Portages   (Caution Allanton weir)

Kms		
0	**Access**	Allanton Bridge. (OS Ref 865545)
2		Ford with footbridge below.

Kms

		100m. Concrete **weir**. 1.5m sloping drop. The 'Gobbler' - *caution* high water. Difficult central chute.
3		Castle. Right.
		Weir. 2m sloping drop. Edington Mill. Left.
6		Bridge.
14.5		**Weir.** 2m sloping drop.
15	**Egress**	Road bridge. OS Ref 958527
17.5		Confluence. River Tweed.

Wooler Water (Harthope Burn)

Langleeford to Wooler

Access:	Langleeford. (OS Ref 949220)
Egress:	Haughhead Ford. (OS Ref 001261) or Wooler. (OS Ref 994283)
Length:	10kms.
Grade:	III
No Portages.	
Local Access Officer:	Mr Peter Clark,
	Windy Gyle,
	Belford,
	Northumberland.
	Tel: Belford 0668 213 289

Introduction

Arising on the eastern side of the Cheviot, this small river starts life as the Harthope Burn.

Higher up the valley walkers to the Cheviot will be familiar with Harthope Linn, a 20 foot waterfall that is awaiting the day when all canoeists are helicoptered in to their access points.

In spate conditions the river offers a swift descent with easy rocky rapids, and the occasional small drop that is unlikely to unseat any riverwise canoeists.

Access

This river is rarely paddled. There are no known access problems.

River Course

A generous amount of rain needs to have fallen on the Cheviots before this becomes a worthwhile paddle. The access point is at Langleeford, where the road up the valley terminates.

Minor rapids take you down through this attractive valley of the Cheviots. The occasional larger rocks or fallen branch, may provoke a little interest.

Several kilometres further on the Carey Burn swells the flow considerably. The river now becomes known as the Wooler Water.

As the neck of the valley is reached the river is forced to wind its way through the hills which now begin to close in on either side, forming 'Happy valley.'

At one point a small gorge is encountered (Racoon Ravine). Here small cliffs soar up on either side as the river goes over a small fall, followed by a brief constriction which is about 0.75 metres wide. This can be quite tricky in low water but quickly washes out in spate conditions.

Soon the valley sides start to open out again as a small ford and footbridge are passed. About 1km downstream a set of steps is formed by a series of small weirs, each with a vertical drop of about 0.35 metres, but the last fall is a little more substantial and should be inspected as a series of rocky slabs lie below.

Most people will wish to egress at the ford which is just downstream, for the river has little else to offer as it makes its way towards Wooler. This has a small weir just after the first road bridge.

Egress at the second road bridge where the B6348 crosses the river about 100 metres below the weir.

Beyond Wooler the river stagnates further before joining a particularly sluggish section of the Till 2.5km further on.

Wooler Water (Harthope Burn) - summary

Langleeford to Wooler

Length 10kms   Grade III   No Portages

Kms		
0	**Access**	Langleeford. (OS Ref 949220)
4		Carey Burn joins left.
		Valley sides narrow as river enters 'Happy valley.'
5.5		Brief **gorge** section. 'Racoon Ravine.'
		Fall. 1m drop into hour glass constriction. Inspect.
6		Ford and footbridge.
		Small rapid below.
7		Succession of small **weirs** each 0.5m vertical drops.
		Final drop is a more significant rocky **fall** 1.0m onto rock slabs.
		Inspection advisable.
7.5	**Egress**	Footbridge. and ford. (OS Ref 001261)

Kms		
9.5		Road bridge. A697. Wooler town left bank.
9.75		**Weir.** 1m sloping drop.
10	**Egress**	Road bridge. B6348. (OS Ref 994283)
12.5		Confluence with River Till.

ADDENDUM
(Northumberland Region)

All the following rivers and streams have been inspected by the author, but only some have been paddled. Most are unsuitable for the average paddler but have been included either to document why nobody bothers to paddle them or to describe an isolated feature of interst such as a waterfall which might tempt some canoeists.

Ashgill Beck

This small tributary of the upper South Tyne has several large falls which can be shot in high water.

Access is either from the B6277 on the Alston to Barnard Castle road or, if you're already paddling the South Tyne you can walk up the Ashgill Beck to the upper falls which lie only 0.75km from its confluence with South Tyne. The confluence is located about 2km above Garrigill in the middle section of the upper South Tyne gorges. (See map upper South Tyne). If access is from the road take care to portage the first bone crushing 10m drop which lies immediately below the bridge.

Bowmont Water

Grade II

A small border river that runs almost due north from the Cheviot hills through Yetholm turning eastwards just south of Coldstream where it is joined by the College Burn to become the River Glen.

Canoeable from Belford or Attonburn, the river offers a steady descent in high water, with continuous if unexciting shingle rapids.

Cauldron Snout

As the young river Tees emerges from Cow Green reservoir it falls about one hundred feet over a Basalt outcrop which forms part of the Great Whin Sill. Your first impression will probably be the right one, that this beautiful silvery cascade looks about as user friendly as a lump of Aldermaston plutonium.

*The author takes an MI 335 over
Cauldron Snout, River Tees
Photo: Stevie Hanson*

Most paddlers will require little prompting to leave their boats tied onto the car. At most water levels it is not really a viable canoeing proposition but has been included to represent the extreme end of what is available to paddlers in the North East.

Considered by many canoeists to be Grade VI, this was recently paddled by the author who managed to descend most of it backwards finishing up at the bottom fall facing in the correct direction only to hit an inconveniently placed rock at the bottom (see photo).

The only tips for canoeing this fall are:

1. Not to shoot it!
2. If you really must have a go, use a short robust boat such as a Topolino.
3. Avoid extremes of water level. Too little water can be as dangerous as too much.
4. In low water the bottom fall has insufficient flow on the right hand side to carry you clear of the rocks and into the plunge pool.

A further difficulty is that there is no public vehicular access to the falls, although the Pennine Way provides a public right of way.

If you want thrills and excitement from shooting large drops most paddlers will find they get much better value from the safer, equally spectacular falls found on the upper Swale.

Chirdon Burn

Grade II/III plus falls
This small river in Kielder Forest has several interesting falls, including Jerry's Linn (OS Ref 745813) a four metre drop which lies just upstream of 100 metres of boulder choked rapids. There are some more falls which lie close to the river's source, although access is difficult.

College Burn

Grade II plus falls
This small Cheviot river runs almost parallel to the Bowmont Water, but several miles to the east.

There are no significant rapids or falls up the valley, although just below Hethpool a small 1.5m waterfall is followed by a much trickier narrow chute beneath an undercut rock. This needs to be portaged.

Not worth making a special trip for.

East Allen

Grade II/III
The best starting point is from Sinderhope Ford or road bridge (OS Ref 844522) which lie just above Holms Linn the largest drop on the river. This 3m waterfall may be shot in the centre/left. Avoid the extreme right where the

Tickling trout on the College Burn

plunge pool is very shallow. Easy rapids then take you downstream through Woods and unspoilt pastureland.

At 5kms Allendale town is reached. As car parking is limited in the town centre those wishing to obtain access to the river at this point are advised to go 2kms downstream to Thornley Gate Bridge with its small weir below.

After 11kms the river merges with its twin sister the West Allen to form the river Allen proper.

River Glen

Grade I - II

Formed from the union of the College Burn and Bowmont Water at West Newton. This river offers a pleasant, easy paddle down from Kilham (OS Ref 886329). After a short paddle the valley sides come down to meet the river at Canno Mill, displaying some interesting glacial features in the form of eskers and drumlins. The weir has been completely dismantled. A good egress point is at Akeld where the A697 crosses the river. Below here the river meanders slowly down the valley to join the Till several miles north of Wooler.

River Nent

Grade II - III plus falls

Canoeable only after heavy rainfall this interesting little tributary of the South Tyne can be paddled from as high up as Nenthead.

But as the first few kilometres contain nothing more exciting than a few watercress beds or an occasional hardy stickleback most paddlers would be advised to start about 4kms downstream at Blaghill road bridge (OS Ref 739469).

After several hundred metres the Nent enters a small patch of woodland with several steps in the bedrock correctly predicting a more promising change of character.

As the river emerges from the wood a large waterfall is encountered on a sharp left hand bend. This is High Force (not to be confused with the High Force of Tees fame). The 3m vertical drop is best shot into the centre. The plunge pool has an approximate depth of 1:75m in the centre/right. Although marginally deeper on the left, the fall has an awkward step in it.

A pleasant bouldery rapid then ensues before the river flattens out for about 1km before the white farmhouse at Gossipgate marks the spot of a 2m vertical drop. The plunge pool is a little less than generous having a depth of 1-1:25m most easily shot in the centre. A road bridge lies just downstream but don't relax as your problems are only just beginning!

In about 100m the river is seen to disappear over a concrete weir with a defunct sluice gate.

A brief inspection will probably be enough to stimulate any latent instincts of self preservation that might be present in the most reckless of wild water paddlers.

The weir consists of a 2m steeply sloping drop onto some rock slabs. You then just have time to take a deep breath before being squirted over Low Force, a 5:5m vertical drop into a rather suspect plunge pool which although having a depth of nearly 2m in the centre shallows rapidly beneath the fall.

Careful inspection of the plunge pool is therefore essential if you don't want a bent boat and a broken spine.

Surprisingly the inspection can be achieved without getting your hair wet by making use of a deep cleft which runs behind the fall. It is reached by a steep footpath on the left bank. Those wishing to portage will find it easier to pass around by the old quarry on the right bank.

The excitement now over several road bridges are then passed as the town of Alston is reached. The best egress point is at the railway station. In the summer months regular steam trains run on a few miles of small gauge track. A convenient footpath leads from the rear of the station car park to follow the river.

In high water conditions many paddlers will wish to continue down to the confluence which lies around the next bend and then to paddle down the South Tyne as far as Featherstone Castle. (See South Tyne for details.)

The Ouseburn

Grade II - III with one 3.5m fall

A few eyebrows may be raised at the inclusion of this small river, running through the centre of Newcastle upon Tyne.

Its delicate fragrance in low water reminds the paddler that effluent is a significant constituent.

In spate conditions this river can be canoed though more as a stunt than a pleasurable canoe trip.

Access is from a small footbridge found by turning right at the bottom of Matthew Bank down Craghall Dene.

After passing beneath Castle Farm road bridge, in about 100 metres a weir with a 1.75m vertical drop prepares you for a large waterfall with a 3.5m drop into a shallow plunge pool. This has several semi submerged rocks on the right. If this is shot your boat is usually never quite the same again. The river is then divided by a large rock in midstream, with tight fast channels running either side. The left being the easiest. The worst is now over with only several easy weirs.

Egress anywhere beyond the Armstrong bridge as shortly afterwards the river disappears into a long, dark tunnel taking the Ouseburn beneath Heaton to re-emerge in Byker before joining the Tyne.

Rookhope Burn

Grade III

This small tributary of the River Wear makes a tasty hors d'oeuvre if you're in the Weardale area after heavy rainfall. There are no difficult rapids but a series of small drops and one rather larger one makes an entertaining run.

Get in about 1/2km before Rookhope village where the road briefly runs alongside the river. Park your car on the right by the footpath sign and get in just below the newish looking footbridge. (OS Ref 944417)

If you miss the access point and end up in Rookhope village simply turn left just past Rookhope Inn where a dirt track road soon leads down to a small road bridge. There is ample car parking space amongst the spoil heaps of the Weardale Leadmining Company. Before getting in pre-inspect the tiny weir which lies 75m downstream. Here a structural timber has broken away from the river bed forming a potentially hazardous obstruction across most of the rivers width except for the extreme right.

Initially there is little of interest but after about one kilometre river banks start to become fringed with larger trees and bushes as the river begins to descend more rapidly as the Rookhope Burn cuts down through the bedrock in a series of little falls towards the valley floor. After about 3km start to keep your eyes peeled for a large caravan site easily visible on the right bank otherwise you risk being inadvertently swept over Broad Law weir. This once beautiful natural fall has been desecrated by the water authorities who have created a gauging weir by dolloping an unsightly lump of concrete over this challenging 4m drop which falls into a magnificent semicircular plungepool. Just downstream two large waterpipes arc overhead to mark the final fall that enables you to finish the paddle with a final flourish. The river enters the village of Eastgate before joining the River Wear.

The Warksburn

Grade II/III

This small tributary of the North Tyne may be canoed in high water from Stonehaugh in the Wark forest down to Wark.

It has a small 1.75m fall at about 2km.

West Allen

Grade II/III

This is very similar in size to the East Allen. Either one can be the larger depending on the pattern of recent rainfall. Both rivers need to be paddled in spate conditions.

The highest reasonable access point is from Ninebanks road bridge (OS Ref 780541) where a large lay-by provides good parking. In about 0.5kms there is a caravan park on the right bank which is just above a fall with a 2.75m vertical drop which provides an exciting start to the paddle. This is usually

Shooting Whitfield Weir on the West Allen
Arrows indicate the positioning of the metal reinforcing rods

shootable on the extreme RHS but a tree has blocked this chute for the past few years. The river then meanders through the beautiful wooded grounds of Whitefield Hall. Aged cedars and huge beeches soar skywards reducing the admiring paddler to lilliputian proportions.

Once the wood has been left behind some easy paddling follows through open countryside before Whitefield Church is seen on the left bank with its tall spire. Just downstream a stretch of slack water shows that Whitefield Weir has been reached. This drops some 4.5m in two steps. This can be a dangerous weir so that careful inspection is required particularly to locate the metal reinforcing rods sprinkled across the weir. (These have been marked on the photo above.) The weir is most easily shot on the left although many paddlers will prefer a portage.

150 metres downstream lies Whitefield road bridge which has by comparison a relatively benign weir beneath it. This is a popular starting point for groups wishing to warm up on the 3kms or so of fast Grade II/III water which leads down to the confluence with the East Allen. This then forms the main River Allen which then flows down to the River South Tyne.

Shooting Richmond Falls, River Swale

THE YORKSHIRE RIVERS

River Aire

Arising in the Pennine Hills of West Yorkshire, the Aire begins auspiciously enough at Airehead just south of Malham Tarn.

In high water the river is canoeable from Hanlith Bridge near Kirby Malham.

From here all the way down to its confluence with the Ouse the river descends at a fairly gentle pace with no major rapids or falls.

The only interruptions to your tranquil journey will come from the occasional weir. These tend to become progressively larger and more frequent as you progress down the valley. All the weirs are shootable although some are dangerous in high water, when they should be portaged. Sadly, man's interference does not stop here, for as the river threads its way through the great conurbations of Leeds and Bradford, large quantities of effluent are dumped into the river so that by the time the Aire has passed through Keighley it should be considered a significant health hazard.

Probably the best canoeing lies between Inghey Bridge and Hirstwood, Shipley. Here the river is a reasonable size and flows through some pleasant countryside, whilst remaining fairly unpolluted.

For those who wish to take up the challenge of the larger weirs and are prepared to put up with the unpleasant odour, the river still passes through some quite attractive countryside right up until Leeds city centre is reached.

Beyond Leeds station the river becomes a navigation so that you'll be sharing the water with much larger vessels. From here the river slowly makes its way to Castleford, where it is joined by the equally grimy Calder before meeting the Ouse near Goole.

The industrial archaeologists amongst you will find many features of interest as you journey downstream.

Most of the mills that lie scattered along the river valley have converted to house new industries, a few have fallen into disrepair, but several such as Thwaite Mill have been renovated and are well worth a visit.

Armley Industial Museum houses many interesting items and the famous Cistercian monastery at Kirkstall Abbey is also worth investigating.

Access

Apart from its upper reaches the river is frequently canoed, usually without problems.

The Aire becomes a navigation below the city station so that a British Waterways pass is required on the rest of the river.

Local Access Officer: J. Ackroyd,
                             Suncote,
                             Edge Bottom,
                             Denholme,
                             Bradford.
                             Tel: 0274 832 850

Kirby Malham (Hanlith Bridge) to Inghey Bridge
Length 19.5kms   **Grade** I   **No Portages**

After heavy rainfall this stretch becomes canoeable providing an easy run through attractive countryside with nothing more hazardous than a small weir or cattle fence.

Those paddlers in the area wishing to unload some adrenalin might like to go a little further up the valley to shoot Janets Foss, a four metre waterfall on Gordale Beck below Gordale Bridge (OS Ref 913634) but don't disturb Janet the Fairy Queen, who inhabits the small cave beneath the fall.

Most paddlers will want to get into the upper Aire at Hanlith Bridge just below the cattle fence. This is the first road bridge after Airehead.

The river now bubbles and gurgles contentedly as clear water takes you downstream. Apart from several cattle fences the first major hazard is Airton Weir which lies just below a footbridge. This two metre drop should present no difficulties.

At 12km the Leeds - Liverpool Canal crosses the Aire and accompanies the river all the way down to Leeds where it eventually joins the river just beyond Leeds railway station.

Some paddlers might wish to plan circular journeys down river and up canal. Those passing through Skipton on the canal may refresh themselves at the waterside pubs or bistros along the canal banks.

Inghey Bridge is a convenient double bridge where its disused forbear now makes a good parking spot. (OS Ref 962517)

Inghey Bridge to Kildwick Bridge
Length 12kms   **Grade** I   **No Portages**

Inghey Bridge (near Skipton) is a popular starting point as the river is soon swollen by the Earby Beck.

Occasional shingle rapids and deep slow moving stretches provide trouble free paddling down to Kildwick Bridge.

Beneath the bridge a tiny weir with a small vertical drop is the nearest you'll come to seeing any white water.

Kildwick Bridge to Apperley Bridge
Length 28kms   **Grade** I   **No Portages**

After getting in at Kildwick Bridge it is worth making the most of the countryside. Gradually the villages dotted along the hillside link up to form continuous chains and then begin to encroach down towards the river eventually forming the towns of Keighley on the right bank and Riddlesden on the left.

The river now becomes quite polluted and the valley more urbanised.

At 12.25km Marley Weir is worth carefully inspecting on account of the metal stakes and debris across the top of the weir. It is usually shootable on the left hand side where several stakes have been removed.

The remaining weirs are usually straightforward although each needs to be inspected especially in high water.

Occasional tracts of woodland and countryside still make this quite a pleasant paddle if the various unsavoury smells of the river can be ignored.

Below Baildon Bridge and weir is a longer stretch of countryside with cattle and horses all part of the rural scene. However, the enormous sewerage works at Esholt remind you that humanity is not too far away. Apperley Bridge is a double road bridge providing a good egress point. The upstream bridge is usually less busy so that it can be used for roadside parking.

Apperley Bridge to Thwaite Mill
Length 19.5kms   **Grade** I (excluding weirs)   **No Portages**

One strongly suspects that Rudyard Kipling might have visited the Lower Aire when he was inspired to write about the 'great grey-green, greasy Limpopo river,' for the Aire now consists of deep, flat, murky stretches of water punctuated by weirs, most of which are straightforward but many are difficult or dangerous in high water.

Worth noting is Newlay Iron Bridge constructed in 1819, and its weir 25 yards beyond which is best shot slowly at the extreme edges where small platforms at the base guide you past the main stopper.

Apart from a quick detour through Kirkstall Forge factory complex with its whirring extractor fans and hum of industrial machinery, open scrub land and fields accompany you for several kilometres until Kirkstall Abbey is seen on the left.

Below Kirkstall Bridge the river soon divides. Canoeists should keep to the right, where the river has several weirs including Boomer Weir, its 3m drop being the largest on the Aire. This weir should be portaged in spate conditions, otherwise shoot at the periphery.

Museum Weir is a little further on and should be shot on the left as there is considerable debris with several islands on the right hand side.

The Dark Arches, River Aire

If you've got the time, pop in to have a look around the industrial museum on the right bank. (It's usually closed on Mondays.)

The final hazard you have to face are the 'dark arches' as the river Aire passes beneath Leeds railway station. A small sloping drop leads into the 100m long tunnel. There is just sufficient light for reasonable visibility.

All the central arches are easily shootable, 3rd, 4th, 5th from the right.

The first two arches from the right can easily be seen to end in blind alleys.

The water is usually fairly fast and shallow. In high water standing waves occur.

Beyond the arches the Leeds-Liverpool Canal joins on the right and the river becomes a navigation.

Several ornate iron bridges are passed, including Crown Point Bridge just above Leeds lock and weir. A small track leads down to beneath the bridge making it a suitable point to egress as there is little of interest downstream until the Thwaite Mill and weir is reached. There are good car parking facilities here, and the mill is now open to the public. With luck you should find the waterwheels turning!

Surprisingly, the mill was working right up until 1975 when floods damaged the weir. Although there has been a mill here since the 17th century the present mill was built by Thomas Hewes in 1823. Its prime use was as a grinding mill for flint and china stone for the pottery industry.

The Aire - summary
Hanlith to Inghey Bridge
Length 19.5kms   Grade I   No Portages

Kms

0	**Access**	Hanlith Hall Bridge. (OS Ref 900610)
		50m cattle fence.
2.5		Footbridge and cattle fence.
3		Airton road bridge. Village right.
5.5		Small **weir**. Bridge just beyond.
6.75		Bell Busk **weir**. 1.75m sloping drop.
7		Small road bridge.
		Otterburn Beck joins right. Just above railway bridge.
9.25		Fallen tree across river. Portage, high water.
9.5		Road bridge.
9.75		Small **weir**. 1m sloping drop. Shoot slot on right hand side.
12		Aqueduct. Leeds/Liverpool Canal.
		50m railway.
14	**Egress**	Gargrave Bridge and town.
14.25		**Weir**. 1.5m steep sloping drop.
		Scattered rocks beyond.
19		Rail bridge.
19.5	**Egress**	Inghey Bridge. (OS Ref 962517)

Inghey Bridge to Kildwick Bridge
Length 12kms   Grade I   No Portages

Kms

0	**Access**	Inghey Bridge. (OS Ref 962517)
		(Skipton town left)
		250m Earby Beck joins right.
3.5		Carleton Bridge.
4.5		Railway bridge.
8.5		Cononley Bridge.
12		Concrete road bridge. A629 T.
	Egress	Kildwick road bridge. OS Ref 012457
		Small **weir** beneath 0.35m vertical drop.

Kildwick Bridge to Apperley Bridge
Length 28kms   Grade I (excluding weirs)   No Portages

Kms

0	**Access**	Kildwick Bridge. OS Ref 012457
3		Silsden Bridge.
8.5		Road bridge. Riddlesden. Left. Keighley right.
12		Marley rail bridge.
12.25		Marley **Weir**. Inspect. 1m sloping drop.
		Iron stakes across weir which collect debris.
		Easiest on left.
12.5		Castlefields **Weir**. 0.75m long sloping drop.
14		Bingley **Weir**. Oblique 1m drop.
		Shoot at an angle in centre.
		50m road bridge.
16		Cottingley road bridge.
17.5		Railway bridge.
17.75		Broken **weir** below and stepping stones.
18		Seven Arches canal aqueduct.
19.75	**Egress**	Left bank. Bradford Rowing Club. Small track at the end of coach road leads down to river. OS Ref 130384
19		Hirst **Weir**. 1m sloping drop.
20		Roberts Park left.
		Saltaire **Weir**. 1.75m sloping drop.
		Shoot far right in high water.
21.5		Baildon Bridge.
		25m Baildon **Weir**. 1.25m sloping drop washes through on right.
22.5		Railway bridge.
24		Buck Mill footbridge. Minor rapid below.
		Buck Wood right.
26		Esholt sewerage works bridge.
27.5		Rail bridge.
28	**Egress**	Apperley Bridge. OS Ref 195380
		Two bridges 50m apart.

Apperley Bridge to Thwaite Mill

Length 19.5kms   Grade I (excluding weirs)   No Portages

Kms

0	**Access**	Apperley Bridge. OS Ref 195380
2		Rail bridge.
3.5		Rail bridge.
4		Horsforth road bridge.
6		Rodley **Weir**. 2m sloping drop.
7		Rail bridge.
7.25		Newlay Iron Bridge. Constructed 1819.

Kms

	25m Newly lane **weir.** 2m sloping drop.
	High water shoot slowly at extreme edges.
8	Kirkstall Forge factory complex. Two rail bridges.
8.5	Forge **Weir.** 1m drop. Shoot extreme right.
9.5	Kirkstall Abbey left, with weir 100m beyond, 2.25m sloping drop.
	Island below.
10	Kirkstall Bridge.
	100m stadium and sports ground left.
	River divides. *Keep right.*
	50m Island weir 0.5m vertical drop. Caution stakes centre right.
10.5	Boomer **Weir.** Horseshoe shape with 3m steeply sloping drop.
	Best shot at periphery.
	Dangerous in spate.
12.25	Museum **Weir.** J shaped 2.25m sloping drop. Shoot 5 - 10m from
	left bank.
	(Islands and debris right hand side.)
13	Rail bridge.
14.5	City centre. Succession of road bridges.
15.5	The **'dark arches'** River passes beneath Leeds station.
	The *first two* arches from the right are blind alleys.
	Shoot through arches 3 to 5 from the right.
	Tunnel is about 100m in length.
15.75	Leeds/Liverpool Canal joins right.
	River becomes a navigation.
16	Victoria Bridge. Ornate iron bridge.
16.5	Leeds Bridge.
	Crown Point Bridge. Alt. Egress point beneath
Egress	the bridge. Track leads up to Clarence Road from right bank.
	100m **weir.** 1.5m sloping drop. washes through far right. Leeds Lock,
	right hand side.
18	Road bridge.
19.5 **Egress**	Thwaite Mill and **weir.** 1.75m sloping drop. inspect.
	Stakes across top of dam.
	Now the mill is restored, and worth a visit. OS Ref 328312.

The Calder

Access:	Charlestown road bridge (OS Ref 973265) Hebden Bridge from Hebden Water, Mytholmroyd (OS Ref 012263) or Sowerby Bridge (OS Ref 063236)
Egress:	Lay-by off A644 just beyond M62 junction. (OS Ref 167221)
Length:	24.25kms
Grade:	I - II (excluding weirs)
OS Map:	Blackburn and Burnley (No. 103) Leeds and Bradford (No. 104)
Local Access Officer:	Dave Wood, 23 Mortimer Avenue, Batley. WF17 8BX Tel: 0924 441040

Introduction

The Calder is another of Yorkshire's industrial rivers. It flows down from the Pennine hills of upper Calderdale in an easterly direction through the small industrial town of Hebden Bridge, before skirting around Halifax as it passes through Sowerby Bridge to reach Dewsbury and then Wakefield. Here the river starts to edge northwards to finally merge with the Aire at Castleford.

One of its larger tributaries the Hebden Water provides an exciting run in high water.

The character of the river is largely determined by the innumerable weirs once built to provide water power for the mills of Calderdale.

Some of the weirs further downstream also give depth to the Calder where it is used as a navigation. All the weirs are shootable although some can be dangerous in spate conditions, whilst in low water they provide the paddler with a cold water jacuzzi in freshly treated sewage.

For this reason the river is best paddled in moderate to high water, when its less savoury constituents are a little more diluted.

Although the river is marginally less polluted than the Aire, during the drier summer months one does sometimes wonder whether a muck spreader has preceded you downstream. Most paddlers would be well advised to clean themselves afterwards with the strongest carbolic soap Boots can provide. Those unlucky enough to go for a swim should immediately be autoclaved!

Whilst much of the upper Calderdale is a mixture of woodland and typical Pennine countryside the canoeist is often unable to appreciate the fine views, being hemmed in by high stone embankments, especially on the most attractive section just above Hebden Bridge.

A much better view of the surrounding countryside can be made from the canals which follow the Calder for most of its journey, and these provide scope for some pleasant circular tours.

Despite the industrialisation the river is extremely rich in bird life, with grey wagtails and kingfishers accompanying you for much of the journey.

Probably the best paddling is from below Mytholmroyd, for the river has now been swollen by the Hebden Water and flows through some attractive countryside, although this is only a brief rural excursion as Sowerby Bridge is soon reached. This is now well known to competition canoeists as a slalom site.

From here there is still some worthwhile paddling with easy rapids and many weirs down as far as the M62 road bridge.

The river then flattens out apart from the occasional weir.

Access

One of the few spin-offs from the river carrying such a heavy load of human effluent is that the Calder stands little chance of becoming a prime sporting river, so that there are no significant access problems. The river is also a navigation below Sowerby Bridge.

River Course

The Calder is canoeable in high water from above Todmorden although there are several difficult weirs to negotiate and the high stone walls restrict ones view. If you wish to start this high up a far better option is to use the canal, which has been restored, from Todmorden to Hebden Bridge. You can then transfer your boat at the aqueduct in Hebden Bridge back to the river.

For those paddlers wishing to start on the river at average winter levels, the highest practical starting point is probably at Charlestown which lies midway between Todmorden and Hebden Bridge.

The first hazard lies at 1km with a 250m long tunnel. This has a few scattered rocks which may have to be dodged in low water.

Several tributaries then swell the flow, first with Colden Water and then the Hebden Water a little further on.

The low bridge which crosses the river just beyond the confluence is the canal aqueduct.

At 2.5km Walkley Clog Mill may create a diversion for those with time on their hands. It is easily recognised from the river as the chimney is fused to one corner of the factory building rather than standing free. The mill is open to the public and provides refreshments.

In 4.5km Mytholmroyd is reached. This is a popular starting place with an access point just opposite the garage on the A646 to Hebden Bridge. (OS Ref 012263) Some may think the town's name has a rather Celtic ring to it but the term 'royd' means a clearing and is tagged onto many place names in the area.

The river now meanders peacefully through several kilometres of pleasant open countryside which should be savoured, as the riverside soon starts to become more industrialised. Brearley Weir provides some entertainment just above Luddenden Foot - a village with another curious name that also sports a fine iron bridge, which has a small broken weir with some easy rapids below. These lead up to a low lattice girder bridge that needs to be portaged in very high water.

Below this the river passes through a large factory complex with the phenolic smell of heated Bakelite that momentarily distracts the nose away from the less pleasant riverside odours. Here there is a V-shaped weir easily slid down on the left or shot dead centre in high water.

The double weir a little further downstream should present no problems, but in high water dangerous stoppers form on both weirs. In high water these are shot on the far right. About two kilometres further downstream Sowerby Bridge slalom site should provide a little distraction with its small weir and two rocky chutes. After another weir and several more kilometres paddling, coils of rusting wire on the left bank show that the Standard Wire Works factory has been reached. Here there is a crescent shaped weir which must be shot on the left as the right hand side has a steep sloping drop which hides an unpleasant stopper in high water.

The prize for the least pleasant weir probably goes to Elland Power Station weir. This offers you its fish slide and powerful stopper on the right and a vertical 1.5m plunge on the left. This guarantees total body immersion and a sinus washout with the circulating effluent of Halifax town. Those who feel their immune system could not cope with such an onslaught should portage along the right bank.

Several straightforward weirs and the town of Brighouse are reached before the M62 weir and road bridge are reached. The egress point is 0.5km beyond on the left where a layby off the A644 comes to within 50m of the river. (OS Ref 168221)

The Calder - summary
Length 24.25kms Grade I - II (excluding weirs) No Portages

Kms		
0	**Access**	Charlestown. (OS Ref 973265) Get in above small road bridge and below weir.
1		Tunnel 250m in length. Sufficient light for visibility.
		Peppered with small rocks.
		Central stanchion about halfway.
1.25		Colden Water joins left.

1.5		Road bridge. Hebden Bridge town.
1.75	**Access**	Hebden Water joins left. (Access via Hebden Water)
		50m low bridge. (Canal aqueduct)
2		Road bridge.
		50m Hebden Bridge **Weir.** 1.5m vertical then sloping drop.
		Easiest far right down gently sloping drop.
		Can slide down weir abutments.
2.5		Small bridge.
		25m Walkley Clog Mill left.
4.5		Small **weir.** 0.3m vertical drop.
	Access	50m Mytholmroyd. Two road bridges. (OS Ref 012263)
6		Road bridge.
		25m Brearley **Weir.** 2m sloping drop. Central cut takes most of flow.
8.5		Road bridges. Luddenden Foot.
		50m Broken **weir.** Minor rapid below.
8.75		Low bridge carrying pipes. May need portaging in spate.
9.5		Factory complex either side of river.
		V shaped **weir** 1m vertical drop on right.
		Sloping drop on left. Shoot centre in high water.
10		**Double weir.** 2.25m sloping drop. Shoot far right in high water. Inspect in spate.
		25m 1m sloping drop.
10.5		Hollins Mill **Weir.** 2.25m sloping drop.
11	**Access/Egress**	Sowerby Bridge. Town. Road bridge and Slalom site. OS Ref 063236.
		25m small **weir** below. 1m sloping drop weir cut away right hand side with playful boil.
		Ryburn adds water right.
		Two further **small drops** along Slalom course.
11.5		Gasometer left.
		250m Mearclough **Weir.** Angled 1.5m sloping drop.
		Usually shot extreme left.
		Caution in high water.
12.5		Standard Wire Works factory and **weir.**
		Convex crescent shaped weir. Shoot left hand side.
		2m gently sloping drop. Right hand side very steep drop with difficult stopper below.
13		Viaduct plus bridge.
13.5		Copley **broken weir** with rapids below.
16.5		Elland.
18		Elland Power Station. Right.
18.5		E.P.S. **weir.** 1.5m vertical drop. *Inspection advisable.*
		Difficult fish slide on right with powerful stopper.

Kms

	Usually best to go over main drop except in high water.
	Easy portage right bank.
20	**Weir.** 2m sloping drop.
22.5	Brighouse road bridge. Sugden Mill and **weir.**
	2m sloping drop.
22.75	Road bridge. Small **weir** below.
	1m drop. Awkward stopper. Shoot far left hand side.
	50m Canal joins River Calder.
23.5	M62. **Weir** and lock. 2m sloping drop.
	100m. M62 road bridge.
24.25	**Egress** Left bank. Walk up to car park off A644. (OS Ref 168221)

The (Yorkshire) Derwent

Malton to Howsham ·
Length 18.5kms   **Grade** I   **No Portages**

Introduction

The River Derwent offers canoeists trouble free paddling through attractive countryside on placid water.

After descending the southern side of the North York Moors the river becomes canoeable from Yedingham, but here the river is frequently canalised and the countryside flat.

Probably the most scenic paddle lies between Malton and Howsham where the river winds its way through undulating wooded hills and two weirs provide a little sport. Howsham to Stamford Bridge is another popular stretch. This also incorporates two weirs in the trip.

Further downstream the river passes through flat countryside again as it meanders slowly across the Vale of York to join the Ouse.

Access

The Derwent recently featured in the National Press when attempts were made to re-open this river as a navigation.

Unfortunately this was refused after lobbying by conservationists and anglers. Despite this the river is frequently used by canoeists, usually without problems.

Local Access Officer: Mr R. McTurk,
31, Lamplough Crescent,
Bishopthorpe,
York.   Tel: (0904) 708399

River Course

Arising on Fylingdales Moor the river descends rapidly as a small stream flowing in a southerly direction.

Just below Hackness, a canal or sea cut directs the headwaters down a canalised system to the sea. A small amount of water is allowed down the old river course through sluice gates. This drastic procedure was done to prevent flooding further downstream.

From here the river is squeezed down the picturesque Forge valley. This is a wooded vale rich in bird life which has now been turned into a local nature reserve.

A small weir with a 1.5m sloping drop occurs just above West Ayton.

The river can be canoed from here although this is only for the most intrepid paddlers, as the river now twists and turns with the river banks overhung with trees and branches often forming an impenetrable barrier requiring many portages.

From here the river gradually turns away from the coast from just below Scarborough, flowing south westwards towards the Ouse basin.

After about 8km the river becomes straightened and canalised. High dykes on either side obscure much of the surrounding countryside. The river opens out a little at Yedingham which is the highest practical starting point. Here the river is shallow, flowing at a gentle pace (nevertheless surprisingly fast considering the complete flatness of the Vale of Pickering).

Just above Malton the river is joined by the Rye. Paddlers wishing to join the Derwent at Malton can either get on at Howe Bridge, which is 1.5km upstream on the Rye, or use the bottom road bridge in the centre of Malton. Here the station yard may be used to park vehicles. A public footpath leads down to the river on the left.

Those wishing for a shorter paddle can get on the water at Low Hutton about 5km downstream. Here a road leads right down to the waters edge terminating near a footbridge. Now the river is deep and slow moving with pleasant wooded hills rising up on either side. Here touring paddlers should be in their element, with nothing more threatening than the birds and the bees! But eventually all good things must come to an end!

The ruins of Kirkham Priory on the left warn of an approaching weir. This has an easy 2m sloping drop, but keep well clear of the perilous sluice gates on the far left.

The next landmark is Howsham Hall lying on the left bank.

Just below here is the well known Howsham Weir with a 1.75m sloping drop. Slaloms are sometimes held here in the summer months.

Several hundred metres beyond is the bridge which is a suitable point to egress. (OS Ref 733625)

The Derwent - summary
Low Hutton to Howsham Weir
Length 12kms   Grade I   No Portages

Kms		
0	**Access**	Yedingham Bridge. (OS Ref 893796)
9		Footbridge followed by small bridge. Nearly halfway to Malton!
12.5		Confluence with River Rye.
		(Access point Howe Bridge 1.5km upstream.)
18		A64. Road bridge.
21		Several road bridges. Malton town right. Norham left.
	Egress/Access	Use the bottom road bridge which is less busy and has a public footpath down the left bank.
27.5		Rail bridge followed by suspension footbridge.
	Access	Low Hutton village. Right.
		Attractive wooded vale.
34		Road bridge. Kirkham Priory left.
		200m **weir.** 2m sloping drop.
		(Avoid dangerous sluice on the left)
39.5		Howsham **Weir.** 1.75m sloping drop.
40	**Egress/Access**	Howsham Bridge. (OS Ref 733625)
47		Buttercrambe Bridge. Village and **weir.** 1.5m sloping drop.
52.5	**Egress**	Stamford Bridge and **weir.** 2.25m vertical plunge.
59		Road bridge. A1074 (T)
64.5		Elvington road bridge.
81.5		Derwent Bridge. Bulwith village left.
91.5		Loftsome Bridge. A63(T). Haughthorpe Hall. Right.
95		Confluence with Ouse at Barmby-on-Marsh.

The Esk

Introduction
In mega water this short Yorkshire river will provide a thrilling paddle and is likely to add a few extra grey hairs to your crown.

Beginning life on Westerdale Moor the Esk runs along the northern flank of the North York Moors to Whitby. The river initially flows northwards to Castleton where it is joined by several tributaries, before turning eastwards towards the sea. The river is canoeable from Castleton in high water, although the pace is initially slow, and its path tortuous.

At 10km Crunkly Gill is reached. This is the first of three bouldery rapids, each set in a wooded vale that takes you on an exciting journey down to Grosmont.

From here the river becomes more placid again as the river makes its way towards the attractive seaside town of Whitby.

The river is accompanied up the valley by the railway, so that canoeists may use the train for a ferry. Check the timetable first as there are only about five trains a day.

Non canoeists and steam train enthusiasts may wish to ride on the North York Moors railway which runs steam trains from Grosmont towards Pickering.

Access
Occasional problems occur in the Egton Bridge/Grosmont area, although by Yorkshire standards it is relatively trouble free.

Local Access Officer: Mr Don Raspin,
28, Cotswold Drive,
Skelton,
Cleveland.
TS12 2JN
Tel. 0287 50668

Castleton to Egton Bridge
Length 19.75km   **Grade** I - II Castleton to Crunkly Gill   **No Portages**
                Grade III - IV Crunkly Gill to Egton Bridge

This section needs to be done in high water to avoid being grounded in the rapids further downstream. Ideally the depth gauge beneath Egton Bridge should be over the one foot mark to ensure a comfortable trip.

Starting off below Castleton Bridge the paddle begins rather inauspiciously as the water is deep and slow, with the river twisting and turning as it runs through tranquil pasturelands. Any attempt to paddle swiftly is soon thwarted by the overhanging trees which frequently meet in the middle, forming dense thickets which have to be prised apart.

Few paddlers will enjoy this stretch and those seeking to paddle the rapids which lie downstream should get in at Houlsyke road bridge (OS Ref 734074) or better still where the road from Lealholm to Houlsyke briefly runs close to the river after passing beneath the railway. (OS Ref 749076)

Shortly after this a wooded embankment rises up on the left hand side. A few ripples begin to disturb the pacid flow as the gradient steepens with dense deciduous woodland now rising up on either side. Here and there rocks begin to decorate the river bed. Soon a heavenly vista of boulders, rocks, and fallen trees begins to unfold before your eyes, pure nectar to the white water paddler. Whilst there is no one particular hazard requiring special mention,

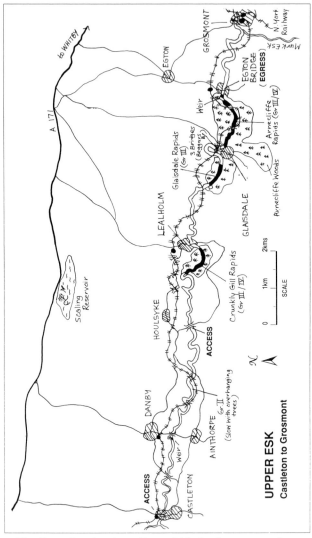

UPPER ESK
Castleton to Grosmont

'The Churn' found on Inner Farne. A blind gully creates an impressive 40ft geyser when there is a powerful north-easterly swell

Photo: Roy Egelstaff

constant attention and deft paddling are required to weave a safe path downstream.

These Grade III - IV rapids continue for nearly one kilometre before culminating in a small broken weir. The woods now begin to thin as the river loses it ferocity, and the rocks gradually disappear with easier rapids taking you downstream towards Lealholm.

A set of stepping stones occur just before the village is reached.

Just above the road bridge a large tranquil pool allows paddlers to regain their composure. On the left bank a compact but well stocked nursery specialising in rockery plants and shrubs may distract the more green fingered canoeists.

Below Lealholm several kilometres of gentle paddling take you past two rail bridges, before a small broken weir is reached with an old mill house on the right that sports an intact iron water wheel.

This marks the start of Glaisdale Rapids (Grade III) which are slightly shorter and easier than those encountered at Crunkly Gill. Again these bouldery rapids lie in a wooded valley and after about 300 metres lead down to a small broken weir.

A placid stretch briefly intervenes as the river passes by the village of Glaisdale.

Here three bridges lie within 150 metres and include the arched stone 'Beggars Bridge' which lies on the coast to coast walk.

Soon woods begin again to mark the start of a long series of rocky rapids at Arncliffe Wood (Grade III - IV) every bit as challenging as those found at Crunkly Gill and will keep you entertained for over one kilometre. In high water this makes for a thrilling paddle of almost Alpine quality as you dodge rocks and fallen trees in quick succession.

Eventually the rapids fizzle out leading up to a weir split into three by two islands.

There is a 1.5m sloping drop with stepping stones 100 metres beyond.

Some flat water follows before egressing at Egton Bridge. (OS Ref 804052)

Egton Bridge to Whitby
Length 15.5km   **Grade** II   **No Portages**

The river now flattens out, especially below Grosmont. The only significant hazard being Sleights Weir. The lower reaches of the river are often used by canoeing groups, especially for basic instruction.

After launching below Egton Bridge, several small rocky falls provide some interest, along with several easy rapids.

Once Grosmont is reached the pace slackens further.

The river is criss-crossed by numerous rail bridges as it goes down the valley.

The Needle's Eye, Berwickshire

Crunkly Gill Rapids on the Esk

At 9.5km Sleights Weir with its 2m near vertical stepped drop should be carefully inspected. The fish ladder on the left has been shot, but it tends to collect debris (and canoes).

Two kilometres beyond Ruswarp Weir is rather easier, being shot close to the rather curious central rib which collects most of the water.

Below here the river is tidal.

Egress on either bank at Whitby Harbour.

The Esk - summary

Castleton to Egton Bridge

Length 20km   Grade   I - II Castleton to Crunkly Gill   No Portages
            Grade III - IV Crunkly Gill to Egton Bridge

Kms		
0	**Access**	Castleton road bridge. OS Ref 685084
1.5		Concrete road bridge. Numerous stanchions.
		Inspect gaps for trapped debris.
2.5		Danby **Weir.** 1.75m sloping drop. Shoot right.
		50m footbridge.
		100m road bridge.

Kms		
3		Low footbridge. Caution in high water.
3.25		Rail bridge.
4.5		Rail bridge.
		100m arched stone bridge with crest of arms.
6.5	**Access**	Concrete road bridge. Near Houlsyke. OS Ref 734074
		50m Small **weir.** 0.5m vertical drop
9.5		Wooded vale.
		Bouldery **rapids.** Grade III - IV at Crunkly Gill for 1.0km.
11.5		Lealholm road bridge.
14		Railway bridge.
15		Railway bridge.
15.5		Wooded vale. Old Mill House. Right.
		Glaisdale **Rapids** - Grade III for 300 metres.
		Small broken weir at bottom.
16		Road bridge.
16.5		Rail bridge.
17		3 bridges. (Road, stone bridge and rail bridge) Glaisdale village.
17.25		Wooded vale.
18		Rail bridge.
		Arnecliffe Wood **Rapids** Grade III/IV for 1.5km.
18.5		Rail bridge.
19.5		**Weir.** 1.5m sloping drop. Split by islands.
		50m Stepping stones.
19.75		**Egress** Egton village and road bridge. OS Ref 804052

Egton Bridge to Whitby
Length 15.5km   Grade II   No Portages

Kms		
0	**Access**	Egton Bridge. OS Ref 804052
		100m. Minor rocky **falls.** 0.5m drops.
		250m. Minor rapid for 100 metres.
1		Footbridge.
1.5		Viaduct.
2.5		Ford with footbridge beyond.
		Murk Esk joins right.
		Road bridge. Grosmont village. Right.
3		Disused wooden bridge.
		Small weir. 0.25m drop.
		Concrete stanchions below.
3.5		Railway viaduct.
		(6 more railway bridges over next 7km.)

Kms

9.5		**Sleights Weir.** 2m near vertical stepped drop.
		Usually shot far right. Avoid awkward fish ladder.
		100m road bridge and footbridge.
11.5		Ruswarp **Weir.** 1.75m sloping drop.
12		Railway and road bridge at Ruswarp.
13		Viaduct.
14.5		High level bridge. A171
15.5	**Egress**	Whitby Harbour. Road bridge.

River Nidd

Following its adaptation for industrial and social reasons, canoeists are the one group of people not well catered for by the River Nidd!

Sadly, this once beautiful river has been decapitated by two reservoirs which usurp the headwaters of the river to the tune of 23 million gallons a day.

Although the valley remains extremely beautiful and unspoilt, the entire catchment area of Angram and Scar House reservoirs is now used to supply drinking water without the barest trickle being allowed past the dam to moisten the parched river bed below.

Eventually a small rivulet forms some miles below the Scar House dam but suddenly this water disappears as well! This time siphoned off down Goyden Pot into a system of underground tunnels well known to the caving fraternity. But all is not lost, for the river soon reappears further downstream where it then flows into Gouthwaite reservoir. By contrast, no water is drawn off here, the reservoir's use being confined to regulating water flow down the Nidd.

The river becomes canoeable a few miles below the dam at Wath.

Most of the river is slow moving with occasional shingle rapids. The only excitement coming from weirs which occur at regular intervals. All are shootable, although some require careful inspection.

The best paddling is from Ripley down to Knaresborough when the river has become a respectable size. Below here the river flattens out as it crosses the Vale of York to join the Ouse at Nun Monkton.

Access

Surprisingly canoeists do not appear to be the most popular of river users especially on the sections above Ripley Bridge and below Knaresborough.

It is advisable if doing the bottom section to egress just above Knaresborough.

Local Access Officer:	Chris Hawkesworth,
	The Mill,
	Glasshouses,
	Pateley Bridge, N. Yorks.
	HG3 5QH
	Tel. (0423) 711624

Wath to Ripley Bridge
Length 24.5kms **Grade** I - II (II/III with weirs) **No Portages**

The river is rather small and shallow at this point, with much of the riverside being decorated with abusive notices towards canoeists! There are no major rapids, but several weirs provide some entertainment. The highest access point lies several miles below Gouthwaite Dam at Wath road bridge where there is convenient roadside parking in the form of a lay-by. OS Ref 144677.

A short paddle brings you down to a small weir above Pateley Bridge which is easily slid down. Just below the town is a wooden footbridge which has a small weir beneath.

At 6km a lattice girder bridge marks the home of Chris Hawkesworth's Whitewater Centre at Glasshouses Mill seen on the left.

Several kilometres beyond, a pair of weirs are encountered, the first with a 1.75m sloping drop is straightforward, but the second needs to be carefully inspected. A series of metal reinforcing rods can easily be seen protruding from the base of the vertical step. These probably represent more of a hazard to your boat than any serious threat to life or limb. The next weir at Summerbridge is easily managed.

At 19kms Birstwith Weir is slightly more substantial. Its 2.25m drop occurs in five steps. Most plastic boats should bounce down with impunity. In high water it usually washes through on the left, but avoid arguing with the concrete wall on that side.

As Hampsthwaite Church comes into view there is sometimes a wire or chain spanning the river at this point, about 100m above the road bridge.

From here it's plain sailing down to Ripley Bridge. Egress downstream left bank. (OS Ref 288597)

Ripley Bridge to Knaresborough
Length 14kms **Grade** I - II (II/III with weirs) **No Portages**

This is one of the best stretches on the Nidd, as there is good access at Ripley Bridge and although there are no major rapids the river passes through some attractive countryside with the weirs again providing most of the sport.

Many groups prefer to egress at the wooden footbridge just above Knaresborough. This avoids the large weirs in town and reduces conflict with

165

the commercial interests in the city centre which hire boats on the flat water above the weir.

The old Ripley Bridge is now disused running alongside its concrete replacement carrying the A61. It thus offers good access with easy parking. From here the river passes through an attractive mixture of woodland and pastureland.

Several easy weirs are encountered before Knaresborough is reached.

Those wishing to continue beyond the wooden footbridge will find a small weir immediately beneath. From here a long stretch of flat water takes you through the centre of town, first going beneath a road bridge and then a disused railway viaduct.

Just beyond, a refurbished mill house on the left warns of a weir. Inspection is advised, although the 3.25m drop should not cause problems unless the river is in spate. There is a small vertical drop with a long plateau before a steep, sloping drop, completes your triumphant descent!

A little further down Mother Shipton's Cave is seen on the right, reputedly the home of a 15th century witch who prophesied many modern inventions. This is near the dropping well where inanimate objects become coated with limestone, which explains the curious string of greyish coloured consumer durables that surround the cave!

There are still several more weirs a few kilometres downstream which can usually be pre-inspected from your boat. After this the river starts to flatten out as it wriggles across the Vale of York to meet the Ouse.

River Nidd - summary

Wath to Ripley Bridge
Length 24.5kms   Grade I - II (II/III with weirs)   No Portages

Kms		
0	**Access**	Road bridge. Downstream right bank. (OS Ref 144677)
3	**Weir**	1.5m sloping drop.
3.5		Pateley Bridge.
5		Footbridge.
	Weir	immediately below. 1.5m vertical then sloping.
6		Lattice girder iron bridge.
		Glasshouses Mill. Left.
7		Footbridge.
9		Old Mill visible. Left bank.
		Weir. 1.75m sloping drop.
		250m **weir.** 1.75m vertical then sloping. **Inspect** carefully.
		Metal reinforcing rods protrude.
11		Summerbridge **Weir.** 1.75m sloping drop.
		200m Water pipe spans river.

Kms

11.25	Road bridge. Summerbridge town. Left.
19	Birstwith **Weir**. 2.25m drop in 5 steps. Inspect.
21	Road bridge. Hampsthwaite church visible right bank.
24.5	A61 road bridge.
	50m Old Ripley. Killinghall road bridge
	50m broken **weir**. Keep far right.
Egress	Left bank below bridge. (OS Ref 288597)

Ripley Bridge to Knaresborough
Length 14kms   Grade I - II (Grade II/III with weirs)   No Portages

Kms

0	**Access**	Ripley - Killinghall road bridge.
		Downstream left bank.
3.5		Viaduct
4.5		Old mill houses. Left.
		Weir. Small vertical drop then sloping. 2.25m.
6		Small weir. 0.25m.
8		Footbridge.
9		Small weir.
9.25	**Egress**	Wooden footbridge. (OS Ref 343575)
		Weir. 0.75m irregular vertical drop.
10		Low road bridge.
		Knaresborough town centre.
10.25		Viaduct.
10.5		Refurbished mill. Left.
		High angled **weir**. 3.25m drop.
		Initial step with long plateau
		Leading to steep sloping drop.
		Inspect.
11.5		Road bridge.
13		Old mill house left. **Weir** 2m sloping drop. Shoot left.
13.25		Mill House. Right.
		Weir 2m sloping drop.
14		Road bridge.
	Egress	Usually left bank above bridge. (OS Ref 362562)

River Swale

Introduction

Falling at nearly 80 feet per mile in its upper reaches, few people will wish to challenge its reputation as one of England's most exciting white water rivers.

The Swale arises from the union of Birkdale Beck and Sliddale Beck which drains an area of the northern Pennines. From here it flows due east, falling rapidly in a series of horrendous waterfalls that most will wish to portage. As Muker is reached the river loses some of its virility, beginning to flow horizontally rather than vertically, with the gentle but sustained pace that makes it such a popular white water river.

The most commonly paddled section is from Reeth to Richmond where one is helped along by Marrick Priory Rapid (Grade II/III). Here one is surrounded by the beautiful Swaledale countryside, so carefully quilted by the impeccable dry stone walling which gives the countryside such a characteristic appearance. Here one can finish the paddle by shooting the famous Richmond Falls. The river now turns south eastwards and its pace gradually slackens as it snakes its way across the Vale of York to Boroughbridge where it joins the Ure.

It should be noted that below the very awkward top section there are no rapids above Grade II/III and whilst the Swale provides a swift descent with continuous minor rapids some experienced white water paddlers may find, that apart from Richmond Falls, there is little to get their teeth into below Muker, especially in high water when many of the minor rapids become washed out.

In these conditions those paddlers who want some excitement, but don't feel up to the challenges of the top section might be better off doing rivers such as the upper Wharfe or Tees.

Hoggarths Bridge to Muker

Length	7.5km
Grade	III (excluding falls) V (including falls)
Portage	Rainby Force (OS Ref 886015)
	Lower Kisdon Force (OS Ref 898010)

If you like the idea of being put in a canoe, and then strapped to the front of a runaway steam train as it is about to enter its terminus, then this stretch is for you!

For those lesser mortals whose threshold of excitement is marginally

The Upper Swale with Wain Wath Force in the background

lower, simply portage the big drops and this becomes quite a pleasant Grade III paddle, with several small drops to provide some thrills.

This is also one of the prettiest and most unspoilt parts of the river valley. The only drawback is that several of the portages are rather tricky.

The river must be paddled in high water and preferably by paddlers who know one end of their boat from the other. A penchant for shooting waterfalls would be a definite advantage as there are seven drops over two metres, with several of these being five metres or more!

Most people will wish to get in at Hoggarth's Bridge where the B6270 crosses the Swale about 3km above Keld.

Those wishing to extend the paddle may get on the Whitsundale Beck at Ravenseat. (OS Ref 863033) See addendum for details.

Below Hoggarth's Bridge, easy shingle rapids and the occasional small step in the hard limestone bedrock take you downstream to the first of the larger drops, Wain Wath Force at 1.5km. This modest two metre fall can be shot by the centre or right hand chutes although caution should be exercised in high spate.

A few more rocky ledges take you downstream into a rather curious gully where the river has sculpted a series of basins in the limestone banks as it passes beneath Park road bridge.

Breakout below the road bridge to avoid going over Rainby Force which is about 50 metres below.

Under most conditions, water tends to use the right hand chute landing

Upper Kisdon Force, River Swale

onto solid rock making a portage mandatory. In high spate the left hand chute opens up, squirting water into a deep plunge pool allowing this four metre drop to be shot.

The quickest route for this awkward portage is to clamber down the rocks immediately to the right of the fall.

Two hundred metres below Rainby Force the river drops a further three metres in a series of steps that take you downward on a rather bumpy ride.

The Swale now enters a small gorge with towering cliffs hemming you in first on one side then the other.

In between the larger drops, occasional rocks and boulders lie scattered along the shingle rapids to keep your mind on the river and stop you worrying too much about what lies ahead!

Just as you begin to relax again a right hand bend reveals a stepped double drop with neither of the two to three metre drops having the comfort of a plunge pool.

Careful inspection of the first drop will reveal a steep chute on the extreme right of the fall. There is no soft option for the second drop which produces a bone shaking descent pretty well wherever you go. If you can do the first drop this brings you down to a ledge on the right which allows you to portage the second drop quite easily.

A brief boulder garden provides a little light relief before the gorge opens out as you pass beneath a footbridge carrying the Pennine Way. Just beyond, Eastgill Beck is seen forming a pretty waterfall as it cascades down the hillside to meet the Swale.

The valley sides now start to steepen again in a rather foreboding manner.

Shooting Lower Kisdon Force

A few larger rocks partially obstructing the river course are easily dodged but suddenly you feel your heart trying to claw it's way out of your chest, as a series of falling horizons greet the eye.

This is the upper fall of Kisdon Force, a fairly straightforward three metre drop into a deep plunge pool (but not made any easier knowing that the lower force is just 100 metres downstream).

This should be shot on the far right which avoids the rocky ledge which occurs across the centre and left of the fall. This is easily seen in low water but masked in high spate.

The lower force is a healthy six metre plunge into a generous plunge pool. One look at this drop will be enough to convince most paddlers to portage this difficult fall. On the left water flow is directed onto a slightly undercut cliff face whilst a rocky ledge sticks out nearly two metres on the right. By choosing a perfect trajectory you can just clip the edge of the ledge before wiping your nose against the cliff face.

The fall is most easily shot in low spate about 1 - 2 metres to the right of the centre tongue. The fall is actually easier than it looks, but since it looks impossible this may not be much of a consolation to most canoeists!

By any standards this is a dangerous fall and paddlers are advised to portage it whatever their abilities and experience.

Even the portage is not without difficulty. Scrambling down the cliffs on the right bank is probably simplest as it avoids a lengthier portage along the footpath. You can now relax for there are no further falls or difficult rapids although it is a further three kilometres before Muker Beck joins on the right and the road briefly runs close to the bank. (OS Ref 920977) Alternatively, some may wish to paddle another few kilometres further on to reach Annerside Bridge.

Muker to Grinton (Nr Reeth)
Length 17km   **Grade** II   **No Portages**

This constitutes a pleasant, fast ride down the Upper Swale with no major rapids or falls, but only the pretty Swaledale countryside to occupy the canoeist's attention.

Access is obtained by going down Muker Beck, getting in just above Muker Bridge, travelling down the beck for two hundred metres before joining the Swale.

After about half a kilometre the river turns right and leads into some shallow rapids which in spate produces some impressive standing waves.

At the second road bridge there is a good play stopper which is worth savouring as it is the only one of any size on this stretch.

Several more road bridges punctuate an otherwise straightforward paddle before egressing at Grinton Bridge. (OS Ref 047985)

Grinton Bridge to Richmond
Length 19.5km   **Grade** II/III (Richmond Falls IV)   **No Portages**

This is probably one of the best stretches of the Swale to paddle, although again it is best done in high water.

It includes several good rapids, those at Marrick Priory and some below Marske Bridge. However, these are all below Grade III, so that experienced paddlers seeking excitement should look elsewhere, especially in high spate when they become a series of standing waves and other more exciting rivers become paddleable. (Wharfe, Allen and Tees, etc.)

Access is achieved by getting in just below Grinton Bridge on the left bank. OS Ref 047985.

Fast Grade II water takes you down through the pretty Swaledale valley.

At three kilometres Marrick Priory becomes visible on the left as the river gradient steepens, with an island dividing the rapid, which then continues around a right hand bend to some slack water.

These Grade II/III rapids last for about 300 metres and should present no problems to the experienced paddler.

A most interesting feature of this part of the river is the large number of ditched cars which represent the main hazard to canoeists. One wonders whether the local population are particularly bad drivers or a car wash got a bit out of hand. Anyway, set in such unspoilt countryside it provides a sad reminder of the unnecessary desecration of the environment by human beings.

In eight kilometres one passes below Marske road bridge, which soon heralds the onset of another series of minor rapids.

At 12km another road bridge is reached with a small rapid just below.

The gradient of the river now begins to level off as the outskirts of Richmond are reached, visible on the left bank as you pass beneath first a footbridge and then a road bridge.

On the final stretch there is a magnificent view of the Castle on the left bank.

Richmond Falls
In another 0.5km a concrete jetty can be seen as the river turns a left hand bend this warns paddlers that Richmond Falls have been reached. Land on the left above the jetty to pre-inspect, but experienced paddlers who know the falls usually prefer to shoot the small, rocky ledges at the top, egressing on the central promontory which allows a better view of the main fall, which must be shot anywhere along the right except in high spate, when a powerful stopper forms here. (See diagram)

In high water the falls are best shot at an angle off the central promontory, this usually takes you past the stopper.

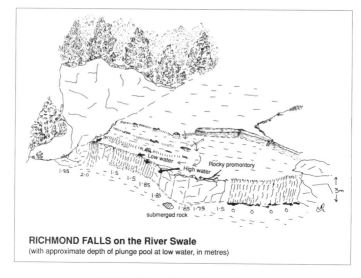

RICHMOND FALLS on the River Swale
(with approximate depth of plunge pool at low water, in metres)

After having shot the falls there are 100 metres of rocky rapids before calmer water is reached.

Egress on the left bank, walking back up to the car park. (OS Ref 173006)

Some may wish to go 3 - 4 km downstream to Easby Abbey, where there are some good rapids with 1 or 2 small play stoppers which seem to be as rare as hens' teeth on the Swale.

Richmond to Catterick Bridge

Length 8.5km   **Grade** II/III   (Richmond Falls. Grade IV)   **No Portages**

This is a short, but good stretch of river incorporating Richmond Falls (See previous section for details) and Easby Rapids where slaloms are held.

After finding the car park at Richmond Falls, get in above or below the falls depending on your inclinations.

For those not wishing to do the falls, there are some narrow steps which lead directly down to the bottom of the falls, so that you can ferry glide across to take advantage of the 100 metres of rocky rapids immediately below.

At 0.5km you pass beneath a road bridge followed by some minor rapids. Easby Abbey is seen on the left at 2km, the river then sweeping around a right bend with the water becoming more turbulent in high water, producing standing waves with a few small stoppers. The river passes beneath a disused railway bridge, with some more rapids, finally sweeping around a left bend, narrowing slightly, with some turbulent eddies.

At 8km the river passes beneath a series of bridges, starting with a large concrete superstructure carrying the A1 followed by a disused railway bridge and finally the stone road bridge at Catterick, which has an excellent play stopper beneath it, which can provide some fun before egressing downstream on the right bank. OS Ref 228995.

From here the Swale has no further rapids of any significance, slowly meandering to join the river Ure near Boroughbridge some 90km downstream.

River Swale - summary

Hoggarth's Bridge to Muker
Length 7.5km Grade III (excluding falls) Grade V (including falls)
Portages Rainby Force (OS Ref 886015)
Lower Kisdon Force (OS Ref 898010)

Kms		
0	**Access**	Hoggarth's Bridge. (OS Ref 871014)
1		Road bridge.
1.5		Waterfall. **Wain Wath Force.** 2m drop. pre-inspect. Most routes feasible.
1.75		Park Bridge.
		50m **Rainby Force** Portage. 4m vertical drop, on to solid rock. Can occasionally be shot in very high water. Left side. (see text)
2		Several rocky ledges. Usually shootable.
2.5		**Double drop.**
		1st fall. 2.75m drop in 3 steps.
		Shoot extreme R.H.S. Inspect.
		2nd fall. 3m in 3 steps.
		Shoot centre or portage over rocky ledge right bank.
3		Footbridge. Eastgill beck joins left.
3.5		**Upper Kisdon Force.** 3m drop. Inspect carefully. Deep plunge pool. Avoid rocky shelf on left. Shoot extreme RHS.
		100m **Lower Kisdon Force.** Rocky ledge RHS. Shoot 1-2m to the right of centre tongue. Portage right bank. 6m vertical drop.
4		Footbridge.
6		Footbridge.
7		Muker Beck joins right.
7.5	**Egress**	B6270. 0.5km before Muker. (OS Ref 920977)

Muker to Grinton Bridge.
Length 17km   Grade II   No Portages

Kms		
0	**Access**	Muker.
		Bridge of Muker Beck. (OS Ref 911978)
		Paddle 200m down to confluence with Swale.
0.5		Minor rapid around right bend.
4.5		Stone road bridge.
8		Stone road bridge. Good play stopper beneath right arch.
11.5		Stone road bridge.
17		Grinton road bridge.
	Egress	Downstream. Left bank. (OS Ref 047985)

Grinton Bridge to Richmond
Length 19.5km   Grade II/III Richmond Falls (IV)   No Portages

Kms		
0		Grinton Bridge
	Access	Left bank downstream. (OS Ref 047985)
3		Marrick Priory. Left. 300m of Grade II/III **Rapids.**
		Series of standing waves in high water.
9		Marske road bridge.
		0.5km downstream succession of **Minor Rapids.** Grade II/III.
15.5		Road bridge where A6108 crosses river.
17		Footbridge. Richmond comes into view. Left.
18.5		Road bridge. Splendid view of Castle. Left.
19.5		**Richmond Falls.** Grade IV 2m Vertical drop. **Inspection advised.**
		Shoot centre right. (low water)
		Just right of central prominence (high water)
		(See text and diagram for details)
	Egress	Left bank. (OS Ref 174006)

Richmond to Catterick Bridge
Length 8.5km   Grade II/III (Richmond Falls IV)   No Portages

Kms		
0	**Access**	**Richmond Falls.** (Above or below!) OS Ref 174006
		Falls. (Grade IV) 2m vertical drop. See text for details.
		Rapids immediately below for 150m.
0.5		Road bridge.
2		Easby Abbey. Left.

Kms

		Succession of **Rapids.** Grade II/III for 1 km.
2.5		Disused railway bridge.
		Minor rapids below.
6		Small bridge carrying road track.
7		Village of Brompton-on-Swale. Visible left.
8		Concrete road bridge carrying A1.
		200m disused railway bridge.
8.5		Catterick Bridge. Interesting play stopper beneath.
	Egress	Right bank below bridge. (OS Ref 228995)

River Ure

Introduction

Scenically the Ure is one of Yorkshire's finest rivers, arising on Abbotside Common in the Northern Pennines where it flows in an easterly direction down the picturesque valley of Wensleydale to Leyburn. From here it turns south eastwards, passing through Ripon before meeting the Swale just after Boroughbridge.

A few miles after this the Ure is joined by a tiny tributary known as the Ousegill Beck. From here the Ure becomes known as the Ouse. The river then meanders slowly across the Vale of York, collecting all the large rivers of the area including the Wharfe and Derwent as it flows past Selby to Goole. Here, it changes name again to become the River Humber, flowing through the city of Hull before meeting the sea at Grimsby.

There are two sections of interest to white water paddlers.

The first of these begins just below Aysgarth Falls. (These are well worth a visit if you've not seen them) down to Wensley Bridge. This has several Grade III rapids, with one set of small falls to shoot. (Redmire Force)

The second, slightly easier section is from Masham down to Sleningford Mill Rapids, which incorporates the short but exciting Hackfall Rapids. (Grade III)

The rest of the river is more suited to novice and touring paddlers who wish to take advantage of the long trouble free stretches of water found throughout most of the Ure. For the most part the river has only the gentlest of gradients to help you on your way.

At times the Ure can be a frustrating river to paddle, for many of the good rapids are separated by long stretches of slack water.

Access

A further complicating factor is the difficult access situation, particularly around Masham, so that canoeists from outside the area would be well advised to check with the local access officer, especially during the fishing season.

This friction is a great pity for such a fine river deserves canoeists!

Local Access Officer: Mr Rob Ringer,
Brampton Hall School,
Brampton by Sawdon,
Scarborough. N.Yorks. YO13 9DB
Tel. 0723 859161

Appersett to Aysgarth Falls

Length	20.5kms
Grade I/II	Aysgarth Mills Rapids (Grade II/III)
Portage	Aysgarth Falls (OS Ref 010886)

High water is required to make this canoeable. After putting in just below Appersett Bridge on Widdale Beck 100 metres of paddling will take you down to the confluence.

Easy Grade I/II rapids will take you down through one of the most attractive parts of the valley.

In one kilometre a small stream joins from the left, this comes from Hardraw Force allegedly England's highest waterfall which can be visited from the village of Hardraw which lies nearby.

At 3.5km Hawes road bridge and town is reached. Shortly after this the gradient increases slightly and a series of Grade II rapids are peppered with small rocks.

Several more road bridges are passed before a metal footbridge is reached at 19kms, which is sometimes used as an egress point. Here there is good access to both banks with plenty of car parking space. (OS Ref 995889) but most will want to continue downstream as the only rapids of significance lie 200 metres further on. These grade II/III rapids consist of a series of rocky ledges for 150m with an old mill just visible on the right.

A short stretch of slack water follows for about 0.5km before the river turns sharply left and the thunderous roar of the falls which greet your ears should have no difficulty in convincing you that this is the time to get out of your boats as Aysgarth Falls have been reached.

Portage 200 metres along the left bank to the car park.

Aysgarth Falls to Wensley Bridge

Length	10.5kms
Grade	III
Optional Portage	(i) Rocky Fall 150m below Lower Force at Aysgarth. (OS Ref 018888)
	(ii) Redmire Force. (OS Ref 045901) (In high water)

This is probably the most difficult stretch on the Ure, although there is nothing here above Grade III. In very high water particular caution should be exercised at Redmire Force, which needs careful inspection and may require a portage.

Visitors to the area will no doubt want to have a good look at Aysgarth Falls, which consist of four major drops, the first two occurring just above the bridge, the Middle and Lower Forces about 150 metres below the bridge. Unfortunately the falls have no significant plunge pools so that they are not a viable canoeing proposition (however tempting they may look).

The Old Mill across the bridge houses an excellent pottery shop and cafe.

After leaving your car in the National Trust car park close to Aysgarth Falls, follow signs directing you downstream to the 'Lower Force.'

About 50 metres below the 'Lower Force' a narrow footpath takes you down between a cleft in the rocks to the water edge on the left bank.

Below the main falls 150 metre of good Grade III rapids take you down to a small 1.25m stepped drop which is worth inspecting. Those in plastic boats can probably bounce down with impunity despite the lack of plunge pool. Others may wish to portage along the right bank.

From here the river splits around an island with bouldery rapids continuing on either side.

The gradient soon eases off with some flat water paddling before Grade II/III rapids lead up to Redmire Force.

This consists of three small falls, the first drop (1.2m) is usually taken just left of centre, the slightly larger middle fall can be taken in the centre or following the main flow of current down a steep chute on the far right, the latter route leads on to some shallow rocks and is best avoided in low water. The final 0.35m drop will hardly be noticed.

From here slow stretches alternate with occasional shingle rapids. In addition, three brief but slightly more substantial Grade II/III rapids will provide some light relief.

At 8.5km Lord's Bridge is passed, a private bridge to the nearby estate. A few kilometres beyond is Wensley Bridge which provides a suitable egress point, although the bridge is narrow with much road traffic. (OS Ref 092895) Downstream from here the river enters a sluggish phase which is best avoided.

179

Wensley Bridge to Masham
Length 24.5kms   **Grade** I/II Squirrel Bank Rapids II/III   **No Portages**

This is one of the flatter stretches of the Ure. At times it is little more than serpigenous canal, although Squirrel Bank Rapids may help to arouse paddlers from their slumbers as they approach Masham.

Most touring paddlers will want to get in at Middleham Bridge on account of its easier roadside parking, but for the sake of continuity we'll continue on downstream from Wensley Bridge. Here most of the river is made up of long, deep, slow stretches of water, with occasional shingle rapids. Just above Middleham Bridge the river forms a gigantic loop, almost doubling back on itself to form an ox bow lake.

At 4.5km Middleham Bridge comes into view, a rather curious folly made of iron with four castellated turrets at each corner.

Middleham village and Castle are just visible high up on the hillside to the right. A flat stretch then ensues until Ulshaw road bridge is reached, when several shingle rapids breathe new life into the river. Two kilometres beyond this on the left is an old mill which marks the site of a dismantled weir (which is still shown on some OS maps).

The river soon returns to its slothful character but eventually at 21km Squirrel Bank Rapids are encountered along with Clifton Castle which is clearly visible on the left bank, set amongst a pleasant woodland park.

Initially there is an easy shingle rapid which then splits around an island leading to a small boulder garden. (Grade II/III)

After a further 3km Masham Bridge is reached. Egress right bank below the bridge. (OS Ref 225812)

Masham to (West Tanfield) Sleningford Mill Rapids
Length 11.5kms   **Grade** II   Hack Fall (Grade III)   Sleningford Mill Rapids (Grade III)
No Portages

This popular stretch of water has two good rapids and several weirs to entertain you, although these are separated by fairly long stretches of slack water. The first of these rapids is Hack Falls which provides some 75 metres of Grade III white water about 2km below Masham. Another stretch of easy water follows before a series of rocky ledges below West Tanfield Weir comprise Sleningford Mill Rapids. This is a longer but slightly easier Grade III rapid.

Nowadays Masham is probably better known nationally as a flash point for access disputes than for its canoeing. In particular the local populace seem keen to acquaint paddlers with the local geology, so keep your helmets well fastened! Because of this problem and the relatively long, slack stretches of water that separate these rapids, many canoeists prefer just to paddle West

Sleningford Mill Rapids on the Ure

Tanfield Weir and Sleningford Rapids on their own using local access, in the form of nearby roads and a 'canoe friendly' campsite, especially in the fishing season when Masham is best avoided.

The town is also famous for being the home of Theakston's brewery. Those unfamiliar with 'Old Peculiar' should drop into the brewery pub to taste one of the finest and strongest beers in the north east!

To get onto the water, drive over the bridge into Masham for about one hundred metres turning left into a car park by the riverside.

Initially there is a rather dull stretch of water, but just as you're beginning to wonder if you have accidentally joined the Grand Union Canal the river has several shingle rapids as it enters a wooded vale. High up on the skyline a small, ruined castle can usually be made out. Hack Fall is then revealed on a sharp left hand bend. The name is rather a misnomer, as there is no fall but simply a turbulent rapid about 75 metres long. Although rather a disappointment in low water it provides a good play area when the water comes up a little with convenient breakouts and several good stoppers on the way down. Make the most of these rapids as another few kilometres of slack water follows, before Mickley Weir is reached. This has a 1.25m sloping drop, easily shot on the left.

One hundred metres below a small weir with a negligible drop of less than 0.25m is easily paddled through, but if taken sideways especially on the far left, tends to submerge the boat with most of the water flowing over rather than under the deck.

In 2km a small rapid leads up to West Tanfield village easily visible on the

181

left. After the road bridge a weir is reached in 0.5km. This has a 1.25m sloping drop which must be shot on the far right to avoid a powerful stopper on the left.

Beyond this a series of rapids are formed by a succession of small drops and ledges for about 0.5km to form Sleningford Mill Rapids. Several good stoppers are to be found here, especially towards the bottom end of the rapids close to the small island opposite the campsite. These rapids are good in medium water but become washed out in spate, becoming interesting again in high spate.

Egress just below the island on the right bank to the campsite, or scramble up the left bank to the road. This site is very popular amongst canoeists especially in the summer months when it is used as the slalom course.

There are no further rapids of significance beyond this and the only excitement provided is by the occasional weir.

River Ure - summary

Appersett to Aysgarth Falls
Length 20.5kms   Grade I/II (Aysgarth Mill Rapids Grade II/III)
Portage Aysgarth Falls (OS Ref 010886)

Kms		
0	**Access**	Appersett road bridge. On Widdale Beck.
		150m. Confluence. (OS Ref 858907)
1		Stream from Hardraw Force joins left.
3.5		'Haylands' road bridge. Hawes visible on right bank.
11		Yore Bridge. Bainbridge visible. Right bank.
11.25		River Bain joins right. Flowing from Semer Water.
12		Askrigg seen left.
13.5		Worton Bridge.
14.25		Small **weir.** 1m sloping drop.
19	**Egress**	Metal footbridge. Good access to roads.
		Left bank. Os Ref 995889.
		200m series of rocky ledges for 150m. Grade II/III **Rapids.**
20.5	**Egress**	Above **Aysgarth Falls.** (not shootable)
		Portage left bank down to car park. Left. (OS Ref 010886)

Aysgarth Falls to Wensley
Length 10.5kms   Grade III   Optional Portage
(i) Rocky Fall 150m below Lower Force at Aysgarth. (OS Ref 018888)
(ii) Redmire Force. (OS Ref 045901)

Kms

0	**Access**	Use N.T. car park.
		Walk downstream following sign to 'Lower Force'.
		Get in 50m below fall. Left bank.
		Grade III **rapids** for 150m. leading up to **rocky fall.**
		1.25 stepped drop. Inspect.
		Rapids continue for a further 100m downstream.
3.5		Two sets of Grade II/III **rapids** lead up to Redmire Force.
4		**Redmire Force.** Grade III. Inspection advised especially in high water.
		Top fall 1.2m vertical drop. Left of centre.
		Middle fall 1.2m vertical drop. Shoot centre or far right.
		Bottom fall. 0.3m Anywhere.
		Several brief Grade II/III **rapids** over next 3km.
8.5		Lords Bridge. (Private)
10.5	**Egress**	Wensley Bridge. (OS Ref 092895)

Wensley Bridge to Masham

Length 24.5kms   Grade I/II (Squirrel Bank Rapids. Grade II/III)   No Portages

Kms

0	**Access**	Wensley Bridge. (OS Ref 092895)
4		Middleham Bridge (Alternative access).
9		Ulshaw Road bridge.
10		Old mill left. Site of dismantled weir.
16		Road bridge.
21		Clifton Castle. Left. With Squirrel Bank **Rapids.** (Grade II/III)
24.5	**Egress**	Masham road bridge. OS Ref 225812

Masham to (West Tanfield) Sleningford Mill Rapids

Length 11.5kms   Grade II   Hack Fall Grade III
Tanfield Weir and Sleningford Mill Rapids. Grade III   No Portages

Kms

0	**Access**	Masham road bridge. (OS Ref 145872)
4		Minor shingle rapids lead into wooded vale.
5		**Hack Fall.** Grade III rapids. Inspection from right bank.
		Several good breakouts and play stoppers.
7		Mickley **Weir.** Angled 1.25m sloping drop.
		Easiest on the left.
		100m small weir. 0.25m drop.
9		Minor Grade II **rapids** on left bend.

Kms		
10.5		West Tanfield Bridge. Village. Left.
11		**Weir.** 1.25 sloping drop.
		Powerful stopper on left. Shoot far right. Then move over to left for deepest water.
		50m Sleningford Mill Rapids begin. Grade III
		Series of **rocky ledges** for 0.5km
11.5	**Egress**	Below Island. (OS Ref 281785)
		To campsite right, or roadside left.

River Washburn

Access:	Below Thruscross Reservoir Dam. OS Ref 156574
Egress:	A59 road bridge at Blubberhouses. OS Ref168554
Length:	3km
Grade:	II - III
No Portages.	
OS Map:	No. 104. Leeds & Bradford.
Local Access Officer:	Contact Washburn committee members (see below)

Introduction

This small Yorkshire river is well known to competition canoeists as it is extensively used during the summer months for intermediate slalom, whilst in winter white water races are held here.

The source of the Washburn lies along the eastern border of the Yorkshire Dales arising on Pockstones Moor. The river course is soon punctuated by a series of four man made reservoirs, which are used by Yorkshire Water Authority to supply drinking water to the Leeds area.

What is left of the river then flows towards Otley where it joins the River Wharfe.

For most of the year this river wouldn't warrant a second glance, but on competition days when water is released from Thruscross the topmost reservoir, the river swells to a respectable size, providing some 3km of white water down to the second reservoir.

The Washburn at full flow is a heart warming sight, especially during the summer months, which are usually a lean time for white water paddlers.

For those who wish to use the river but are not competing it is usually

River Washburn, the access point below Thruscross Dam

possible to sneak on to the river just before or after competitions.

The Washburn provides a stretch of continuous fast water over 3km of no great technical difficulty, being virtually free of obstructions, with only one fall of any significance.

Although no one particular section of the river would probably warrant grading much above Grade II the unremittingly fast flow, with no patches of slack water, combined with extensive tree lined banks which make rescues and breakouts difficult it seems appropriate to slightly upgrade this stretch of water to a II/III.

The river flows through an attractive woodland park, so those unable to paddle may enjoy a pleasant riverside walk or picnic.

Access

Information about its use may be had by looking through the B.C.U. slalom and white water year books or by contacting members of the Washburn User's Committee.

Secretary: H. Pashley,
10 Crawshaw Grove,
Sheffield.
S8 7EB
Tel. 0742 747874

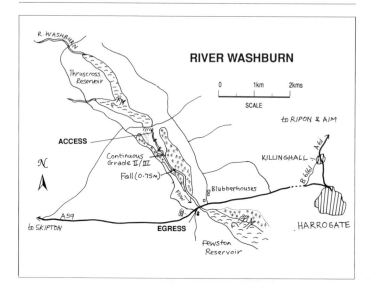

River Course

The small road which takes you up to Thruscross Dam is found by travelling some 15km along the A59, from Harrogate and just beyond a small concrete road bridge which crosses the Washburn, turn right down a road signposted 'West End.'

After about 3km this road takes a little dip to cross a small stream and just beyond this there is a small road off to your right which takes you to the point of access at the base of Thruscross Dam. (OS Ref 156574)

After getting in 200m below the dam, you soon pass beneath a footbridge, followed 100m later by a 0.5m drop and small stopper. At 300m a second footbridge leads into a sharp left hand turn, which will test the lock of those in racing boats. Several hundred metres of easy, fast grade II/III water leads up to a 0.75m vertical drop, with a large eddy below.

Beneath this fall is an irregular stopper which is quite safe to play in, but looks angry enough to put most slalomists off with their paper boats.

From here fast water takes you uneventfully down a further 2km to egress just downstream of a concrete road bridge, which has a small car park immediately adjacent to it on the right bank. (OS Ref 168554)

River Washburn - summary
Length 3km   Grade II/III   No Portages

Kms			
0	**Access**	Base of Thruscross Dam.	
		Right bank. OS Ref 156574	
		100m	Footbridge.
		200m	Small **weir** with stopper (0.5m drop)
		300m	Footbridge. Followed by sharp left bend.
		600m	**Weir.** 0.75 vertical drop.
			Easily shot in the centre.
			Small irregular play stopper.
3	**Egress**	Concrete road bridge on A59.	
		Downstream. Right bank. (OS Ref 168554)	

River Wharfe

This is one of Yorkshire's most exciting rivers for after heavy rainfall the gentle meandering flow is quickly transformed into a turbulent, foaming rapid, capable of providing plenty of unsolicited adventure.

The river's character is largely determined by the porous nature of the limestone geology which allows most of the water to disappear into the ground but following a downpour there is a quick run off which causes a rapid rise in water level within a few hours of the rain starting.

Conversely the river falls equally quickly often within 12 hours of the cessation of rainfall. This extreme lability catches many paddlers unaware, who hear the Wharfe is in spate one day and arrive to find it a trickle the next!

The surest way of checking water levels is to phone Buckden Outdoor Centre which lies on the banks of the Upper Wharfe. Rick Halsall the Local Access Officer is always happy to offer advice.

The river rises on Oughtershaw Moor from the union of Oughtershaw Beck and Greenfield Beck at Beckermonds.

Fast water takes you south eastwards passing through Hubberholme and Buckden. This is one of the best and most popular stretches for white water paddling.

From here the gradient eases, although some excitement is provided by Conistone Falls and the Ghaistrills, which lie just above Grassington. Below here several difficult rapids have to be negotiated. Firstly, Linton Falls followed by Appletreewick Rapids and the notorious Strid. Soon after this the safety of Bolton Abbey is reached. The river then loses its excitement apart from the occasional weir as it passes through Otley and Wetherby before running across the Vale of York to join the Ouse.

The lower part of the Wharfe provides some good paddling for touring canoeists on the fairly easy water between Bolton Abbey and Tadcaster.

Access
Regularly canoed usually without problems. Some harassment on the lower stretches particularly between Barden and Otley.

Local Access Officers:

Source to Grassington	Rick Halsall, Buckden Outdoor Centre, Buckden. N. Yorks. Work: (075676) 254 Home: (075676) 296
Grassington to Barden	Mark Markham, 22 Wrenbury Crescent, Cookridge, Leeds. Tel: 0532 675235
Barden to Otley	John Morgan, 77 St Richards Road, Otley. Tel: 0943 464826
Otley to Cawood	Peter Arter, 4 Wetherby Road, Tadcaster, LS2 4JN. Tel: 0937 833876

Beckermonds to Hubberholme
Length 6.5kms   **Grade** III/IV   **No Portages**

This part of the Upper Wharfe offers one of the best sections for white water paddling in the region.

It provides virtually continuous rapids for 6-7kms, which although exciting are unlikely to cause major problems to the competent paddler.

Spate conditions are required, so the river must be paddled during or just after heavy rainfall.

To get there drive up the Wharfe valley on the B6160, turning off at

The waterfall just below Beckermonds, River Wharfe

Buckden towards Hubberholme, going a further 8kms up the valley until Beckermonds is reached. Here a small farm track branches off to the left leading down to a group of houses as the main road turns sharply right to climb a steep hill. Follow the farm track off to the left for a short distance, parking your car just before the small road bridge, getting in just below the bridge close to the confluence of Oughtershaw Beck and Greenfield Beck. (OS Ref 874803)

Swift water and several minor drops soon bring you down to the most challenging but not unduly difficult fall on this stretch. Here the water falls over two metres, where several small drops funnel water down a central cleft. Whilst impractical in low water it is easily shootable in high water going either side of the cleft, usually to the right.

Just as you start to relax again a footbridge comes into view. Above this lies a small Strid where water is directed into the slightly undercut right bank. This is overhung by a small but awkwardly placed bush. Inspection may be required, although one is usually swished down uneventfully.

The river continues to fall steadily through a series of rocky ledges. These become a little more concentrated just above the road bridge, although there is nothing here to impede your progress.

Easy rapids continue with nothing above Grade III but some vigilance is needed as the odd sheep fence or piece of wire straddles the river across its lower reaches.

Egress just below Hubberholme road bridge as the rapids soon peter out.

Hubberholme to Kettlewell
Length 10.5kms   **Grade** I - II   **No Portages**

A rather disappointing piece of water after the excitement of the Upper Wharfe.

The river takes broad meanders across the valley, with nothing more than shingle rapids to augment your paddling.

Access is from Hubberholme road bridge. (OS Ref 926783) Egress at Kettlewell road bridge. (OS Ref 968723)

Kettlewell to Grassington
Length 11kms
Grade II/III   Conistone Falls Grade III   Ghaistrills Grade III   **No Portages**

A popular stretch of water which although easier than the topmost section has several interesting rapids.

Get in just below Kettlewell Bridge (OS Ref 968723) where an easy Grade II rapid leads down to several sets of small, rocky ledges. These soon become washed out in high water.

At 1km some stepping stones can usually be squeezed through by all but the largest boats.

The River Skirfare soon adds a considerable quantity of water from the right. (This can be canoed in spate although there are no significant rapids.)

Kilnsey Crag now becomes visible on the right, the limestone cliff jutting out into the valley. Its famous 40ft overhang is well known to climbers.

Shortly afterwards Conistone road bridge is passed. An area of slack water leads up to Conistone Falls (Grade III). Most will want to inspect this 2m drop, which occurs in two steps. It is shootable at most levels, usually in the centre.

Another few kilometres of flattish water bring you to the Ghaistrills.

In low water the river is forced through a narrow Strid for about 20 metres. It is usually unobstructed with little turbulence. In high water this becomes flooded out with no more than a few standing waves as testimony to its existence.

Below the Strid lies a short Grade III rapid, which can be difficult in low water. Most of the flow is channelled close to the right bank, but this leads on to a series of rocks, which are difficult to avoid. In high water you are able to sneak around the relatively rock free left bank.

Grassington Bridge is about 0.5km further downstream. Egress on the left bank. (OS Ref 998639)

Shooting Linton Falls, River Wharfe

Grassington to Bolton Abbey

Length	20.5kms
Grade	III Linton Falls IV (V Spate)
	Strid III-V (When Shootable)
	Linton Falls OS Ref 001634
	Strid OS Ref 064566
Optional Portage	

This section has the most difficult rapids on the Wharfe, although they are split up by fairly lengthy stretches of easy water.

Access is from Grassington Bridge. (OS Ref 998639)

A short flat water paddle will soon bring you down to a high weir with a 2.25m steeply sloping drop. A concrete chute on the far right makes the descent almost too easy, but don't worry there's plenty of excitement around the next corner!

In 200m an angled weir with a 1.5m drop is easily shot on the left. Immediately below lies Linton Falls (Grade IV) which must be carefully scrutinised, especially in high water when it becomes Grade V. In very low water it becomes unshootable due to a dog's leg channel.

At average water levels there is a 2m drop with a turbulent chute on the

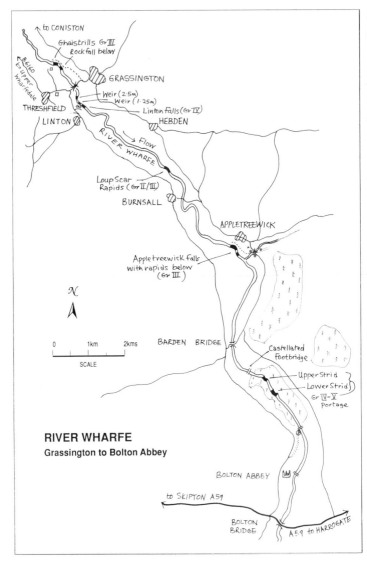

RIVER WHARFE

Grassington to Bolton Abbey

far right, which avoids the main fall.

Alternatively the centre channel will lead over the main drop.

A common pathway lead through a stopper with an extremely uninviting boil below before calmer waters are reached. The small stopper at the bottom can be played in at most levels.

In high water the right hand channel is usually the least perilous route, although many would be advised to portage along the left bank. The river then takes a rest for several kilometres before an S bend in the river is reached, where a limestone crag is exposed on the left bank, and some fast, broken water forms Loup Scar Rapids Grade II/III for about 100 metres.

Calmer waters gradually bring you down towards Burnsall Bridge with the picturesque village easily visible on the right bank.

A longish paddle of some five kilometres now follows before Appletreewick Rapids Grade III are encountered. Here the river splits around an island with most of the water flowing to the right where there are usually several stoppers.

In high water these develop an insatiable appetite for canoeists so that pre-inspection is advisable. In low water they're fun to play in.

Around the next corner lies a brief rapid before the river slows down again.

Barden road bridge lies several kilometres downstream. This is followed one kilometre later by a stone footbridge with battlemented walls which bear more of a resemblance to fortification than a footbridge.

Below here the pace quickens slightly, perhaps warning incipient travellers of adventures to come.

At one kilometre the river narrows with water being funnelled through a small hour glass constriction with a 1m drop. This is the Upper Strid, usually at its most difficult in low to medium water, but can be shot in most conditions.

Two hundred metres below lies the Strid proper. It consists of a deep, narrow channel cut into rock with both banks deeply undercut where the river has scoured away at the softer rock, producing small pockets and basins. The word 'Strid' is derived from 'stride' as the 2 - 3 metre gap may be jumped, although its sinister reputation comes from those hopefuls who failed to complete this feat, falling into the turbulent quagmire never to be heard of again. To our knowledge, those drownings that have occurred here have always been to non canoeists.

The Strid is shootable in very low water and most easily in high water. At medium levels water becomes deflected sideways by a large rock at the entrance to the Strid, making it virtually impossible to negotiate the narrow gap that leads into the Strid. In high water these features wash out when the rapid is little more than Grade III-IV. Provided common sense is used most paddlers should easily be able to cope with the Strid at high water levels.

Below this minor rapids take you down to a footbridge and car park which is a convenient place to finish.

Bolton Abbey and road bridge is a further 3kms downstream. (OS Ref 073528)

River Wharfe - summary
Beckermonds to Hubberholme

Length 6.5kms   Grade III/IV   No Portages

Kms		
0	**Access**	Beckermonds Bridge. (OS Ref 874803)
		50m Confluence with Greenfield Beck.
		250m 1m. Vertical drop.
0.5		**Rocky fall.** 2m stepped drop through central cleft. Inspect.
1.5		Footbridge. Small **Strid** above.
2		Road bridge. Preceded by series of small **drops.**
3.5		Yockenthwaite Bridge.
6.5		Hubberholme road bridge. (OS Ref 926783)
	Egress	Below Bridge.

Hubberholme to Kettlewell

Length 10.5kms   Grade I-II   No Portages

Kms		
0	**Access**	Hubberholme road bridge. (OS Ref 926783)
2		Buckden road bridge and town. Left.
6		Starbotton village. Left.
10.5	**Egress**	Kettlewell road bridge. (OS Ref 968723)

Kettlewell to Grassington

Length 11kms   Grade II/III   Conistone Falls III   Ghaistrills   III
No Portages

Kms		
0	**Access**	Kettlewell road bridge. (OS Ref 968723)
1		Stepping stones.
3.5		River Skirfare joins right.
5.5		Conistone road bridge and village. Left.
7		**Conistone Falls.** 2m drop in 2 steps. Inspect.
		Shoot centre.
10.5		**Ghiastrills Strid.** (Grade III) Inspection advised.
		River forced through narrow channel 2m wide,
		25m long. Usually unobstructed and straightforward.
		50m Tricky **Rapid.** Easiest in high water. Keep Left.
		Avoid tempting looking right channel which leads onto rocks below.
11	**Egress**	Grassington Bridge and town. Left. (OS Ref 998639)

Grassington to Bolton Abbey Bridge

Length 20.5kms   Grade III   Linton Falls IV - V OS Ref 001634
                                                              Strid III-V (When possible) OS Ref 064566

Optional Portage

Kms		
0	**Access**	Grassington Bridge. (OS Ref 998639) Can walk 500m upstream to put in at the Ghaistrills.
0.5		**Weir.** 2.5m steeply sloping drop. Easily shot far right, down gently sloping chute.
		200m angled **Weir.** 1.5m sloping drop.
		Shoot left and land on bank to inspect falls below.
		250m **Linton Falls.** Grade IV (Can be V in spate)
		Careful inspection necessary especially in high water.
		2m drop. Two routes. Right channel forms a steep turbulent chute.
		Left channel leads to single vertical plunge of 2m.
		Below small stopper with unpleasant boil behind.
4		Footbridge.
4.75		Loop Scar **Rapids.** Grade II/III on S bend.
5.5		Burnsall road bridge and village right.
10		**Appletreewick Falls.** Grade III Inspection advised.
		Dangerous in high water as large stoppers form.
		River splits around island.
		Shoot right side.
		Initial drop leads to Stopper.
		75m rocky rapid for 50m.
13		Barden Bridge.
14		Stone footbridge with castellated walls.
		Minor rapids below.
14.75		**Upper Strid.**
		River narrows to channel 2-3m wide.
		With 0.75m fall with turbulent stopper below.
		(This can be circumnavigated to the left in high water)
15		**Lower Strid.** (Grade III-V)
		Rocky fall 1m into narrow channel.
		Narrow deeply undercut banks with several further constrictions for 75m.
		May be shot in high water when Strid washed out.
		Otherwise **Portage.**
17.5	**Egress**	Egress point. Footbridge to cafe and car park.
19		Bolton Abbey right. footbridge.
20.5	**Egress**	Bolton Bridge. (OS Ref 073528)

Taking on The Strid in high water, River Wharfe

ADDENDUM
(Yorkshire Region)

All these rivers have been inspected by the author, but only some have been paddled.

Arkle Beck

Grade III

In high water this river offers 6km of pleasant, bouldery rapids. Canoeable from the road bridge just above Langthwaite. (OS Ref 000036) down to Reeth road bridge or you can continue on downstream to join the Swale as it makes its way towards Richmond.

Ribble

Grade III/IV

Although just outside the remit of this Guide, this westerly flowing Yorkshire river has been included on account of the excellent photograph we have of one of our team thoughtfully inspecting the river bed as he descends Stainforth Force upside down. (Photo - frontispiece.)

196

Heavy rainfall is again needed to make this stretch canoeable, although Stainforth Force is most easily shot in low water.

Access is from Helwith Bridge. (OS Ref 811695). After several kilometres there are about 100 metres of bouldery rapids. Another few kilometres bring you down to the next hazard about 100 metres below a stone hump backed road bridge. This is Stainforth Force, a three tiered drop, with each step being about 1.5m high. The river now flattens out before a weir is reached two kilometres further on. The 1.75m vertical drop is usually shot via the fish ladder on the extreme left. This weir should be carefully pre-inspected and in high water a portage is often a wise choice. There is one more weir before the safety of Settle road bridge is reached. (OS Ref 817641)

Rye

Grade II/III
After recent rainfall the more adventurous tourer should try this paddle set in the spectacular steep wooded Rye valley as the river descends off the North York Moors.

Canoeable from Haunby road bridge (OS Ref 543893) down to Helmsley. (Ideally the gauge beneath the bridge should be between 0.3m and 0.6m.) In full spate the river becomes dangerous as you tend to be swept into the tree lined banks.

In very low water you risk an arduous portage from the weir just above Helmsley where much of the water is lost underground.

The river now flattens as it crosses the Vale of Pickering to join the Derwent just above Malton.

Skirfare

Grade II
In high water this river offers a speedy, if unexciting, descent from Arncliffe or even Litton.

Most paddlers continue beyond the confluence with the Wharfe down to Grassington.

Whitsundale Beck

Grade II/III. Plus 2 falls
This tributary of the Upper Swale needs plenty of water. Access is from Ravenseat (OS Ref 863034).

After about 250 metres a 1.25m fall leads to a higher 2.25m stepped drop that requires inspecting, as there is no plunge pool. Plastic boats can bounce down on the left side. Most of the excitement is now over although you can now appreciate the spectacular scenery of Ravenseat Gorge, before you join the Upper Swale several kilometres further downstream.

FLAT WATER AREAS
Available to Canoeists

This list is not comprehensive but includes some of the most commonly used lakes and reservoirs in the region.

Bolam Lake

This small lake set in attractive woodland is owned by the National Trust and run by Northumberland County Council. Although rather muddy it is used by both canoeists and windsurfers.

Hemlington Lake

A small lake situated at Hemlington village just south of Middlesbrough. Canoeing permitted. Approximately 400m x 100m wide. OS Ref NZ 480145.

Kielder Reservoir

This is the largest man made lake in Britain. It is located in Kielder Forest and collects the headwaters of the North Tyne. Kielder is now used for a wide variety of recreational purposes, from waterskiing to sailing.

Its original purpose was to provide water for industrial use to the Teeside region, but as water demand has not yet met the projected estimates it does seem to have become rather a white elephant.

Kielder's main use at the moment is as a recreational facility although some electricity is produced from the hydro electric generators in the dam. Output of these generators is of great interest to canoeists as their use has some effect on the water further down the North Tyne. The generators are used to supplement generating capacity from the larger thermal power stations, so they tend to be used only at peak times, particularly in the winter months from 8.00am to midnight, and on Sunday mornings when everybody is having their Sunday roast cooked.

Whilst this might sound straight forward, in practice there are so many other variables involved it is quite impossible to predict when releases will occur. The simplest and best solution is to phone Kielder Dam on the number given below.

It is regrettable that whilst the water authorities have so kindly set up this service they have not provided any background information that enables the average canoeist to interpret the data on Kielder releases. No apology is therefore given for discussing the figures in some detail.

Planned releases are described in 'cumecs' this is sometimes written as m³/sec. A cumec is simply one cubic metre of water flowing past a given point per second. Whilst one cumec might not sound a lot it is about 200 gallons per

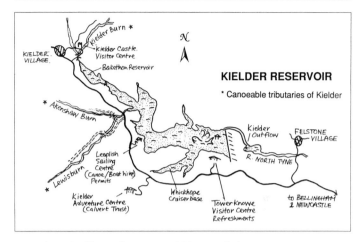

second or 18 million gallons over a 24 hour period.

The minimum 'compensation flow' that Kielder reservoir must release by statue at all times (to prevent the river bed drying up) is 1.3 cumecs.

Two hydroelectric generators are housed in the dam, a small Francis turbine which has a working capacity of 1.5 cumecs which is designed to operate when only the minimum compensation flow is being released. The second much larger Kaplan turbine requires 14.1 cumecs. Thus the maximum release for purely generating electricity will be about 16 cumecs. All these figures are perhaps a little difficult to translate into visual images of the river level but as a very rough guide the following may help:

1) 2 to 4 cumecs. Tyne at a rock bottom. Canoeing not really viable.
2) 5 to 10 cumecs. River low but paddleable. Small top stopper Warden gorge.
3) 11 to 20. Still rather rocky. Good summer level but low to average for winter. Holding top stopper.
4) 21 to 50. High winter level. Powerful top stopper.
5) 51 to 400 plus. Low spate to flood.

At relatively low flow rates the river level rises at about 3 to 4cms per cumec but this drops off in spate conditions to less than 1cm per cumec as the river velocity has increased.

The graph over the page shows the mean daily flow at two points on the North Tyne as a monthly average over an eighteen month period from January 1989. The gauging weir at Ugly Dub lies directly below the dam and is thus measuring the releases from Kielder. Reaverhill gauging weir lies just above Chollerford and is measuring what is going on at the lower end of the

199

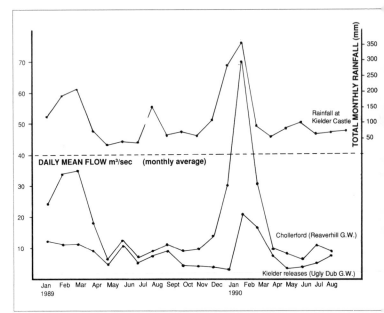

The mean daily flow on the North Tyne

North Tyne.

Comparing the two weirs during the dry summer months shows that the flow rates are very close together and roughly parallel. This is because there is insignificant input from tributaries during dry weather. In these conditions the flow rate at Chollerford will usually be very similar to the amount released from Kielder as indicated by the information service.

By contrast during the wet winter months there is now often significant input from the tributaries so that there now is no longer such a close relationship between Kielder releases and the flow at Chollerford.

This is well illustrated by looking at the flow rates over the four month period from October 1989. During this period Kielder releases were *successively reduced* whilst the level in the lower North Tyne *progressively rose!*

So during wet months you probably get just as good an idea of lower North Tyne levels from just keeping an eye on the weather as you would from phoning the Kielder information service.

During winter time the tributaries are fairly sensitive to rainfall as the ground is saturated. However this does not apply to dry summer months when low to moderate rainfall is usually just soaked up by the soil with little effect

200

Fun on flat water, Kielder

on water levels.

A further complicating factor is the long time delay between releases leaving Kielder and arriving at Chollerford. It takes ten hours fifteen minutes to reach Reaverhill. There is always an additional 'wind up' time of two hours when the flow is gradually increased to the scheduled amount. This is to prevent a bore developing due to a rapid rise in river level. Therefore a full TWELVE hours has to elapse from the scheduled time of the start of a release to the full release reaching Chollerford. (Not the six hours most canoeists optimistically believe.)

Details of the water releases may be obtained from the number below. A recorded message details the times on a weekly basis.

Canoeing is allowed in the lake provided a small fee is paid at the club house located in the Leaplish Sailing Centre. Canoes and equipment can also be hired from the Centre. The facilities have recently been upgraded to include a cafe, showers and a changing room.

After heavy rainfall several of the larger tributaries flowing into Kielder become canoeable. The best of those are the Lewis Burn, Kielder Burn and Carey Burn.

For general advice, hire of canoes, windsurfers and sailing boats.
Contact: Leaplish Sailing Centre,
Kielder Water,
Northumberland.
Tel: 0434 250203

Recorded message for Kielder Water releases: Tel: 0434 240463

Killingworth Lake

A small municipal lake, of importance because of its close proximity to Newcastle- upon-Tyne.

It is very shallow (1.5m) and, therefore, an excellent place for novices to get basic instruction. A small annual membership fee is payable to K.W.S.A. (See Appendix II Club addresses.)

Ladyburn Lake

Opened in 1989 this lake forms part of the Druridge Bay Country Park which was created out of a redundant opencast coal site.

With an annual membership fee of over £20 few canoeists will want to dig so deep into their pockets unless they are already members of the Watersports Association which also caters for windsurfers and waterskiers.

As the lake is a popular venue for wild fowl to overwinter watersports are only allowed from April to September.

The Park offers free public access to the lakeland area and three miles of coastal dunes along Druridge Bay.

There is also a full-time warden who operates from the visitor centre. This is located on the eastern shore of the lake, following the A1068 northwards out of Ashington through Widdrington towards Amble. A few miles beyond the turn off to Red Row the Park lies adjacent to East Chevington opencast site.

Queen Elizabeth II Silver Jubilee Lake

Otherwise affectionately known as 'Ashington Pond.'

This small lake was created out of an old colliery spoil heap. It was run by Wansbeck Council for recreational purposes, being primarily used by windsurfers and anglers. Canoeists are also welcome provided they pay a small launching fee.

The lake is well signposted from the main road. Follow the A189 out of Newcastle towards Ashington. Continue straight over several roundabouts as the A189 by-passes Ashington on its way to Lynemouth. Just beyond the second roundabout the road passes beneath a small concrete railway bridge. This is soon followed by a road off to the left which will bring you to the lakeside after about 0.5km.

Recently a hotel and a sailing club have been built by a private company who have taken over the sporting facilities from the council.

Wardens Office. Queen Elizabeth II Park. Tel: (0670) 856968

Scaling Dam

A small man made reservoir between Guisborough and Whitby fed by the Roxby Beck. OS Ref 750130.

Canoeing allowed with some reluctance by Northumbria Water.

Selset Reservoir

A medium sized reservoir situated in the Lune Valley, approximately four miles south west of Middleton-in-Teesdale. OS Ref NY 910216.

Used mainly for sailing. Permission is required from Selset Sailing Club.

Pettico Wick Bay, St Abb's

SEA CANOEING
The North-East Coastline

Contributors

Geoff Burk (Tyne to Flamborough Head)
Geoff Wood (Newbiggin area)
Vic Brown (Amble area)
Peter Hawkey (Nat History of the Farnes)
Rob Eglestaff (Berwick Caves)
Martin Melling (Tidal theory)

THE NORTH-EAST COASTLINE

Introduction

The North-East coastline with its wide variety of coastal scenery should be able to offer you an exciting trip whatever your skills and canoeing interests.

These vary from committing open sea crossings to magnificent coastal excursions with sweeping sandy beaches providing abundant surf at many locations.

This beautiful coastline is matched by the equally varied and rich wildlife which cannot fail to impress even the most fanatical paddler. However, it is sad that in our overcrowded island the sheer concentration of wildlife on places like the Farnes is now virtually unique.

To share your trip with a playful dolphin or hold court with a multitude of heavily whiskered seals forever nudging closer to your boat, is a thrilling experience every bit as exciting as shooting a difficult rapid and certainly something to be savoured and remembered.

Many visitors to the area will also wish to see the chain of well preserved castles that lie along the coast providing reminders of the bloody conflicts that once raged along the border areas.

Probably the most spectacular trips are those to the Farnes and around St. Abbs Head, although there is also good paddling along the Yorkshire coast around the high cliffs at Saltburn and the beautiful eroded chalky shoreline of Flamborough Head.

Good surfing is available. The most commonly used beaches being at Longsands, Tynemouth, and at South Shields.

Using the Guide

The description of the coastline has been divided into two halves. The Northumbrian coast is described from Tynemouth northwards, working its way up the coast to St. Abbs Head in Berwickshire.

The Co. Durham and Yorkshire coastline is described from South Shields going southwards down to Flamborough Head.

The emphasis of the book has been to outline the main geographical and historical features of the coastline of interest to sea canoeists. Whenever possible we have tried to detail the best launching points, and provide information about tides and sea hazards.

Paddlers requiring more extensive navigational and tidal information should refer to the relevant admiralty charts and sea pilots which are listed in the bibliography.

Likewise the theory of sea canoeing is not within the remit of this Guide. However, it is felt a brief discussion of some aspects of tidal theory and safety at sea would be of some practical assistance to paddlers, especially to those fly-by-night river canoeists who occasionally venture on to the sea.

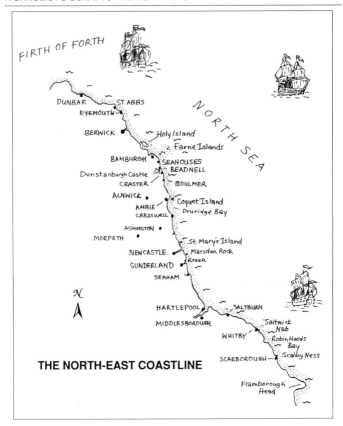

FIRTH OF FORTH

NORTH SEA

DUNBAR — ST.ABBS
EYEMOUTH
BERWICK
Holy Island
Farne Islands
BAMBURGH — SEAHOUSES
BEADNELL
Dunstanburgh Castle
CRASTER — BOULMER
ALNWICK
AMBLE — Coquet Island
CRESSWELL — Druridge Bay
ASHINGTON
MORPETH
St.Mary's Island
NEWCASTLE — Marsden Rock
SUNDERLAND — ROKER
SEAHAM

N

HARTLEPOOL — SALTBURN
MIDDLESBOROUGH
Saltwick Nab
WHITBY — Robin Hoods Bay
SCARBOROUGH — Scalby Ness
Flamborough Head

THE NORTH-EAST COASTLINE

Safety at Sea

As the sun blazes down on a calm, azure sea, (as we frequently get in the North-East) it is extremely tempting to make the most of the weather by setting out with little more than your Hawaiian T shirt, trendiest shades and a bottle of sun tan oil.

The reality is, that however brilliant the weather may look there is often something unpleasant lurking over the horizon. This usually manifests itself with the sudden descent of a dense sea fog, or the apparently spontaneous arrival of a sea squall.

Whilst the shoreline may look a few paddle strokes away, with adverse tidal or weather conditions, tired company and the occasional capsize, it could prove an endless journey by which time weather conditions could easily have got out of hand.

In the North-East you should always hope for the best but prepare for the worst!

Planning

You may wish to inform the local coastguard of your intended trip and obtain a local weather report along with tidal information.

For longer trips and in unfamiliar water it may be worth perusing the sea pilot and obtain the local admiralty chart for the area.

Local canoeists should be consulted whenever possible.

Equipment

Apart from the canoeists' usual regalia, the sea canoeist should carry several additional items of equipment, of which distress flares are probably the most important. These should usually be of several types, but should include red parachute flares which shoot to over 500 feet for attracting attention, and smaller penflares as a means of locating you once rescue is at hand.

Smoke distress signals can also be used, although they are somewhat limited in windy conditions. Whatever their type the flares must be in an accessible position, i.e. not beneath a tight spraydeck! A plastic whistle is also worth carrying.

Split paddles are always a good idea, especially with larger groups and on long trips.

Headgear is a more contentious issue amongst sea canoeists. Helmets do make identification easier in the water, minimise heat loss as well as providing protection whilst landing on rocky shorelines. Woollen hats may also be helpful especially in colder weather. Wide brim sun hats and sunglasses will add to your comfort in fine weather.

A compass is an invaluable navigational aid should fog descend and for longer offshore trips.

Emergency equipment is otherwise similar to river canoeing. This should include spare food and drink, hypothermia kit, first aid and, of course, money! Even at sea, landing on islands or launching from harbours seems to involve parting with your precious shekels. On longer trips sufficient equipment should be carried to enable you to bivouac in an emergency. A stove or means of making a fire is also strongly advised.

An efficient towing line is also recommended in case of paddle loss or enfeebled individuals requiring assistance.

Having a reliable base contact with all the names, addresses and phone numbers of expedition members is also a good idea. If the trip becomes inappropriately overdue allowing for prevailing conditions they should have instructions to contact the coastguard.

Basics of Tidal Theory

An understanding of tides is essential for successful sea canoeing. They are caused by the gravitational pull of the sun and the moon. Since the moon is much nearer than the sun, it has the greater influence. The biggest tides occur at full and new moon and are called SPRINGS, the smallest tides occur at half moon and are called NEAPS. All you really need to tell you where you are in this lunar cycle is your diary; Full Moon or New Moon and a few days after you're on SPRINGS, First Quarter or Last Quarter and a few days after and you're on NEAPS. Another way of getting this information is from your Tide Tables (30p from your local fishing tackle shop or free from some chandlers, try Cosalts on North Shields Fish Quay).

If you are still following this then you have the makings of a sea canoeist. You will also have noticed that the diary method is a rough guide, the tide tables give you more accurate information.

The next thing you need to know is the direction of the tidal stream. Basically this runs more or less parallel to the coastline but on this coast; north when ebbing and south when flooding. When flooding the tide is rising and so coming towards High Water. When ebbing it is falling and so moving towards Low Water. This movement from High Water to Low Water takes a little over six hours and is often referred to as "a tide". The speed of a tidal stream during a tide is not constant, it starts from nothing and accelerates gradually to it's maximum flow in the middle of the tide and then decelerates to nothing again. These periods of no movement when the tide is turning are called slack water. They can be quite long at neaps and very short at springs. A rough guide to estimating the rate of flow

MOON PHASES G.M.T. — 1988

JANUARY		FEBRUARY	
Full Moon	4	Full Moon	2
Last Quarter	12	Last Quarter	10
New Moon	19	New Moon	17
First Quarter	25	First Quarter	24
MARCH		APRIL	
Full Moon	3	Full Moon	2
Last Quarter	11	Last Quarter	9
New Moon	18	New Moon	16
First Quarter	25	First Quarter	23
MAY		JUNE	
Full Moon	1	Last Quarter	7
Last Quarter	9	New Moon	14
New Moon	15	First Quarter	22
First Quarter	23	Full Moon	29
Full Moon	31		
JULY		AUGUST	
Last Quarter	6	Last Quarter	4
New Moon	13	New Moon	12
First Quarter	22	First Quarter	20
Full Moon	29	Full Moon	27
SEPTEMBER		OCTOBER	
Last Quarter	3	Last Quarter	2
New Moon	11	New Moon	10
First Quarter	19	First Quarter	18
Full Moon	25	Full Moon	25
NOVEMBER		DECEMBER	
Last Quarter	1	Last Quarter	1
New Moon	9	New Moon	9
First Quarter	16	First Quarter	16
Full Moon	23	Full Moon	23
		Last Quarter	31

1988
TIDES and DEPTHS AT NORTH SHIELDS
(All times are G.M.T.)

		JANUARY 1988					FEBRUARY 1988		
		Morn.	H	Aft.	H		Morn.	H	Aft.	H
		hr m	M	hr m	M		hr m	M	hr. m	M
	1F	01 07	4.4	13 44	4.5	1M	02 44	4.4	14 56	4.6
	2Sa	02 02	4.5	14 29	4.6	2Tu	03 21	4.5	15 29	4.7
	3Su	02 49	4.6	15 07	4.7	3W	03 55	4.6	15 59	4.7
SPRINGS						4Th	04 26	4.6	16 27	4.8
	4M	03 29	4.7	15 42	4.7	5F	04 57	4.6	16 55	4.8
	5Tu	04 07	4.7	16 14	4.8	6Sa	05 26	4.5	17 25	4.8
	6W	04 42	4.7	16 47	4.7	7Su	05 57	4.4	17 56	4.7
	7Th	05 18	4.6	17 18	4.7					
	8F	05 51	4.5	17 51	4.6	8M	06 29	4.4	18 29	4.6
	9Sa	06 28	4.3	18 27	4.5	9Tu	07 04	4.3	19 10	4.5
	10Su	07 06	4.2	19 04	4.4	10W	07 47	4.2	19 59	4.3
						11Th	08 37	4.1	21 01	4.1
NEAPS	11M	07 48	4.1	19 51	4.3	12F	09 41	3.9	22 20	4.0
	12Tu	08 36	4.0	20 44	4.1	13Sa	11 01	3.9	23 54	4.1
	13W	09 31	4.0	21 46	4.1	14Su	***	***	12 25	4.1
	14Th	10 34	4.0	22 58	4.1					
	15F	11 40	4.1	***	***	15M	01 14	4.3	13 31	4.4
	16Sa	00 11	4.3	12 45	4.3	16Tu	02 15	4.6	14 23	4.7
	17Su	01 20	4.5	13 42	4.5	17W	03 05	4.9	15 10	5.1
						18Th	03 50	5.1	15 53	5.3
SPRINGS	18M	02 19	4.8	14 33	4.8	19F	04 34	5.1	16 35	5.5
	19Tu	03 12	5.0	15 21	5.0	20Sa	05 18	5.1	17 19	5.5
	20W	04 02	5.1	16 07	5.2	21Su	06 00	4.9	18 04	5.3
	21Th	04 49	5.1	16 52	5.3					
	22F	05 37	5.0	17 39	5.3	22M	06 43	4.7	18 50	5.1
	23Sa	06 25	4.8	18 27	5.2	23Tu	07 27	4.5	19 41	4.7
	24Su	07 13	4.6	19 17	5.0	24W	08 16	4.2	20 37	4.3
						25Th	09 14	3.9	21 49	3.9
	25M	08 04	4.4	20 11	4.7	26F	10 33	3.8	23 27	3.7
	26Tu	08 58	4.2	21 11	4.4	27Sa	***	***	12 07	3.8
	27W	10 02	4.0	22 21	4.1	28Su	00 55	3.9	13 14	4.0
	28Th	11 15	4.0	23 43	4.0					
	29F	***	***	12 31	4.1	29M	01 51	4.1	14 01	4.2
	30Sa	01 00	4.1	13 31	4.2					
	31Su	01 59	4.2	14 19	4.4					

during a tide is called the twelfths rule. It states that during the first hour $^1/_{12}$ of the tide flows, during the second hour $^2/_{12}$ and the third hour $^3/_{12}$. This same pattern applies to the second half of the tide in reverse 3,2,1.

Hour of Tide
1 2 3 4 5 6
Flow of Tide
1 2 3 3 2 1

Another good source of tidal information is your chart. At various places on the chart you will find a little diamond with a letter in it thus.

Accurate measurements have been taken here to determine the rate and direction of the tidal stream throughout the tide. This information is given in a table somewhere on the chart. (See 2nd chart page 210)

The time that a tidal stream begins to flow relative to High or Low Water can vary depending on the location. e.g. At the mouth of the River Wear the tidal stream is said to turn exactly on local High and Low Water whereas off the Tyne there is a 40 min. delay. Off the Farnes (Longstone) the stream runs on for well over an hour after local High and Low Water at Seahouses. This iinformation can be obtained from the chart or the Admiralty Pilot (a book of detailed information relevant for navigating vessels along the coast).

The weather can also have an effect on the tides. Prolonged northerly gales for example can increase both rate and duration of a flood tide on this coast.

Let's do a little calculation to make sure you understand these basic ideas of tidal prediction. Say you wanted to go for a paddle from South Shields on January 1st 1988......you really are a keen sea-canoeist! You decide to go

Tidal Streams referred to H. W. at River Tyne

Hours		Lat. 55°36·3' N. Long. 1°39·3' W. Direct'n	Rate Sp.	Np.	Lat. 55°39·5' N. Long. 1°44·0' W. Direct'n	Rate Sp.	Np.	Lat. 55°44·9' N. Long. 1°48·2' W. Direct'n	Rate Sp.	Np.	Lat. 55°45·8' N. Long. 1°56·1' W. Direct'n	Rate Sp.	Np.
Before H.W. R. Tyne	6	306°	1·7 kn.	0·9 kn.	340°	0·5 kn.	0·3 kn.	233°	1·1 kn.	0·6 kn.	326°	0·5 kn.	0·2 kn.
	5	329°	0·4	0·2	011°	0·1	0·1	277°	0·8	0·4	315°	0·2	0·1
	4	118°	1·1	0·6	147°	0·4	0·2	241°	0·2	0·1	090°	0·1	0·0
	3	127°	2·2	1·1	156°	0·8	0·4	151°	0·4	0·2	133°	0·3	0·2
	2	125°	2·4	1·2	158°	1·0	0·5	107°	0·7	0·4	43°	0·6	0·3
	1	127°	2·2	1·1	160°	1·0	0·5	105°	0·8	0·4	43°	0·8	0·4
H.W.		124°	1·7	0·8	166°	0·7	0·4	105°	0·8	0·4	87°	0·7	0·4
After H.W. R. Tyne	1	126°	0·8	0·4	173°	0·3	0·2	103°	0·7	0·4	1·6°	0·6	0·3
	2	335°	0·6	0·2	310°	0·2	0·1	098°	0·4	0·2	34°	0·8	0·4
	3	314°	1·4	0·7	330°	0·8	0·4	323°	0·1	0·0	31°	0·8	0·4
	4	306°	2·2	1·1	336°	1·0	0·5	293°	0·6	0·3	316°	0·9	0·5
	5	300°	2·6	1·3	338°	1·0	0·5	290°	1·0	0·5	319°	0·8	0·4
	6	303°	2·3	1·2	340°	0·8	0·4	235°	1·1	0·6	315°	0·7	0·3

afloat at 10.00am. Looking up your tide table tells you that the nearest high water is at 1344. For our planning purposes we can round this up to 1400. Working back to our launch time of 1000 we can see that during our first two hours of paddling the tidal stream will be running at its peak rate, hours 3 and 4. At 4.5 metres the tide is about half way between neaps and springs. So given this information and provided that the wind is not an overriding factor it would be an easier paddle to go south to say Roker taking advantage of the favourable flood tide. Of course there are other alternatives which you can consider for yourself. This has been a very brief and hopefully simple introduction. If you want to delve further then the following reading is recommended; *Sea Canoeing* by Derek Hutchinson. *Sea Touring* by John Ramwell. *BCU Coaching Handbook*. Sea Canoeing Chapter by Nigel Foster.

THE NORTHUMBERLAND COASTLINE

Tynemouth to Newbiggin

Although much of the industry and population of Northumberland is found in this south eastern corner of the county, there are several excellent surfing beaches, however the coastline between Blyth and Lynemouth is more industrialised and therefore best avoided.

When the prevailing wind is from the west, shelter can often be sought close to shore especially where the coast is high at Tynemouth, Whitley Bay, Seaton Sluice and Newbiggin.

Tides; Although of no great strength it is worth noting that on this stretch of the coast the tide floods from the south and ebbs north. The Tidal Constant from Dover is 4.40 hours.

On an ebbing tide there is usually quite a powerful drift northwards up the beach at Long Sands towards the rocks at the northern tip of the bay. (Saddle Rocks and Crabhill)

Paddlers are advised to try and keep south of the Plaza.

Tyne Estuary

Probably the best launching point is from Priors Haven which lies at the mouth of the Tyne just inside the North Pier in the little bay occupied by Tynemouth sailing and rowing clubs.

Offloading may be done by the shore, but use the car park just above the bay.

This access point is particularly useful in rough weather when heavy surf on the beaches may prevent you breaking out.

After rounding the North Pier the craggy ruins of Tynemouth Priory are easily seen above the cliff tops juxtaposed with the sleeker outlines of the coastguard station which also lie within the Priory grounds.

The natural splendour of the cliffs has been at least partially destroyed by the concrete buttressing built along the cliff tops to provide support for the gun emplacements put there to protect the harbour during World War II. Several of the guns remain in place today.

The high cliffs of the Priory soon give way to a small, sandy bay. Whilst easy to effect a landing it can only be accessed by a steep set of steps coming down from the Gibraltar Rock Pub.

Beyond the bay lies Sharpness Point. Here a group of rocks and shoals extend out into the sea, which when passed reveal the long curving beach of Long Sands.

Long Sands Beach, Tynemouth

Access to the beach is usually achieved at its southern end, where a tarmac spur branches off from the sea front opposite the Grand Hotel to lead down to the beach.

Although only a short distance, the road is wide, providing convenient car parking space close to the beach. However keep a watchful eye on your belongings as there have recently been a large number of car thefts here.

Long Sands is probably the best surfing beach in the area, certainly the most popular. Gently shelving it can produce surf when everywhere else is dead or dumping.

After two kilometres of rocky coastline the south end of the three kilometre Cambois beach is reached, marked by the three red conical topped storage hoppers for the bauxite used at the aluminium smelter at Lynemouth.

Another obvious landmark almost midway along this beach is the Blyth Power Station, with its twin pairs of tall chimneys which line up on an east west heading. Again this sandy beach is paralleled by the road and is gently

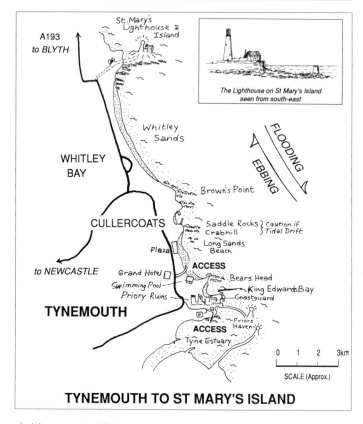

A193
to BLYTH

St. Mary's
Lighthouse &
Island

The Lighthouse on St Mary's Island
seen from south-east

Whitley
Sands

FLOODING

EBBING

WHITLEY
BAY

Brown's Point

CULLERCOATS

Saddle Rocks } Caution if
Crabhill } Tidal Drift

Long Sands
Beach

Plaza

ACCESS

to NEWCASTLE

Grand Hotel

Bears Head

Swimming Pool

King Edwards Bay

Priory Ruins

Coastguard

TYNEMOUTH

Priors
Haven

ACCESS

Tyne Estuary

0   1   2   3km

SCALE (Approx.)

TYNEMOUTH TO ST MARY'S ISLAND

shelving except at high water, but beware of the outfall pipe from the power station. At the north end of the beach prior to reaching the mouth of the River Wansbeck is the Buccaneer Pub nestling among the dunes. The mouth of the Wansbeck has a very pronounced bar which can lift the smallest sea into waves and indeed can be very dangerous to small boats, several lives having been lost here. At high tide it is possible to paddle into the mouth and the large mooring pool beyond, but at low water the entrance is almost dry.

The north side of the mouth is occupied by a large caravan site, so access by car is possible. From here begins a two kilometre paddle in the shadow of tall cliffs topped off at their mid point by the first of the group of great measured mile pylons used by ships to calibrate instruments and engine speeds during sea trials.

Rounding Spittal Point you enter Newbiggin Bay, easily recognised by the church out on its northern point. In rough seas the dumping waves on the beach can be avoided by landing behind the breakwater below the church.

Beyond Newbiggin the four pairs of chimneys belonging to the Alcan Aluminium Smelter can easily be seen along with the single, tall chimney of the Alcan Power Station.

Short sea trips can also be commenced from Tynemouth. The usual round trips being northwards to St Mary's Island or across the Tyne Estuary down to Marsden Rocks.

At the southern end of the bay lies the outdoor swimming pool, the unofficial headquarters of Killingworth Canoe Club, whose members will usually be found there or in the waves.

The palatial outlines of the 'Plaza' dominate the centre of the beach. Originally built as a dance hall it has resorted to the usual mish-mash of cheap seaside tourist entertainments, from gaming halls to selling fish and chips. Its one redeeming feature is housing an excellent roller skating rink.

To the north the beach curves round to a rocky reef, saddle rocks and several smaller shoals.

In rough weather and on an ebbing tide there is a strong drift up the beach on to these rocks and paddlers are advised to keep to the southern half of the beach.

Around saddle rocks lies Cullercoats Haven. A small beach, protected by the concrete arms of north and south breakwaters. It houses a Lifeboat Station, Marine Research Laboratory and the club house of Poseidon Sub-Aqua Club.

Whitley Bay and St. Mary's Island

To the north of Cullercoats lies a rocky promontory known as Browns Point. This short stretch of rocky coastline has sunk several vessels whose remains lie in the murky water below.

Soon the rocky shoreline gives way to the long, sandy beach of Whitley Sands. Again, plenty of pubs, fish 'n chips, and amusement arcades line the length of this popular holiday resort.

Dominating the skyline along the sea front are the undulating waves of twisted metal work belonging to the Rollercoaster beneath which are the exotic looking pleasure domes of Spanish City, Whitley Bay's permanent fairground. There are numerous points for vehicular access although parking is restricted above the promenade.

At the northern extremity of the beach the distinctive outline of St Mary's Lighthouse can easily be seen.

St Mary's Island has now become a popular tourist attraction. It is joined to the land by a causeway which is covered at high tide. The impressive lighthouse has now been decommissioned and a visitor centre opened there which is run by North Tyneside Borough Council.

213

Blyth and Newbiggin

Around the headland of Seaton Sluice starts the four kilometre long Blyth South Beach. Surf sometimes runs well here, but beware of the outfall pipes along its length. The road here runs parallel with the beach about 2 - 300 metres beyond the sand dunes, an awkward portage. At the north end of the beach can be seen the entrance to Blyth harbour, the South Pier being of open pile construction and the North, concrete with a lighthouse at the end. The harbour is used by commercial shipping, and the harbourmaster does not allow the entry of canoes for safety reasons.

Rounding the North Pier care must be taken when passing the outlying reefs of Seaton Rocks and the Sow and Pigs as they can be nasty when a north sea is running.

Druridge Bay

Cresswell to Hauxley

Once Newbiggin and Lynemouth are passed the industrial landscape of Northumberland is suddenly left behind as Snab Point is rounded, to reveal the long, sweeping, arc of Druridge Bay with 10km of golden, sandy, dunes stretching out as far as the eye can see.

Occasionally used by local canoeists, few paddlers will wish to travel this far to surf, as there are other more accessible beaches closer to Tyneside. The best area lies between Druridge village and Cresswell when north westerly swells create good surf. To the north the rocky reef's at Bondicarrs are surfable to those in plastic boats and are good sport in a variety of conditions.

Whilst never crowded, the beach always seems to have the occasional jogger, beachcomber, or dog exercising its owner.

For those interested in wildlife a series of small lakes and reed beds have been created as nature reserves, as this part of the North-East coastline is on the migratory route for wildfowl journeying south from the Arctic to North Africa.

Of course, such beautiful countryside is bound to attract the attention of developers and regrettably Druridge Bay is no exception. In fact, it has now become one of the most well known places in Northumberland following the national publicity about its proposal as a site for a nuclear power station. Despite vociferous and sustained opposition, the scheme refuses to be killed off, like Hercules battling with the giant Hydra, no sooner do you cut off one head than it grows two more!

Whilst most of us accept the necessity of having some nuclear power stations, surely not in the middle of Northumberland's most beautiful beach!

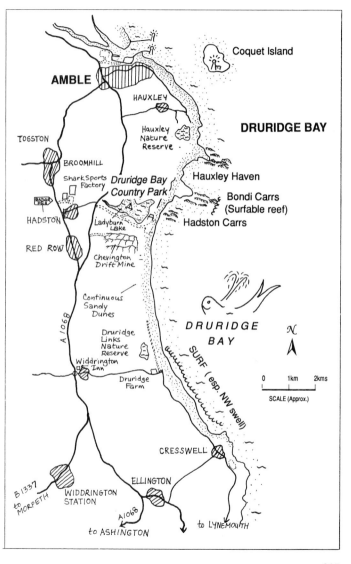

Access

There are four main access points along the bay.

(i) Cresswell

This small hamlet overlooks the beach on the southern most tip of the bay.

Whilst there is a rather scruffy car park in the centre of Cresswell, a far more pleasant car park with a good footpath down to the beach lies at Cresswell dunes. This is 250m to the south of the village opposite the large caravan park. (OS Ref 299931)

(Be sure to lock your car.)

(ii) Druridge Farm

Lying in the centre of the bay, Druridge Farm probably offers the most convenient access site.

It lies about two kilometres north of Cresswell, where the road takes a 90° dog's leg turn with an unlocked but gated tarmac road continuing alongside the beach for several kilometres.

The land is owned and run by the National Trust who levy a small car parking fee on visitors. (OS Ref 276960)

(iii) Druridge Bay Country Park

The Park lies about 6km to the north of Widdrington just off the A1068, opposite the village of Hadston and a few hundred metres beyond the entrance to East Chevington open cast mine.

If you get lost just head for the enormous spoil heaps which dominate the countryside for miles around.

A tarmac road winds down through the Park to a visitor centre and car park, which is only about 50 metres from the shoreline.

(See also Ladyburn Lake, Flat Water Areas)

(iv) Hauxley

This is a small mining village with a redundant pit on the northern extremity of Druridge Bay.

The surrounding area has been converted to a nature reserve. This part of the beach is rather windswept and bleak.

Amble to Beadnell

Amble

This small seaside town lies at the mouth of the river Coquet about 25 miles from Newcastle.

It is situated just around the headland forming the northern tip of Druridge Bay.

Inland lies the historic town of Warkworth with its splendid castle, medieval bridge and Norman Church.

About 2km offshore lies Coquet Island which provides an excellent short sea trip.

Launching; The easiest access is from the sandy beach known as 'little shore' (See Map).

An alternative is to follow signs to the Marina off the A1068 where there is a large public car park close to Coquet Yacht Club.

Canoeing in the Harbour; Currents flow strongly in the harbour, particularly on the ebb, on spring tides, and when the river is in spate. Care is needed when passing the many boats moored in the river.

Going upstream, past the Marina and the Yacht Club, you will notice (at high tide) a creek running northwards up the coast behind the sand dunes. This is the old course of the river and can be paddled up for about half a mile. It is a good place for spotting birds - you will see numerous varieties of waders and ducks. It is only accessible near high water.

Following the main river takes you to the weir (covered at half-tide), which can provide some white water amusement. (Take care at the northern edge - the concrete 'jetty' is severely undercut.) You can paddle up past Warkworth (another small tidal weir), round the magnificent Castle, and up past the Hermitage (a Chapel on the northern bank cut out of a sandstone outcrop - interesting to visit), to the Coquet Lodge weir. There may be anglers in the fishing season. There is usually not much current on this section, particularly if the tide is rising.

The Castle and the Hermitage are English Heritage properties, and may be an added attraction for any non-canoeing members of your party.

Surfing; When the sea is rough, and the tide is low, there is fantastic beginners' surf inside the harbour. The wave basin is flat sand, and the waves run in beautifully - not too big, and with an easy return route in the deep water channel. More challenging surf is found in the harbour entrance, but it is prudent to keep to the shallower water if the tide is ebbing. On a rising tide it is much safer, as a capsized canoeist is swept back into the harbour instead of out to sea!

There is also good surfing on the beach to the north of the harbour. You can paddle the North Breakwater, or carry canoes over the landward end.

Sea Hazards; Tides flow quite strongly in the vicinity of Amble. An ebb tide can create a confused sea in the harbour mouth, particularly with an incoming swell or wind. There is a strong flow in the channel to the south west of Coquet Island, with a significant chop when the flood tide meets a southerly wind. When the river is in spate, flood water can be seen running right out beyond the northern edge of the Island.

When there is a swell running, you may find breaking waves quite far from shore. There is shoal water (Pan Bush), to the east of the harbour (marked with a red buoy to seaward.) You can see the bottom here on a low tide. An

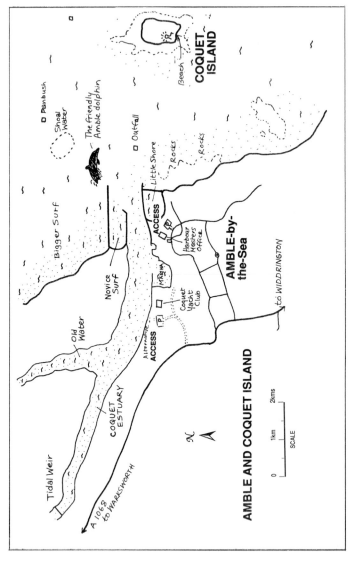

COQUET ISLAND

Beach

□ Panbush

Shoal Water

The friendly Amble dolphin

□ Outfall

Little Shore

Rocks

Rocks

Bigger Surf

ACCESS

Harbour Masters Office

AMBLE-by-the-Sea

to WIDDRINGTON

Novice Surf

MARINA

I.P.

Coquet Yacht Club

Alternative ACCESS

Old Water

Coquet Estuary

A 1068 to WARKSWORTH

Tidal Weir

N

SCALE

0   1km   2kms

AMBLE AND COQUET ISLAND

R.A.F. boat was capsized here with great loss of life a few years ago. Rocks run out for about half a mile to the north of the island, and there are two sets of rocks running out from the coast to the south of the island - Bondicarrs and Hauxley Carrs. There is a buoy marking the seaward end of the Hauxley Carrs.

Coquet Island (Puffin Island)

This small island lies just to the south of Amble Harbour, about 2km offshore.

The island is now owned by the R.S.P.B. and kept as a bird sanctuary.

Although the island is small, there is a large population of puffins who lend the island its nickname. Other residents include, seals, rabbits, the three lighthouse keepers (soon to be replaced by an automatic system) and the famous Amble dolphin, who has taken up residence in the surrounding coastal waters. He is extremely friendly so don't forget to take your camera if it is waterproof!

The dolphin is usually located about 100 metres offshore directly opposite the Harbour entrance. If you're swimming in the water and wish to 'play' with Freddy it is usually best to appear non threatening by adopting a fairly passive posture in the water by floating upright or on your back. When Freddy approaches don't suddenly reach out to grab him as if he were a lifeline otherwise you risk just frightening him off. He will always make it quite plain when he feels you can be trusted and it's time for play. It's usually a good sign when he rolls onto his back pointing his Ventral fins into the air! (See colour photo)

In the past probably its most famous resident was St Cuthbert who occupied the Benedictine cell which is located close to the lighthouse.

Landing on Coquet Island is not permitted as it might disturb the nesting birds. However, circumnavigation of the island makes an excellent short sea trip.

Alnmouth

This pleasant seaside village lies about 6km to the north of Amble. It provides a large, sheltered, estuary pool for pottering about at high water.

The beaches at Alnmouth and just to the north offer good surf when there is a south westerly swell.

Above Alnmouth the long, sweeping, sandy beach gradually gives way to a rockier shoreline. Here overfalls at Seaton Point and beyond create reef breaks which are surfable.

Boulmer

As the northern point of Alnmouth Bay is rounded, a bright orange windsock behind the shoreline indicates that the helicopter base at R.A.F. Boulmer has been reached.

A few houses scattered close to the shoreline form the village of Boulmer.

This has a long seafaring history of smuggling and heroic rescues along this treacherous stretch of coastline.

The next bay is Howick Haven, the northern point has a large hole in the outcrop of dolerite through which the sea sucks and surges known as the 'rumbling kern.' This is best visited at low tide. It also provides a sheltered beach suitable for a bivouac.

A little further north a detached house lies close to the shoreline. This was a Victorian bathing house built by the Grey family. The Greys resided in Howick Hall, a large mansion lying just inland. The gardens are open to the public during the summer months.

Craster

This small seaside village lies a few miles further up the coast. It has a small harbour, with two small jetties offering a safe haven in rough weather. Several small reef breaks lie immediately offshore at Muckle Carr and little Carr.

Landing on the rocky shoreline, even in good weather, is best avoided.

A small cove, the 'Hole in the Dyke' provides an alternative landing spot lying at the southern tip of the village just before the houses begin. It is about 50m below the old school building which is now home to Kevin Danforths Adventure Centre, River Deep, Mountain High.

The town is well known for curing kippers. Its fishing traditions are maintained with a small fleet of cobles that still go out for lobsters and herring. During the summer months most of the population seem to be tourists living in holiday homes. There is a car park and tourist centre in the town.

Dunstanburgh Castle

The craggy outlines of this ruined castle perched on top of a basalt outcrop, dominates the next few miles of coastline, forming an impressive landmark.

Built by the Earl of Lancaster in 1313, it was abandoned in the 16th century after the development of artillery made it redundant.

It is open to the public and is run by English Heritage.

Just offshore at Castle Point, the reefs at Thorn Carr produce haystacking waves when there is a swell. These waves can sometimes be surfed but those wishing to stay dry should give these reefs a wide berth.

Embleton and Newton Haven

After Castle Point is rounded a succession of attractive sandy beaches and sheltered bays make an excellent place for windsurfing, sailing and canoeing.

The first of these is Embleton Bay which is a good spot for surfing. This leads into Newton Haven. A sheltered natural harbour ringed by rocky islets and reefs that makes a good trip for novice sea canoeists.

There is good access and car parking at Low Newton by the Sea.

Beadnell

This small seaside town lies at the northern tip of a sheltered bay with a pleasant beach that is much used by windsurfers and canoeists.

There is good surfing especially with a south-westerly swell.

Parking is very restricted in the town itself. To gain access to the beach follow signs to the car park which lies 50 metres from the shoreline.

Seahouses & Bamburgh

Seahouses

In the summer months this pleasant seaside town becomes a mecca for tourists. Many of whom converge on the small harbour seeking boat trips to the Farnes.

The charm of this small town is somewhat tempered by the cheap commercialism that seems to spring up wherever tourists are to be found. Ice cream vendors and candyfloss stalls are cheek by jowl with the traditional industries of fishing and lobster potting.

Parking is very restricted in the town centre and harbour, so that its convenience for access is limited. Those who do launch from the harbour at high tide will find that there is little more than a muddy pool at low water. This often makes your last few yards the most perilous of your journey!

Bamburgh

Well known because of the famous Castle that overlooks the village.

Like Dunstanburgh it is built on a solid basalt outcrop forming part of the Great Whin Sill.

In the centre of the village lies the Lord Crewe Arms Hotel. Opposite this a small tarmac road 'The Wyndings' leads northwards along the shoreline to terminate at the golf course after about 2km.

'The Wyndings' offers good access for those journeying northwards to Holy Island or beyond.

Those passing this way should certainly visit the Castle who's furnishings and paintings seem to resemble more of a stately home than a fortification.

Originally a wooden fort was built in AD 547 by King Ida of Northumbria, but this was later destroyed by Viking raids.

Rebuilt by Henry I, it was much used during the Wars of the Roses.

Lord Crewe, Bishop of Durham bought it in 1704 and began restoring it.

This work was later completed by the Tyneside inventor, Lord Armstrong, who bought it at the turn of the century.

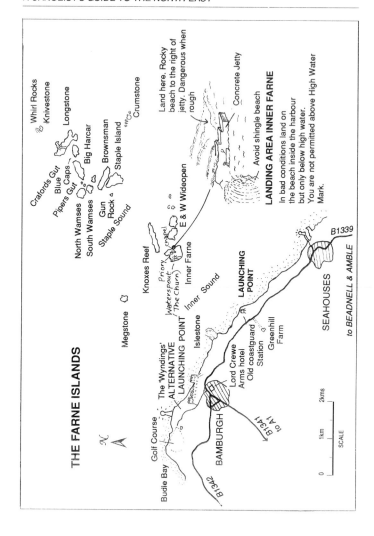

THE FARNE ISLANDS

Whirl Rocks
Knivestone
Longstone
Crafords Gut
Blue
Pipers Gut Caps
Big Harcar
North Wamses
Brownsman
South Wamses
Staple Island
Gun Rock
Crumstone
Staple Sound

Land here. Rocky beach to the right of jetty. Dangerous when rough

Concrete Jetty

Avoid shingle beach

LANDING AREA INNER FARNE

In bad conditions land on the beach inside the harbour but only below high water. You are not permitted above High Water Mark.

E & W Wideopen

Knoxes Reef

Megstone

Priory
Chapel
Waterspout
(The Churn)

Inner Farne

Inner Sound

Islestone

The 'Wyndings'
ALTERNATIVE
LAUNCHING POINT

Golf Course

Budle Bay

LAUNCHING POINT

LAUNCHING POINT

Lord Crewe Arms hotel
Old coastguard Station

Greenhill Farm

SEAHOUSES

B1339

to BEADNELL & AMBLE

BAMBURGH

B1342

B1341
to A1

SCALE

0   1km   2kms

The Farne Islands

Introduction

The Farnes must rate as one of Britains best sea canoeing areas. They consist of a group of 15-28 islands, depending on the state of the tide, lying off the north Northumberland Coast between 1.5 and 5.5 miles from the mainland. They are the eastern end of the Great Whin Sill and have a distinctive wedge shape appearance with the high cliffs at the south-west tapering off into the sea at the north-east side, the result of the last glaciation which deposited a layer of boulder clay capping the islands. The islands are the home of some 53,000 pairs of breeding birds of seventeen different species which nest on the islands from mid-April to the end of July. In addition a further 140-180 species of passage migrants are recorded annually, mainly during the spring and autumn, in total more than 250 species have been recorded.

In addition to the natural history interest, the islands have an early religious association with St. Cuthbert who lived as a hermit on Inner Farne from 676 to 684 and returned to die there on 20 March 687. It was while St. Cuthbert lived at the Farnes that an early form of bird protection started when he laid down the rules for the protection of the breeding birds and he blessed the eider ducks nesting in his rough cell causing this species to be known as St. Cuthbert's Duck or locally as Cuddy's Duck. There followed a period of monastic occupation when the islands were owned by the Dean and Chapter of Durham from 1255 and a small monastic house, usually a master and two associates, was maintained until the dissolution of the monasteries in 1536. The islands then passed into private ownership some of which exploited the wild-life but later when the Archdeacon Thorp came into possession of the Inner Group, he paid wardens to live there and protect the birds during the breeding season. The Farne Islands Association was then formed which continued this protection on the islands until in 1924 the islands came onto the market. Naturalists through the Natural History Society of Northumberland and Durham launched a public appeal which raised the money to buy both groups of islands and handed them over to the National Trust in 1925. They are now one of the most important nature reserves in Europe and a Government Sanctuary Order gives complete protection to the islands and their wild-life.

Great sea stacks, fast tidal streams and overfalls, together with the abundant wildlife, have attracted many a canoeist to the outlying islands over the years. Whether one is a beginner in the company of more experienced canoeists, or an advanced paddler, the Farnes area has everything to offer and, on return to the mainland, provides some of the best surfing beaches in Britain.

Launching

The most common launch site is that near the old coastguard station, on top of the sand dunes south of Bamburgh Castle and directly opposite Farne Island. Cars may be parked in the pull-in, just off the road leading to Greenhills and opposite the coastguard station. A short kayak-carry down the dunes leads to the magnificent sandy beach immediately south of Islestone, a rocky scar projecting seawards from the coast.

Alternatively launching may be found at Seahouses harbour, but parking is limited.

The "Wyndings", found by taking the golf club road from the centre of Bamburgh, provides another launch site. Parking on top of the dunes avoids congestion often caused by parking by the roadside. The "Wyndings" provides another excellent surf beach, similar to that found below the coastguard station.

Launching from either Seahouses or the "Wyndings" means a longer sea crossing to Farne Island, and careful tidal stream prediction is required to avoid a long, hard slog.

Tidal Streams

Streams may be strong in the sounds between the islands, producing overfalls and turbulence, especially with an opposing wind or swell. An examination of the tide tables will help one calculate the rate of flow, thus ensuring an easier crossing, or, for those with masochistic tendencies, providing great excitement!

Tidal streams run as follows:	
North westerly stream (ebbing) begins.	+06.00 HW Dover
	+01.30 HW Tyne
South easterly stream (flooding) begins.	HW Dover
	-04.30 HW Tyne

In Inner Sound the tidal streams may attain a rate of two knots at springs but, close to Farne Island, this speed may possibly double due to the shallowing bottom, and a tide race exists at both ends of the island.

Staple Sound has a tidal stream of four knots at springs, and produces overfalls at its southern end with a flooding tide meeting an opposing wind or swell. Around Gun Rock and close to Staple Island is a tidal race which can produce large standing waves and very turbulent water.

Piper's Gut, a narrow passage between North Wamses and Big Harcar, together with Crawford's Gut, a narrow passage between the Blue Caps and Longstone, both produce conditions not unlike a fast-flowing river when the tide is running strongly. Both above areas provide excellent amusement for the experienced paddler.

Knivestone and Whirl Rocks, which form the most seaward extremities of the Farne Islands, produce the fastest tidal streams, with spring rates in excess of 4 - 5 knots. Here, the uneven sea bed in conjunction with rapid tides produce great overfalls and very turbulent water. Huge standing waves and small whirlpools make this a canoeing area designed solely for the insane!

Visiting the Farne Island

Longstone Main Rock is open each day throughout the season at present, although circumstances may alter this arrangement at any time. There is no entrance fees to pay at this island at present. The Lighthouse and its jetties are the property of Trinity House and permission to visit must be obtained from them.

Inner Farne and Staple Island are open to visitors from 1st April (or Easter if earlier) until 30th September each year during opening hours which vary, according to the breeding season for the birds, as follows:-

Up to 15th May, after 15th July to 30th September, Staple and Inner Farne are open from 10:00hrs to 18:00hrs daily.

From 15th May to 15th July (both dates inclusive), Staple Islands is open from 10:30hrs to 13:30hrs daily and Inner Farne is open from 13:30hrs to 17:00hrs daily. Should the weather conditions be such that any disturbance would affect the success of the breeding birds, such as driving rain and cold wind, then the islands will be closed without notice during this period.

National Trust members gain free admission but non-members have to pay the current entrance fee to land. (About £2.00)

Whilst canoeists are welcome they must land when the islands are open to the public and at the correct place.

Most paddlers will wish to visit Inner Farne which has a visitor centre incorporating a good photographic display of the common species to be found there.

The landing area which has to be shared with commercial boats lies on the North easterly side of the Island.

Land on the flat rocks just to the *right* of the concrete jetty, **not** the tempting beach on the left. (Except in very rough weather.)

Parties of canoeists planning on visiting the islands could notify the Warden/Naturalist at 8 St. Aidans, Seahouses, Northumberland. NE68 7SR, of their intended visit and which island(s) they intended visiting so the wardens on the islands are prepared for them arriving to help them land their craft safely.

Navigation

Farne Island lies one and a half miles from the coast, with Staple Island a further one and a half miles to seaward; Longstone lies five miles from the coast. A full circumnavigation of all of the outlying islands, including Megstone and Crumstone, may exceed eighteen miles, depending on the route taken.

Navigation around the Farnes is fairly easy, even across the rapid tidal streams, providing one has a basic knowledge of transits and compass work. On ones return journey, the backdrop of the Cheviots and the radio mast near Chillingham provide excellent transit points, with the coastguard station and sand dunes in the foreground.

Weather

Weather conditions can change extremely rapidly off the N.E. coast. An accurate local forecast is essential before undertaking an offshore trip of this type.

Sources for local weather information:

Tyne Tees Coastguard...	091 257 2691
Newcastle Weather Centre.................................	091 232 6453
Marine Call (recorded message only).............	0898 500 453

The coastguard may be contacted on VHF marine radio, Channel 16. Please remember to use correct radio procedure.

The Inner Islands

Inner Farne is the largest of the islands and the nearest to the mainland. Here kittiwakes, shags, guillemots, razorbills and fulmers can be seen nestling on the cliffs during the breeding season (May to end of July) and the large grass meadows hold numerous nesting puffins, arctic and common terns and eiders with a few oystercatchers and ringed plover. There is a nature trail to follow and leaflets are available on the island from the information centre. St. Cuthbert's Chapel is open to the public but Prior Castell's tower is the base for the National Trust Wardens and is not open. This tower was used as the first warning beacon, lit on the roof on stormy nights, but was replaced by beacon towers at Staple island and later Brownsman island. The present day Inner Farne Lighthouse was built in 1809 and made automatic in 1908. At the North-western tip of the island a blind narrow gully forms an impressive fifty foot water spout known as the 'churn' whenever there is a north easterly swell. (See colour photo)

When visiting Inner Farne during the nesting season (May) it is advisable to wear some form of head covering to protect oneself from the terns swooping down defending their territory.

Knoxes Reef is mainly used as a high tide roosting site, although fulmars, eiders and waders do nest there. Large numbers of waders and ducks are also found here during the migration periods in spring and autumn. West and East Wideopen hold good colonies of puffins as well as the usual cliff nesting species. Cormorants have colonised the East Wideopens recently. Big and Little Scarcar are always a good place to see resting immature shags, pale brown plumage instead of the green/black of the adults, preeening and drying their feathers and sometimes grey seals haul-out here.

Megstone, a rocky island lying to the north of the inner group, still supports quite a number of breeding shags, guillemots and some years, cormorants. A few seals breed here in November and often haul-out there at low water. The island is bisected by a narrow gully which can be paddled through at high water.

The outer Islands

Staple Island is an ornithologists' and photographers paradise where the cliff nesting species can provide close-up views of shags, kittiwakes, guillemots, razorbills, fulmars and over 5,000 pairs of puffins burrow their nesting holes into the soil cap. The old beacon tower was partially destroyed by a storm in 1783, the same storm that also broke off one of the Pinnacles leaving three remaining stacks just off the island and are the home of at least 1,000 pairs of nesting guillemots. A nature trail is provided and leaflets can be obtained when landing.

Longstone is always worth circumnavigating as most of the islands seals are to be found concentrated along the north-eastern shoreline.

Conclusion

The Farne Islands provide exciting canoeing, together with spectacular scenery and a chance to see many species of wildlife in their natural surroundings: killer whales and basking sharks have been sighted annually.

The Farnes have something to offer every canoeist, provided that the conditions are right. Night trips around the islands provide an interesting variation with phosphorescence, eerie silhouettes and the wailing of seals on distant islands.

Canoeists will often find themselves paddling amongst herds of seals and rafts of puffins. You can be dive-bombed by overfed guillemots and shags, as they attempt to attain stable flight after launching themselves from their rocky perches. Screaming gulls and perhaps even the occasional dolphin all go to make paddling to the Farnes an unforgettable experience.

Natural history of the Farne Islands
Birds

Eiders are present throughout the year and in the spring the drakes are resplendent in their black and white plumage while the ducks are a dull mottled brown, well camouflaged to do all the incubating of the eggs. Records of this species go back to the 7th century when St. Cuthbert laid down the rules for the safety of the nestling ducks. Both sexes come ashore in early May and

Eider duck on nest, Inner Farne. Photo: Peter Hawkey

the duck makes a scrape in the vegetation which she lines with down plucked from her breast to hold the five or six eggs which are incubated for 26-28 days. Ducks sit so tightly that visitors can pass within a short distance of them. After the ducklings are hatched they are taken down onto the sea and across to the mainland coast to find a good food supply on the shore. Some years over 1,500 ducks breed on the islands.

Mallard and Shelduck breed occasionally but are rarely seen until they are found escorting their ducklings onto the sea.

Four species of terns breed on the islands. Often called sea-swallows because of their swooping flight and long tail streamers, these birds migrate each year between the southern and northern hemispheres, fortunately breeding in ours. The Sandwich terns (4,000 pairs) arrive first, about the beginning of April and are followed by the Arctic (3,500 pairs), Common (500 pairs) and lastly the rarer Roseate (21 pairs). The species can be identified by the various coloured bills and legs. One can be identified by the various coloured bills and legs. One arctic tern was recovered in Melbourne, Australia having travelled 17,509kms and another arctic tern was found breeding at Inner Farne 27 years after it was ringed as a nestling there. Other tern species occur from time to time but the most exciting was the Aleutian tern which appeared at Inner Farne on 28th May 1979, the first ever European sighting of this North Pacific species.

Guillemots (14,000 pairs) and Puffins (25,000 pairs) are much the most

Puffins on Staple Island. Photo: Peter Hawkey

numerous species. Guillemots, with their chocolate brown upper-parts and white breasts, crowd closely together on the cliff ledges and stacks, laying their single egg onto the bare rock, incubating it by holding it on the top of their feet and sitting on it. The eggs are pear shaped, so if knocked it will simply roll in a circle rather than roll off the ledge. Puffins, easily distinguished by their colourful triangular bill, also lay a single egg but they dig out a burrow into the soil-cap where they sit on their eggs and rear their young. The young never come out of the burrows until they are full grown and deserted by their parents, then they leave the islands at night to find the safety of the sea to avoid predatory gulls. Both species can live to at least 25 years old.

Razorbills are less numerous, about 70-80 pairs breeding but not as a colony, using individual nesting sites. Their plumage is black upper-parts and white breast and they have a sturdier bill than the Guillemot which carries a conspicuous white line.

Wading birds breeding include the oystercatcher (30 pairs), with its striking pied plumage and long orange bill which it uses to attack and remove limpets from the rocks for food and the ringed plover (28 pairs), a quiet inconspicuous bird rearing two broods each year.

Kittiwakes (6,000 pairs), breed on most cliff faces, their constant call of its own name identifies them at once. Their cup shaped nests are cemented onto any small cliff projection and their young birds never seem to fall out. The adult birds are easily picked out with their grey upper-parts white head and

Above: Cormorant
Right: Shag
Photos: Peter Hawkey

underparts, yellow bill and black legs. Young birds usually have a black ring around their necks and black wing bars. Outside the breeding season this species does disperse over the seas and Farne ringed birds have been recovered from America in the west and Germany in the east.

Herring gulls and Lesser Black-backed gulls (c1,000 pairs) breed each year and are the predators on the islands taking the unattended eggs and young of any other species. A few Black-headed gulls (c200 pairs), breed among the terns.

Cormorants (300 pairs), are very shy birds and nest close together in a colony for protection. If they were disturbed from their eggs they would be very slow to return thus losing their eggs to gulls and for this reason we never disturb them during the breeding season. Their brown-black plumage, large size and, during the spring, their white thigh plumes make them easy to identify. They feed their young on partially digested regurgitated fish which makes their colony site a rather smelly place. Some years they all breed at one site but in the last decade they have split into three colonies on separate islands.

Shags (1,500 pairs), have a bottle-green-black plumage and during the spring a lovely erect crest on their heads. They are very aggressive so are able to fight off most predators and defend their nest sites on the broader cliff ledges. Like the cormorants they lay small eggs which are quickly hatched out
230

Inner Farne South Cliffs and Stack. Photo: Peter Hawkey

but the young stay in the nest and are tended by their parents for a much longer period than most species.

Fulmars (300 pairs) first nested on the islands in 1935. Each female bird only lays one egg and if predated it will not re-lay. Fortunately they are long lived birds, the oldest known over 40 years old, so there is no threat to this species and the population continues to expand slowly each year. Fulmars do look like gulls but its flight, rather stiff wing beats and a series of long glides interspersed with a few wing beats, and its tubes on the top of its bill help to distinguish it.

Land birds are also recorded on migration, mainly in the spring and autumn. Between 140 and 180 other species are recorded each year and details are given in a yearly report. An occasional blackbird, pied wagtail and starling breed on the islands usually among the buildings or walls.

Brownsman Island is the home of terns, eiders, guillemots, kittiwakes, fulmars, puffins, ringed plover and oystercatchers and the peaty soil-cap is honeycombed with puffing burrows. The beacon tower was built just after the Staple Island beacon was destroyed and in 1810 a paraffin oil burning lighthouse was erected only to be pulled down in 1826, leaving only the cottage, when the Longstone Lighthouse was built. Grace Darling and her father lived in this cottage which is still used today as a base for the wardens looking after the outer island group.

North and South Wamses can be a popular place for grey seals hauling out to rest. The main colony of birds breeding on the North Wamses are cormorants, with guillemots and gulls intermixed among them and shags have colonised the south cliffs of South Wamses in recent years. During the late autumn and early winter these islands are two of the main breeding sites of the grey seals.

Big Harcar is the island where the S.S. Forfarshire was swept ashore during a northerly gale on 7 September 1838 and Grace Darling and her father rescued fifteen survivors, rowing from the Longstone Lighthouse alongside the Blue Caps and Little Harcar at low water to gain as much shelter as possible from the northerly storm. This island has little or no vegetation or soil-cap left yet still supports colonies of gulls, kittiwakes, eider, shags and a few puffins.

Longstone End is the favourite hauling out site of the Grey Seal, more at low water than at other times, many of them playing around in the water between here and Longstone Main Rock. This island also supports small numbers of breeding eiders and puffins and a good place to see wading birds such as turnstone, oystercatcher, redshank and in the autumn and winter months, purple sandpipers.

Longstone Lighthouse is owned by Trinity House but the Longstone Main Rock is open to the public. The adjacent Northern Hares is another grey seal haul-out and winter breeding site as well as being the home to a small number of nesting oystercatchers, ringed plover and a few eider ducks.

Grey Seal, yearling. Photo: Peter Hawkey

Crumstone and Knivestone are storm-washed rocky islands with no breeding birds but again often used by large numbers of seals hauling out when the sea conditions permit. Knivestone is tidal and is the most outer island of the Farnes.

The vegetation growing on the islands peaty soil-caps consists mainly of sea-campion, scurvy grass, silverweed, hemlock, bugloss, ragwort, dock, nettle, various grasses including fescue, Yorkshire fog and common salt-marsh grass. In all some 125 species of plants have been recorded but there is one interesting alien plant, Amsinckia lycopsoides, a species of borage which is a native of Lower California, U.S.A. This plant probably came to the island with imported grain used as chicken feed while the lighthouse keepers were resident at Inner Farne during the early 1900s.

Grey Seals are large animals and the bull seals may measure up to three metres in length and weigh up to 294kgm. They can be seen around the islands throughout the year as many of them haul out onto the rocks where they lie huddled together yawning or scratching. It is only during the breeding season that they spend any lengthy periods ashore. Births start in late October, peak by mid-November and tail off by early December. Each breeding cow produces a single pup which weighs about 13.6kg at birth. The seals' milk is extremely rich, it contains more than 50% fat, so that a well fed pup will put on about 1.64kg per day. After weaning at about 18 days old, when the cow deserts the pup, it should weigh between 36-41kg if it is to survive.

233

Pups are born with a white coat which they moult and obtain their adult grey coat before leaving the islands to fend for themselves. Cows start to breed at 4-5 years old and can live until over 40 years old whereas the bull will not become sexually mature until it is 7-8 years old and will not breed in the colony until it is 12-15 years old when it reaches its peak in strength to gain a breeding territory. Bulls have a much shorter life span reaching only 30 years. Records of grey seals at the Farnes go back for 800 years and the colony is part of the North Sea Colony which also breeds at the Isle of May in Scotland.

The recent outbreak of morbillivirus, closely related to canine distemper, has affected the colony slightly in 1988 when about 21 yearling animals were found dead and about 10% of the expected total of breeding cows did not breed. However this is better result than that of the Common Seals where it is estimated that up to 60% of the population has perished from this disease. This disease will probably occur again until the species build up a natural resistance to the virus.

Common seals are rarely seen around the islands, only occasionally at the Inner group. Porpoises are seen regularly passing through the Inner Sound and the occasional dolphin species is recorded. Killer whales pass through the islands about once a year, usually in July, but they rarely attack the seals.

Holy Island

Lying just to the north of Bamburgh, this small island off the Northumbertland coast can be reached by a small causeway which becomes covered in high water.

The island is usually cut off for about half of each tide, so scrutinise your time tables carefully.

Each year someone gets it wrong and is forced to abandon their vehicle on the causeway, then helplessly watch their beloved car being given the ultimate in car washes as it is gradually submerged, and if it is a powerful Spring tide, to be finally swept off the causeway!

The island is well known for its monastery which was established here in 635 AD by St. Aidan. He was created Bishop of Lindisfarne by Oswald, King of Northumbria.

Soon afterwards St. Cuthbert, a shepherd from the Scottish borders saw a vision of St. Aidan. As a result he came to Holy Island in 664. He was to spend most of his life on the island and at the retreat on Inner Farne.

The Danes, in there usual vandalistic traditions, destroyed much of the original Priory in 875 AD.

The monastery was refounded in the 11th Century, before being destroyed again by King Henry VIII, with the dissolution of the Monasteries.

Some of the quarry stone from the Monastery was used to build the castle,

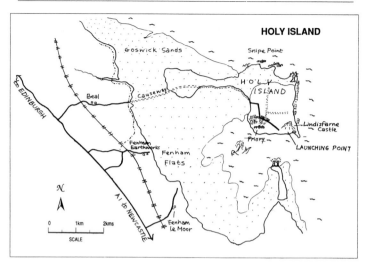

which was established in 1539, primarily to protect the harbour.

Like all the other castles in the area, it is built on basalt from the whin sill outcrop.

The castle was restored by Sir Edward Lutyens earlier this century and is one of Northumbria's smaller but more residential castles. It is now open to the public, and is run by the National Trust.

The island has a small population of about 170, which is mainly dependent on tourism and fishing for its livelihood. Much of the island forms part of a nature reserve, including the intertidal area stretching down to Budle Bay. Public access is allowed only on rights of way.

Sea Trips

The island can be circumnavigated, but the extensive mud flats and salt marshes either side of the causeway, drain remarkably quickly, so that a Spring tide and accurate tidal prediction is necessary to avoid becoming stranded on the flats.

An easier trip for the sea canoeist is to set off from the south eastern tip of the island, rounding Castle Point, to explore the rocky north-eastern shore as far as Snipe Point.

Launching

Turn left in the centre of the village following signs to the Castle.

Put in close to the Lime Kilns which lie just to the east of the Castle.

Tidal Streams

As previously mentioned, these run strongly into and out of Holy Island Harbour.

Time from High Water		
	+ 0510 Tyne	W - going begins
	(-0245 Dover)	
	-0045 Tyne	
	+(0345 Dover)	E - going begins

Berwick to St. Abbs

Berwick

This border town lies at the top of Northumberland at the mouth of the river Tweed. The town was very much in the front line of the conflict between the Scots and English as is testified by the heavily fortified town walls and the fact that it changed hands some 14 times before the English finally wrenched it from the Scots in 1482, by the Earl of Northumberland with a modest army of 22,000 men!

Geographically it should really be in Scotland as most of the Scottish border lies to the south of the Tweed, but at Berwick the border arcs across the river, running a few miles to the north of the town.

Three impressive bridges span the Tweed. The old medieval bridge, with its fifteen arches, was constructed in 1634 and took over 20 years to build!

The splendid railway viaduct, built in 1847 at a cost of £207,000 was designed by Robert Stephenson.

Berwick is now a thriving county town, deriving much of its livelihood from tourism and fishing, mainly in the form of salmon netting.

Launching Points

As the streets are narrow, and often congested during the summer months, the city centre is best avoided.

Good parking and access is found along the southern shore of Tweedmouth, close to the Lifeboat Station, where there is a car park. OS Ref 005551.

Just around Sandstell Point, Spittal beach also offers good access, although parking space along the seafront is limited.

Tidal Streams

Time from H.W. 1½ miles E of breakwater		Notes
	− 0335 Leith + 0010 Dover	S.E going stream begins. Spring rate ¾ knot.
	+ 0235 Leith − 0010 Dover	N.W. going stream begins Spring rate 1 knot.
In the river	+ 0515 Tyne − 0240 Dover	In going stream begins Spring rate fairly strong.
	− 0100 Tyne + 0330 Dover	Out going stream begins Spring rate fairly strong.

Sea Trips Berwick Caves

The usual trip is from Berwick to Burnmouth or Eyemouth (or the reverse direction, depending on the prevailing winds and tides).

The latter is a much better egress point, as the rugged coastline between Burnmouth and Eyemouth, with its seastacks and rocky islets, makes a good contrast with the sheet, red, sandstone cliffs that lie between Berwick and Burnmouth. In addition, the over enthusiastic harbour master at Burnmouth charges canoeists a small fee if launching between the harbour walls. Penniless canoeists are, therefore, advised to launch just beyond the harbour jetty.

After setting out from Berwick harbour, once the northern jetty is rounded, the sandstone cliffs begin to appear. Like a block of red cheddar that has suffered at the hands of some hungry church mouse, each is nibbled away at the base to form a series of dark, foreboding caves, that simply beg exploration. Once the home of desperate smugglers and their contraband. Now you are unlikely to find anything more threatening than an out of breath seal.

Essential equipment for the trip includes some crusty bread to feed the extraordinary number of sea going swans that lie across the Tweed estuary and a waterproof cavers torch to provide illumination in the caves.

The trip is best undertaken two hours either side of the tide so that most of the cave entrances become navigable, but the sea needs to be calm. The high cliffs provide shelter from the wind so that this trip is feasible even when powerful westerly winds blow. This trip includes the famous Needles Eye, a sea stack lying just offshore a few miles up the coast. (see colour photo opposite p161)

A little further northwards Marshall Meadows Bay is easily recognised,

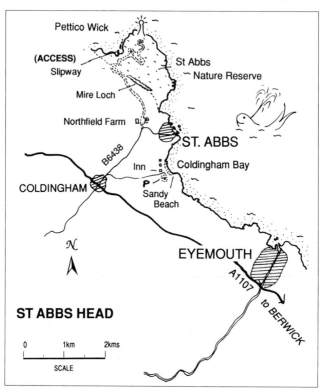

having several caves visible halfway up the cliffs. These were once famous smugglers haunts, although the row of caravans sprinkled around the cliff top rather detract from the romantic associations inspired by their former use.

Burnmouth

A small fishing village and harbour.

From here the red sandstone cliffs are replaced by volcanic rocks and larva flows which spill out into the sea.

Eyemouth

This small seaside town and harbour at the mouth of the Eye Water, makes a good place to finish. There is ample car parking around the harbour and a tourist information centre.

Exploring St Abbs

Eyemouth is also a good starting or finishing point for trips around St. Abbs.

Coldingham Bay

A small, sandy beach for those wishing for a shorter trip around St. Abbs.

It lies about four kilometres up the coast from Eyemouth.

The beach is found by taking the St. Abbs road out of Coldingham (B6438) and turning right just as you leave the village where the road takes a sharp left hand bend.

There is good car parking and a small, but very hospitable Hotel which overlooks the beach.

St. Abbs Head

Here a mass of volcanic rocks juts out into the sea with massive cliffs soaring skywards for several hundred feet. Each is deeply fissured and folded, with every nook and cranny peppered with nesting sea birds. Everywhere the dark igneous rocks are mottled with a pungent whitewash of bird droppings.

Far below huge sea stacks and rocky islets lie along the serrated coastline around which the sea sucks and surges, creating powerful eddies and currents on which the more adventurous canoeist can play. Narrow channels and dark foreboding caverns all invite exploration.

Whatever you interests and levels of skill, this spectacular stretch of coastline has something to offer every canoeist.

At the tip of the headland lies the famous lighthouse, its friendly beam warning ships of the treacherous rocks below.

Just beneath the lighthouse, perched on the rocks like a giant tuba is the now redundant foghorn. No longer needed because of the improved navigational aids used by shipping. The row of cast iron cylinders behind the lighthouse once held compressed air to provide puff for the foghorn.

The rest of the headland and surrounding waters are now a Nature Reserve run by the National Trust.

The clear water and rich marine life make it a popular venue for divers who come here from all over the country.

Distress and Rescue

Coastal rescue equipment is maintained at St. Abbs Head, but no watch is kept.

Nearest Coastguard. Tel. Eyemouth 50348.

(In Emergency dial 999 and ask for Coastguard)

Tidal Streams

The ESE going stream begins	-0345 Leith. H.W. Dover.
WNW going stream begins	+ 0240 Leith - 0600 Dover.

Streams run strongly around St. Abbs Head.

Launching Points

Probably the best access point is from Pettico Wick Bay on the West side of St. Abbs Head. Take the B6438 out of Coldingham, turning left just before St. Abbs is reached, following signs to St. Abbs Nature Reserve. This road takes you through Northfield Farm. After about two kilometres the road dips slightly with Mire Loch on your right, and Pettico Wick Bay just out of sight on your left. Here there is a small car park (for divers only) before the road climbs up to the Lighthouse over the brow of the hill. A convenient slipway and shingle beach provide easy access. (OS Ref 908691)

Most paddlers will wish to egress at either St. Abbs harbour, or Eyemouth if a longer paddle is required.

Coldingham Bay is another alternative. It has a pleasant, sheltered, sandy beach and sports a small Hotel within easy reach of the shoreline.

The coastline is also of interest further northwards towards Dunbar and some may wish to make an extended trip around St. Abbs to Cockburnspath some 15km further up the coast. This trip incorporates the remains of Fast Castle at Telegraph Hill, where legend has it that concealed in a local cave there lies a fortune in gold collected in the 16th century in a vain attempt to free Mary Queen of Scots. There are many caves and sheltered coves in this area, which make excellent bivouac sites and this trip lends itself to a two day excursion.

COASTLINE FROM THE TYNE TO FLAMBOROUGH HEAD

South Shields to Roker

South Shields provides varied canoeing, having a large harbour and several excellent beaches.

Trips up river can provide great interest amongst the vast Tyne dockland area which services a wide range of vessels from small sea-going cobbles to large oil rig structures with their giant podia supporting a huge thorax of curious steel pipes and cylinders like some alien arthropod from a far off galaxy.

Whilst admiring the latest state of the art marine technology, caution should be observed when paddling in a busy port like the Tyne, with its fast tidal streams and manoeuvring vessels. Also, be careful that a larger than average wave or wash does not entangle you with the moorings of stationary vessels.

Launching for trips within the harbour or up river is best from the small beach next to South Shields Yacht Club and the 'Groyne' pier, which has good parking. An alternative is from the foreshore beach within the main piers/harbour area, again with a large car park.

Good surfing, and access for sea trips to the south can be found at the large beach south of the Southern pier. Parking can be found on the foreshore next to 'Gypsy Green Stadium.' This beach offers excellent surf when conditions permit, and is the home of both South Tyneside Canoe Club and the Board Surfing Club. Lifeguards operate on this beach during the summer months.

Coastal trips to the south offer excellent canoeing. Rock dodging amongst the various reefs, gullies and small sea caves that exist provides good sport, especially with a slight swell! The most popular trip is to Marsden Rock, lying 1½ miles to the South. This is a huge sea stack with a natural arch cut through it. The sea stack and surrounding cliffs are home to a wide variety of sea birds that nest on the tiny ledges of the cliff face.

At the base of the cliffs lies the 'Marsden Grotto' a rather uninspiring pub. A lift and steep staircase connect the cliff tops to the beach.

The rocky shoreline continues past Souter Point and Whitburn lighthouse, where it slowly tapers down to low rocky outcrops 1½ - 2 miles further south. The way ahead is usually blocked by the military police when the Firing range is in use. (Red flags are flown and M.P.'s patrol the boundaries.)

The tides along the coast from the River Tyne to the River Wear are very weak, but caution should always be taken when entering or leaving either harbour, as tidal flow, in or out, will produce turbulence and an increase in water speed at the pier entrances.

South from the firing range to the Wear entrance the coast is very low lying, with only the reef at Whitburn, South Bents, projecting southwards, providing a little shelter for a number of small boats owned by locals and fishermen.

Seaburn beach provides some good surf when conditions are right, with a good point break off the south of South Bents reef.

An unusual night paddle from the beach at Roker (between the Piers) to Whitburn, is very worthwhile if done between September - November when the Sunderland illuminations are on. Spectacular lazer shows can be seen from a unique angle (when projected seawards towards you) and the paddle along the full length of the illuminations to Whitburn is very enjoyable.

Sunderland to Ryhope

Local canoe clubs and outdoor centres use Roker as an ideal training area for beginners, as the area within the harbour piers usually affords shelter. (Except in a strong North Easterly.)

Paddling up the River Wear into the Dockland area provides some interest, but caution must be taken with the fairly busy river traffic.

The coast from Sunderland to Seaham provides some interesting sea conditions with a little swell as the bottom is very uneven.

The beaches are often less than inviting due to the coal waste from the local collieries that has been dumped into the sea over many years.

The beaches at Ryhope and north of Seaham harbour provide small reefs and rocky outcrops which allow for some good sport, rock dodging when a little swell permits.

The coastline from Sunderland to Seaham for the most part has a backdrop of heavy industry. From the docklands South of the river mouth to Hendon, large factories and warehouses back onto the beaches, often with large concrete coastal reinforcements along the shoreline.

Further south from Ryhope to Seaham the view from the sea is one of coastal collieries which have discharged and dumped vast quantities of waste into the sea over many years. This practice has sadly destroyed what was once an attractive coastline. Rocky outcrops rising from the beaches and deep ravines or dunes that cut into the grassy banks and low lying cliffs behind provide scenery for the passing sea canoeist.

Canoeing any part of the coast from Sunderland to Hartlepool is quite safe, as long as conditions permit. However, this section like that of the entire North East coast offers limited shelter from heavy seas from any easterly direction, but especially North Easterlies.

Tidal streams up and down this section are fairly weak and should not cause problems.

Seaham Harbour to Middleton

Canoeing this section is very similar to the previous Sunderland to Ryhope stretch, with more coastal collieries and beaches covered in coal waste.

At Blackhall rocks the coastline has rocky outcrops similar to those found at Ryhope.

Further south at Crimdon the coast is much cleaner. Here rocky outcrops give way to large stretches of sand, with high dunes backing onto the beach.

Launching can be best made at Seaham, north of the harbour, and at Crimdon Dene immediately south of the caravan site.

South of Crimdon a paddle seaward is required to avoid the 'pier like' framework supporting Steetby Magnesites water intake pipe, and from here it is advisable to stay seaward of the scars surrounding Hartlepool Headland until the Heugh breakwater can be rounded, as any swell produces rough water and breaking waves over the very uneven bottom. Once the 'Heugh' has been rounded at Middleton, a safe landing is usually available on the beach just within the breakwater. From here an exit can be made with ample car parking on the promenade.

Hartlepool and Tees Bay

The canoeing around Hartlepool/Teeside can be varied allowing dockland paddling, estuary work, coastal paddling, or sea trips around the various large vessels lying at anchor in the bay.

Tidal streams in this area will be found strongest around Hartlepoool Headland, and the Heugh breakwater as well as the entrance of the River Tees between the Piers of the North and South Gare. Otherwise the tidal streams are fairly weak, apart from the obvious tidal flow in and out of the estuary. The River Tees is tidal almost as far as Yarm, which allows for some long estuary paddling through parkland as well as very heavily industrialised areas. If paddling the estuary, ensure you catch the right tide to assist you. There is good access at South Gare by the coastguard station along with ample space for car parking and a pleasant sandy beach.

Rough water will be experienced, with anything more than a slight swell, over Longscar (a reef which is actually a petrified forest) and lies south of the Heugh breakwater and seaward to the North of Seaton Carew. Foul ground off the North Gare also produces breaking waves when a swell exists.

Caution should be taken when paddling in any dockland area, particularly within shipping lanes and near any moving vessel.

Launch sites within Teesbay are limited, with only Hartlepool and Seaton

Carew providing easy access with parking facilities. Access to the river for estuary paddling with parking facilities is best found at Stockton near Church Road, where a launching slip can be found, or further up river at Preston Park or Yarm. Other access points can be found but have limited parking.

Seal Sands, once a large, water filled area within the North and South Gare Breakwaters has been extensively reclaimed and is now the site of large petrochemical works and other industries. However, some water-filled areas still remain for the exploring canoeist. Seals that once inhabited the area in great numbers, (hence the name) sadly left as industry took over and pollution rose. However, odd ones have been sighted in recent years, which hopefully is a good sign.

ℛedcar, Saltburn and Whitby

The coastal resort of Redcar forms the southern edge of Teesbay and provides easy access for the sea canoeist. A sandy beach to the Northern end of town provides surf when a swell exists from the North, although this is usually messy and not too well formed.

Salt Scar, a huge reef, extends seaward of Redcar for a distance of one mile. This reef and surrounding rocks produce large, breaking waves when any sea or swell exists and should be avoided in such conditions.

Launch sites at Redcar with good parking are numerous in calm conditions when it is possible to pick a safe route through Salt Scar and the surrounding reefs.

Canoeing South from Redcar provides sandy beaches backed by dunes and clay banks past Marske and then on to Saltburn, with its pier. Beware of fishermen casting their lines.

The surf around Marske seems to be messy and not well formed mostly, unless conditions are exceptional. Saltburn provides the best surf in this area, with its North facing beach which tends to 'hook up' most swells from the North to East. The surf usually works best just south of the pier, where the beach tends to be more regular. Watch the surf for a while to find the best sections before paddling out, or seek local advice. A surfboard and ski hire operates from the car park, next to the pier during the summer months.

Saltburn

Towards the east end of Saltburn beach the sand turns to rock and the huge Hunt Cliff, dark red in colour and nearly perpendicular, towers over the sea.

The coastline along this section provides almost continuous cliffs from Saltburn (Hunt Cliff) to Sandsend Ness. Canoeing below these spectacular cliffs is excellent, with views of many different species of sea birds amongst their rocky perches. The shape of the cliffs themselves with heights of over 600 feet is truly breathtaking.

Tidal streams around 'Hunt Cliff' and the various headlands to the south can be fairly strong at 'springs' and they run as follows:-

NW	going stream begins	-02.30	TYNE (+2.00 DOVER)
SE	going stream begins	+03.45	TYNE (-4.10 DOVER)

Caution must be observed when contemplating a trip along this area of coastline, as safe landing points are few and far between, and most can become inaccessible in heavy seas.

Rocky outcrops and scars below the cliffs provide excellent canoeing, and when conditions permit it is possible to land on the huge rock ledges and explore below the cliffs. Many fossils can be found in the rocks and it is still possible to see the remains of old mine workings in the cliffs.

Skinningrove

A small bay approximately 1½ miles from Saltburn. Car parking in and around the fishing village is possible, but parking near the fishermens huts on the east side reduces the carry to and from the water.

This section provides good canoeing below high cliffs, among rocky outcrops, with interesting sea conditions produced by the uneven bottom.

Immediately you leave the bay at Skinningrove huge cliffs dominate the coastline with their ruggedness. As each headland is rounded, another comes into view, with its reef and breaking water produced by it pointing seaward like some huge, silver finger saying beware.

Travelling South past Boulby where the cliff attains heights of over 600 feet, and rises just beyond to 700 feet, the reefs below push further into the sea until Staithes is reached. The small harbour provides a good access/egress point.

If approached from along the coastline in rough weather the rocky reef's either side of the harbour entrance will sometimes be seen to produce an impenetrable barrier of continuous surf either side of the harbour entrance. However don't despair for closer inspection from a little further out to sea will reveal the whereabouts of the calmer deep water channel where refuge can be sought.

Continuing South from Staithes the picture is similar to that just covered, although the cliffs are not as high. In half a mile the headland of Old Nab is reached with its reef reducing slightly any waves that break over the headland. Further South tucked in behind another headland, the old harbour of Port Mulgrave lies with its breakwaters showing signs of the incredible power of the North Sea. This old harbour brings to mind all sorts of sea fairing tales, with its remote setting within this rugged coastline of Alum Shale cliffs.

Runswick village lies approximately 1½ miles S.E. of Old Nab and is set to the western end of Runswick Bay, a large bay with reefs guarding both sides. Good access by road is available, but beware, as the village and car

The rising contours of Boulby Cliffs

park lie at the bottom of a very steep hill. (Make sure your brakes are O.K.!) The village has a Life Boat station and Yacht Club. Surfing is possible within Runswick Bay, but is not for the faint-hearted, as the break is over rocky slabs with the occasional large boulder, and usually works when the break at other local surf beaches is too big or 'blown out.'

Kettle Ness forms the Eastern extremity of Runswick Bay, with its reef extending around the point and continuing South for some distance. In calm conditions, when it is possible to land, this area has many fossils within the rocks. Cliffs fronted by reefs continue from Kettle Ness for two miles to Sandsend Ness. South of this point lies Sandsend Village with a large car park for easy access. From Sandsend to Whitby a two mile stretch of sand exists, with good access from the road which runs parallel for one mile. Good surf exists when conditions permit, providing entertainment for beginners and experienced canoeists alike.

Whitby

The town of Whitby and its harbour provides the canoeist with some interesting scenery, with its fish quays and quaint buildings. Further up the river Esk lies the Marina with Sailing vessels of all shapes and sizes. Whitby is a town which is steeped in history of the sea and its connections, with the intrepid explorer Captain Cook. The town also has an ancient Abbey, which stands high on the east side of the river overlooking the town. The tidal streams are strong across the harbour entrance.

Saltwick Nab to Scalby Ness

Canoeing to the South of Whitby provides paddlers with impressive coastal views of the Abbey, standing well above the town and high sea cliffs around Saltwick Nab. These are fronted by large, flat rocks, which become exposed at low water. The flat slabs often have deep gullies which produce interesting sea conditions in a slight swell, making coastal trips more enjoyable especially at high water.

Caution must be exercised when canoeing along this section of coastline, as there are few exit points if sea conditions change whilst at sea. This should be born in mind when planning trips if there is a chance of Easterlies or bad sea conditions.

The cliffs from Saltwick Nab south to Robin Hood's Bay, gradually reduce in size, yet still provide a home for the hundreds of sea birds which bombard the passing canoeist. (In areas like this, with high cliffs and an abundance of bird life, a wide brimmed hat is strongly recommended.)

Robin Hood's Bay, five miles south of Whitby entrance, is a place of great interest, with its large bay which at low tide is ribbed with lines of rocky outcrops resembling the ribs of some enormous whale or prehistoric animal. Access to the bay is via a very steep hill with its quaint fishing village, which is steeped in history and well worth a visit. Approximately one mile further south access is possible at Boggle Hole, although this involves a reasonable walk carrying the canoes down the lane past the Y.M.C.A. before gaining access to the small beach.

Canoeing south from Boggle Hole for the remainder of Robin Hood's Bay, the coast is fringed with scars for a further 1¼ miles to the rocky outcrop of South Cheek. The coastline from South Cheek to Scarborough (approximately nine miles further) takes on a greener look, with high cliffs giving way to steeply wooded areas and very few exit points.

As Scalby Ness rocks are rounded, the coastline changes again as rocky shoreline turns to the sandy beaches at Scarborough North Bay.

Scarborough to Flamborough Head

Good surfing is available around Scarborough, as the seabed is regular and with suitable sea conditions provides good regular surf.

Scarborough is a very popular seaside resort and is well known for the motor Cycle events held at Oliver's Mount. The town is also famous for its Castle, which, standing high on a summit north of Scarborough Bay is one of

Exploring the sea caves at North Landing, Flamborough Head

249

the most striking objects on the North Yorkshire coast.

Canoeing south from Scarborough Bay one leaves the South Sands and within one mile the seabed becomes very rocky, giving way to large scars seaward of White Nab. Rough water may be experienced over these scars when any swell is felt. One mile further south, Cayton Bay is entered, with its holiday resort above the beach. Further south rough water can be experienced over foul ground and rocky ledges at Yons Nab and for a further mile. Four miles south of Cayton Bay, Filey Brigg is reached which is a chain of rocky ledges forming an easterly facing promontory, giving some shelter for Filey Bay. Strong tidal streams exist off the end of Filey Brigg.

Filey Bay is a large, sweeping expanse of sandy beach which continues south for some 3¾ miles, changing its name as you travel south, from Filey Sands, Muston Sands, Hunmanby Sands, Reighton Sands and Speeton Sands. South from Speeton Sands the coastline takes on a very different view, changing from a sandy bay to vertical chalk cliffs, providing a home for thousands of sea birds. This section of coastline to Flamborough Head, six miles south, provides some of the most spectacular canoeing on the North East coast, with vertical chalk cliffs eroded to form natural arches and sea caves. The best time to paddle this area is at high water when one can get close in and paddle right up to the cliffs as long as there is no swell. Most of the caves can also be visited on foot at low tide.

Launching at Flamborough is best made at the North Landing where a carry down the steep lifeboat ramp gives access to the small beach, or alternatively, the South Landing, where a long carry down the lane gives access to a rocky beach cleared in one section for fishermen to haul their boats out.

Canoeing any part of Flamborough Head can only be described as spectacular, so remember to take a good torch for exploration of some truly amazing sea caves. Take care when paddling this area during any swell as the seabed below the cliffs is very rocky and strewn with large boulders.

Tidal streams off Flamborough Head are strong and according to the chart run as follows:-

North going stream begins	+ 01.30 HRS. TYNE
South going stream begins	- 04.30 HRS. TYNE

These times are approximate, for further information consult the PILOT Book.

Eddies occur on both sides of the headland, and rough water can be experienced around the headland during the main tidal flow.

Further south Bridlington Bay offers safe easy canoeing. Cruises to Hornsea are possible with pre-arranged transport. There is an interesting local pottery there. If in the locality, a trip by car to Spurn Point is worthwhile.

APPENDIX I

Regional Access Officers

Where appointed, Local Access Officers should usually be contacted in the first instance. Their addresses are listed under the Access Section for each particular river.

The Regional Access Officer should be contacted when no Local Access Officer is available or the advice is of a general nature.

Northumberland and Co. Durham
Eddie Palmer,
3, Middle Cowden,
Birtley,
Wark,
Northumberland.
Tel. 0660 70318

Yorkshire and Humberside
Mike Twiggs,
38, Badger Gate,
Threshfield, Skipton.
BD23 4EN
Tel. 0756 3101

Scotland
Mary Conacher,
81, Dundee Road,
West Ferry, Dundee.
Tel. 0382 76021

APPENDIX II

Canoeing Clubs and Organisations

British Canoe Union (B.C.U.)
Adbolton Lane,
West Bridgford,
Nottingham.
NG2 5AS
Tel. 0602 821 100

The B.C.U. is the official body that represents canoeing in Britain. In particular, they are concerned with the organisation of coaching, competition and regulation of the sport.

Scottish Canoe Association (S.C.A.)
Caledonia House,
South Gyle,
Edinburgh.
EH12 9DQ
Tel. 031 317 7314

The S.C.A. is the equivalent organisation for Scotland. They publish an annual hand book which includes a diary of competition events plus information on local clubs, and a list of access officers. Good value for one pound.

National Rivers Authority (Northumbria Region)
Eldon House,
Regent Centre,
Gosforth,
Newcastle-upon-Tyne.
NE3 3UD
Tel. 091 213 0266 (24 hour pollution incident hot line)

Formed in 1989 the main functions of this authority is to monitor water quality, control pollution, protect the population from flooding and to protect fish stocks. It also aims to promote other recreational uses for the waterways.

They are supposed to be independent of Government, industry and the water and sewerage business.

Hydrographic data on the regions rivers are also available on request.

Northumbria Water Authority
Northumbria House,
Regent Centre
Newcastle-upon-Tyne.
NE3 3PX
Tel. 0632 843151
Northumbria Water has a public relations officer who will deal with most queries.

Yorkshire Water Authority,
West Riding House,
Leeds.
LS1 1AA
Tel. Leeds 44 8201

or

Dr. D. J. Shillcock,
Fisheries and Recreation Manager,
2l, Park Square South,
Leeds.
LS1 2QG
Tel. 0532 440191

North Tyneside Outdoor Activities Centre,
Holystone Hospital,
Whitley Road,
Forrest Hall,
Newcastle-Upon-Tyne.
Tel. 091 266 3524

Provides low cost outdoor equipment to groups involved in any form of education in North Tyneside. Although primarily for school children, equipment is also supplied to those involved in higher education in the Tyneside area. They have an excellent range of equipment from skis and windsurfers to plastic canoes, minibuses can also be hired.

City of Newcastle-upon-Tyne Outdoor Education Centre,
Fox and Hounds Lane,
Benwell,
Newcastle-Upon-Tyne.
Tel. 091 274 0355

Located at the old site of Pendower Hall School they provide outdoor equipment and run courses mainly for 11-25 year olds. The centre is now run by Graham Little who replaced Rob Egelstaff in 1989.

Local Clubs
The Scottish Borders

Gala Water Outdoor Activities Club
Derek Jones,
School House,
Stow, Galashiels.
Tel. 05783 218

Roxburgh Canoe Club,
Kenny Fraser,
East Booraw Cottage,
By Hawick.
Tel. 0450 78640

Selkirk H.S. CC.
Selkirk High School,
Selkirk.
Tel. 0750 20246

Tweed Canoe Club,
Malcolm Ross,
Dingleton Road,
Melrose.
Tel. 0896 822132

Northumberland and Co. Durham

Barnard Castle Canoe Club,
c/o Linda Smith,
44 The Bank,
Barnard Castle.
This newly formed club now has over 30

members. Strategically placed by the river Tees and with the experienced tutelage of the Smith family this club should do well.

Boldon Canoe Club,
382 Sunderland Road,
Cleadon Park,
South Shields.
NE34 8BW
Tel. 091 454423

This small club run by Dick Rice is mainly interested in surfing. There are some pool sessions for basic instruction with occasional river trips.

Coquet Canoe Club,
c/o Vic Brown,
27 The Turn,
Loansdean,
Morpeth,
Northumberland.
NE61 2DV

A relatively new, rapidly growing club with a wide variety of activities from pool sessions offering basic instruction, to regular river and sea trips.

Derwent Canoe Polo Club,
Neil Cranston,
31, Crammond Way,
Collingwood Grange,
Cramlington.

A specialist club which restricts its activities to canoe polo.

Durham Kayak Club,
Ann Quigley,
9, St. Josephs Close,
Durham.

A large active Club, interested in slalom, river racing, and sea touring. Enthusiastic teaching under the watchful eye of Penny Swaine.

Gateshead Outdoor Activities Centre. (G.O.A.C.)
Whinney House,
Durham Road,
Low Fell,
Gateshead.
NE9 5AR
Tel. 091 487 9356

Although not a club in the formal sense. G.O.A.C. specialise in providing low cost outdoor equipment from Windsurfers to Skis. They have an active canoeing section run by Geoff Newcombe and Keith Elliot. They organise pool sessions for basic instruction and rolling practice. There are regular trips on most weekends either to local rivers or the coast.

Killingworth Canoe Club,
c/o M.W. Hamilton,
44, St. Georges Road,
Cullercoats,
North Shields,
Tyne and Wear.
NE30 3LA

Based in North Shields and not Killingworth as its name suggests. This clubs main activities involve surfing and polo.

K.W.S.A.
Peter MacDonald,
3, Bolam Road,
Killingworth,
Tyne and Wear.
Tel. 091 268 2176

This Club meets regularly at Killingworth lake. Convenient for those living in Newcastle who are looking for an area of relatively clean flat water paddling near the city. Main interests are marathon racing and slalom. Somewhat limited in not having regular pool sessions or regular river trips.

Lemington Canoe Club,
c/o Richard Glover,
The Old School,
Barrasford,
Hexham.
NE48 4AR
Tel. 0434 81348

This newly formed club has a small but active membership.

Newcastle University Canoe Club,
c/o Athletics Union,
Kings Walk,
Newcastle upon Tyne.

Although primarily for students at the University, the club does accept other students in full time education from the Newcastle area, especially those in Polytechnics and Colleges of Further Education. It is one of the most active clubs in the area, with weekly pool sessions, polo and river trips. One of the very few clubs to mount regular overseas expeditions. Usually to the Alps.

South Shields Canoe Club,
c/o Stephen Legg,
174 Hardie Drive,
West Bolden.

Mostly interested in sea canoeing and surfing.

Sunderland Canoe Club,
c/o Ian Gill,
57, Park Avenue,
Roker,
Sunderland.
Tyne and Wear.
SR6 9NJ

An active club interesting particularly in sea canoeing and surfing, but also has pool sessions and organises river trips.

Sunderland Outdoor Activities Centre,
113, Hind Street,
Sunderland.
Tel. 091 5657630

The Kayak Section is run by Pete Button. Although primarily for Schools and those on employment courses, it is open to the public. A variety of BCU courses are run along with some pool sessions and river trips.

Tees Kayak Club,
c/o Bob Scarve,
50, Greenfield Drive,
Earlscliffe.
Cleveland,
TS16 OHE

A large Club which has produced many excellent canoeists. It has a particular interest in slalom competition, along with pool sessions and river trips.

Tyne Valley Canoe Club,
M. Dennison,
Tyne River CTI Park,
Information Centre,
Low Prudhoe,
Northumberland.

This relatively young club is one of the best in the area. It organises regular teaching sessions on the Tyne at Prudhoe. Supplemented by pool sessions for polo and basic instruction. Strongly recommended for those in the Tyneside area.

Yorkshire Region

Bradford and Airdale CC
c/o J.B. Robinson,
Sunways,
Otley Road, Eldwick,
Bingley, Yorks.
BD16 3DA

Mr. D.G. (Dennis) Lees,
Sec. Canoe Camping Club,
18, Meadow Park Drive,
Stanningley, Pudsey,
Leeds, West Yorkshire.
LS28 7TH
Tel. Leeds 551141

Calderdale Youth CC
c/o 1, Montague St.,
Sowerby Bridge,
W. Yorks.
HX6 1EA

Dales Canoe Club,
c/o Dr. F.M. Young,
5, Fortune Hill,
Knaresborough,
N. Yorkshire.
HG5 9DG

Dewsbury Adventure Club,
c/o P. Tolson,
13, Chapel Close,
Thornhill, Dewsbury,
West Yorkshire.
WF12 0DL.

E/Glanford District S/Cou,
c/o Peter R. Gunnee,
17, St. Helens Road,
Brigg,
S. Humberside.
DN20 8BX.

Giggleswick School CC
c/o John Sturgess,
Giggleswick School,
Settle, N. Yorks.
BD24 0DE

Glanford and Scunthorpe C/C,
c/o Mrs S. Pell,
309, Messingham Road,

Bottesford,
Scunthorpe,
S. Humberside.
DN17 2QZ

Grimsby Cleethorpes C/C,
B. Humphrey,
38, Cooper Lane,
Laceby, Grimsby,
South Humberside.
DN37 7AY

Halifax Canoe Club,
c/o M. Spender,
Long Rigging Farm,
Booth, Halifax,
W. Yorks.
HX2 6SZ

Hollowford Centre,
c/o John Bagge,
Hollowford Centre,
Castleton, Sheffield,
S. Yorks.
S30 2WB

Hull and District C/C,
c/o G.M. Edwards,
137, Carr Lane,
Willerby, Hull,
N. Humberside.
HU10 6JT

Huddersfield Polytechnic Canoe Club,
c/o Students Union,
The Polytechnic,
Huddersfield.

The Secretary,
Hull University Canoe Club,
Students Union,
Cottingham Road,
Hull, Humberside.
HU6 7RX

255

Humbersiders,
c/o A. Pell,
309, Messingham Road,
Bottesford, Scunthorpe,
S. Humberside.
DN17 2QZ

Keighley (Fell Lane) SG,
c/o E. Pickles,
6, Raglan Avenue,
Fell Lane,
Keighley, W. Yorks.
BD22 6BJ

Kingston Kayak Club,
c/o D.J. Davis,
8, Saxondale,
Spring Head Estate,
Hull, N. Humberside.
HU4 7SH

Knottingley Canoe Club,
c/o Mr J. Gale,
6, Fieldhead Close,
Baghill, Pontefract.
W. Yorks.
LS16 7EB

Leeds Canoe Club,
c/o M.J. Markham,
22, Wrenbury Crescent,
Leeds, W. Yorks.
LS16 7EG

Leeds University Canoe Club,
c/o Students Union,
The University,
Leeds.

Sheffield Canoe Club,
c/o Andrew R.C. Glasgow,
169, Standon Road,
Sheffield, S. Yorks.
S9 1PH

Sheffield University C/C,
Athletics Office,
Sheffield University,
Western Bank,
Sheffield, S. Yorks.
S10 2TG

Sheffield Polytechnic Canoe Club,
c/o Students Union,
Sheffield Polytechnic,
Sheffield.

Stockton & Thornaby Canoe Club,
c/o Mike Horsley,
20, Thornfield Grove,
Middlesborough,
TS5 5LG
Tel. 0642 822631

Swaledale Outdoor Club,
c/o Carol Williamson,
17, New Road,
Richmond,
N. Yorks.

Trent Valley Canoe Club,
c/o C. Black,
Westlands, Susworth,
Scunthorpe.
S. Yorks.
DN17 3AN

West Yorkshire Canoe Club,
c/o H. Patterson,
11, South Drive,
Sandal, Wakefield,
Yorks.
WF2 7ND

Whitby Canoe Club,
c/o Pat Partlet,
217 North Road,
Darlington, Co. Durham.
DL1 2PU

White Rose Canoe Club,
Mr & Mrs N. Taylor,
73, Gateland Lane,
Shadwell, Leeds.
West Yorks.

York Canoe Club,
c/o Patricia Allen
21, Cranbrook Road,
Acomb, York.
YO2 5JB

The Secretary,
York University Canoe Club,
Athletic Union,
University of York,
York.

APPENDIX III

Outdoor Centres in the North East
with an interest in Canoeing

These are residential centres open to the public:
Haefen House,
Middle Hay Leazes,
Allendale, Northumberland,
NE47 9NP
Tel. Allendale (043 483) 409

Run by Jean and Jerry Tracey. This centre in the wilds of Allendale, runs canoeing courses especially training weekends for white water racers.

Jerry is also Access Officer for the South Tyne and River Allen.

Kielder Adventure Centre,
Low Cranecleugh, Kielder Water,
Falstone, Northumberland.
NE48 1BS
Tel. 0660 50232

Run by the Calvert Trust, this excellent centre specialises in offering holidays for the disabled and their families.

North of England Adventure Training,
Craster, Northumberland,
NE66 3TW
Tel. Embleton (066576) 551

Run by Kevin Danforth, a variety of canoeing, windsurfing and activity holidays are organised. The centre now trades under the name;
River Deep, Mountain High,
2, Craster South Farm,
Alnwick,
Northumberland.
NE66 2ST
Tel. 066576 511

The Old Vicarage,
Forest In Teesdale,
Co. Durham.
DL12 0HA
Tel. 0833 22302

This outdoor centre was originally known as 'Pace' when it was run by Steve Wales. It is now owned by the Rev Anthony Kelton and run by Cliff and Kathy Burrage. Opened in 1990 it offers a diverse range of activities from Archery and Rifle shooting to mountaineering and of course canoeing. Situated on the banks of the River Tees just above High Force it has easy access to some of the best water in the area.

Windy Gyle Outdoor Centre, (B.E.A.R. Sports)
West Street,
Belford, Northumberland.
NE70 7QE
Tel. 0668 213 289

This converted country house opened as an Outdoor Centre in 1980 by Peter Clark. A variety of canoe courses and activity holidays are run from several different centres in Northumberland.

APPENDIX IV

Manufactures of canoe equipment in the North East

Chris Hare Marine, Unit 3a,
Ullswater Road,
Longhill Industrial Estate,
Hartlepool, Cleveland.
TS25 1UE
Tel. 0429 235 737

This small manufacturing company is owned and run by Chris Hare. It is well known for its wide range Open Canadian canoes. They also stock plastic canoes and retail other accessory equipment. Chris is also a keen supporter of Dragon boat racing and the company has now started to make boats for this increasingly popular sport.

McNulty Seaglass,
Commercial Road,
South Shields, Tyne and Wear,
NE33 1RZ
Tel. 091 456 3196
Well known manufacturers of fibreglass sea canoes and Canadian kayaks.

M.I. Designs,
Scanro Ltd., Unit 99/15,
North Tyne Industrial Estate,
Longbenton, Newcastle upon Tyne.
Tel. 091 266 9222
This large company has a finger in many pies. Windsurfers will be familiar with Scanro for the Vinta range of boards

manufactured on Tyneside. M.I. are known for their range of plastic canoes and canoe accessories. They have just introduced a new series of improved designs with the M.I. Slalom 370 and the Adventure 335. The 335 is a robust boat which has the Dancer's easy handling in white water, but will last twice as long. At last here is the North East's answer to the Dancer!

North Shore Designs,
Tanton Hall Farm,
Stokesley, Middlesbrough.
Tel. 0642 710350

This company formed only a few years ago by Richard Agar and Mike Nelson are now the North East's main manufacturers of fibreglass boats. There is also a well stocked retail shop on site. Their friendly service always makes them worth a visit. Lying just north of Stokesley at Tanton village on the B1365 there are only about four buildings, so you can't fail to miss them.

Shark Sports,
Norstrom House, North Broomhill,
Morpeth, Northumberland.
NE65 9UJ
Tel. 0670 760355
Wet suit manufacturers. Although Shark Sports do not usually sell to the public directly they do sell seconds and end of lines on Saturday mornings *only*. Large groups can negotiate discounts. You are

advised to telephone before going to check that stock is being sold off.

Located just off the A1068 follow signs to Red Row. After passing through the village, at about 0.75km follow the large roadside sign which directs you to the Radar pub. The factory lies directly behind the pub on the right hand side of the road. (See map of Druridge Bay, Sea Section.)

Wild Water,
The Mill, Glasshouses,
Pateley Bridge, Harrogate,
HG3 5QH
Tel. 0423 711 1624

Run by Chris Hawkesworth, this firm needs no introduction. They produce and retail a wide range of canoeing equipment.

Manufacturers of outdoor equipment in the North-East

J. Barbour & Sons Ltd,
Simonside,
South Shields, Tyne and Wear.
NE34 9DP
Tel. 091 455 4444

Those wishing to be kept warm and dry whilst watching their friends having a good time on the river should consider this company's famous Barbour jackets. This small family firm manufacture a wide range of outdoor gear. Catalogue from the above address, but goods need to be ordered through local dealers. They have a splendid 'Seconds' factory shop which offers large reductions on most items. Open 10am to 12am on Saturday as well as a few hours mid week. The shop is located at their Simonside factory on the Bede trading estate.

Berghaus, (LD Mountain Centre)
34 Dean Street,
Newcastle-upon-Tyne.
NE1 1PG
Tel. 091 2323 561

The LD Mountain Centre was started in 1966 as a retailing outlet. Difficulty in obtaining suitable outdoor clothing for their shop prompted the owners to start their own manufacturing business. Well known for their rucksacks and anoraks using modern man-made materials such as Gore-Tex their products are always in demand.

Shorebreak Designs Ltd,
High Street,
Staithes, Cleveland.
TS13 5BQ
Tel. 0947 840 711

This small design manufacturing company is located just off the cobbled high street in the centre of Staithes. Its main interest is making windsurfing harness's and related gear although they do produce some neoprene cagoules suitable for canoeist's.

Retailers of canoeing equipment in the North-East

Carlisle Canoes,
Pennywise Shop,
41 Wigton Road, Carlisle.
Tel. 0228 37658

Run by Jim Wilson from his mother's shop much of his business is done by mail order. A comprehensive catalogue is available on request.

C - Trak,
48, Gibson Street,
Newbiggin by the Sea,
NE64 6UY
Tel. 0670 8525 74

Run by Geoff Woodman, this watersports shop specialises in sea canoeing equipment. Located on the main street just as you enter the outskirts of Newbiggin. The shop is next to the West-end post office on the left of a left hand bend. These instructions should be carefully noted as the façade is cleverly disguised as a shop selling knitting wool.

Diving Centre Ltd.,
159, Westgate Road,
Newcastle upon Tyne.
NE1 4AN
Tel. 091 232 7983

Good for wet suits, although they do sell canoes and equipment.

Four Seasons,
44, The Bank,
Barnard Castle, Co. Durham.
Tel. 0833 37829

Owned and run by Russell and Len Smith, this shop has a fine range of canoes, canoe equipment and mountaineering gear. In fact, just about everything you need to take on the elements. Len is also the Access Officer for the Tees and will throw in plenty of good advice on the river.

Fox and Hounds Marine Ltd.,
166, Brinkburn Street South,
Newcastle upon Tyne,
NE6 2AR
Tel. 091 276 1161

Although primarily a chandlers for yachtsmen, they stock canoeing accessories from buoyancy aids to paddles. Fibreglass and resin is also available for those with glass fibre boats. The shop is located just behind the Byker Wall.

Newcastle Windsurfing Centre,
7/9 Tyne Street, City Road,
Newcastle upon Tyne.
NE1 2BE
Tel. 091 2325556

A friendly comapany, full of trendy gear from wet suits to bermuda shorts.

Robin Hood Watersports,
152 Leeds Road, (A62)
Heckmondwike, West Yorkshire.
WF16 9BJ
Tel. 0924 443 843

The shop is easily found by taking junction 27 off the M62 and following the A62 signposted to Huddersfield. The shop is about 2½ miles down the road on the left. It stocks most types of canoe gear and also offers a wet and dry suit repair service.

Storrar & Bax,
21a Coast Road,
Newcastle-upon-Tyne.
Tel. 091 266 1037

This shop is primarily a Chandlers although some canoeing gear is stocked. The shop has a good selection of pulleys, and dry suit seals which for some reason are difficult to obtain in Newcastle. Their range of canoes is somewhat limited.

Trident Sailmakers,
18 - 24, High Street,
Gateshead,
NE8 2AQ
Tel. 091 490 1736

Trident are easily located being on the

Gateshead side of the Tyne Bridge, just where a small road filters off to take you down to the Swing Bridge. Their shop sells canoes, windsurfers, yachting chandlery as well as manufacturing and retailing canoe clothing.

Wet and Wild Adventure Sports,
619 Anlaby Road, Hull,
HU3 6SU
Tel. 0482 54076

Owned and run by Rod and Sue Dubber their shop has a wide variety of canoeing gear to suit most paddlers tastes.

Wilderness Ways,
2, St. Nicholas Buildings,
Newcastle upon Tyne.
Tel. 091 232 4941

One of a number of outdoor shops in the North East, Wilderness Ways sell a wide variety of outdoor equipment. They have a good range of canoes and accessories. They sponsor a number of clubs and events in the North-East which should encourage custom. The shop is located in the centre of town between the Central Post Office and the High Level Bridge.

Their other five stores are located at;
LEEDS: 17 Eastgate. Tel: 0532 444 715
MIDDLESBROUGH: 100 Newport Road.
Tel: 0642 248 916

YORK: 9 Colliergate. Tel: 0904 639 567
HARROGATE: 71 Station Parade.
Tel: 0423 562 874
CHESTERFIELD: 26 Park Road.
Tel: 0246 201 437

Wild Trak Mountain Store,
60 - 62, St. Andrews Street,
Newcastle upon Tyne.
NE1 5SF
Tel. 091 261 8582

Good range of reasonably priced canoes and equipment.
The shop has a central location off Newgate Street by the Co-operative store.

The Watershed,
Unit 1, Elliot Terrace,
Mill Lane Industrial Estate,
(Off Westgate Road)
Newcastle-upon-Tyne.
Tel. 091 272 2225

At last! Newcastle has its own specialist Canoe Shop owned and run by Dean Maragh. Opened in October 1990 his shop is well worth a visit. It is located in the Trading Estate just behind the bowling alley opposite Newcastle General Hospital. A specialist in Prijon boats and equipment he would probably try to sell you an ice cube if it was made by them.

APPENDIX V

The Coastguard

They provide a variety of important services for the sea canoeist. Although their primary function is to mount and co-ordinate the marine rescue services, they also have valuable information about local sea hazards and can provide up to date weather information. Surfers also make regular use of the Coastguard as they will happily describe surfing conditions on the Tynemouth beaches.

Plans of intended sea trips may be notified to the Coastguard so that they keep a close eye on your progress.

Whilst the regional headquarters are based in the Priory grounds at North Shields, there are also sector bases at

Berwick-upon-Tweed, Seahouses, Amble, Seaton Sluice, Sunderland, Redcar, Whitby, Scarborough, Hartlepool and Flamborough Head.

Headquarters for the North East Region:-   H.M. Coastguard,
Priory Grounds,
Tynemouth, Tyne and Wear.
NE30 4DA   Tel. 0632 572691

APPENDIX VI

The fishing seasons

In order to try and reduce conflict with anglers a knowledge of the close seasons (when fishing is not allowed) can sometimes be helpful. There is some slight regional variation between river boards but most are similar to those detailed below:

Northumberland & Tyneside (Includes all Northumberland rivers except the Tweed and its tributaries.)		Yorkshire Ouse and tributaries	The Tweed and tributaries
Coarse Fish	15th Mar - 15th June	28th Feb - 1st June	15th Mar - 15th June
Trout	1st Nov - 21st Mar	1st Oct - 14th Mar	1st Dec. - 31st Jan
Mig. Trout	1st Nov - 3rd April	31st Aug - 2nd April	——————————
Salmon	1st Nov. - 31st Jan	1st Nov. - 31st Jan	1st Dec. - 31st Jan

It should also be noted that in Scotland there is no fishing on Sundays.

APPENDIX VII

High Water times relative to River Tyne entrance

From H/W time at Tyne entrance	Add/Subtract	Hrs	Mins
Blyth	-	0	6
Holy Island	-	0	45
Berwick	-	1	0
Sunderland	+	0	7
Hartlepool	+	0	12
Middlesborough	+	0	13
Whitby	+	0	26
Humber Immingham	+	2	16

APPENDIX VIII

Bibliography

The following guides will provide further reading for rivers in and around the North-East.

(i)   *Rivers of Cumbria* by Mike Hayward. Cordee 1988.
(ii) *Guide to the Waterways of the British Isles.* British Canoe Union 1980.
(iii) *Scottish White Water.* Lochhead and Todd. B.C.U. 1986.
(iv) *Canoeists Guide to Yorkshire Rivers.* Edited by Geoffrey Wood.
      (New edition edited by Mike Twiggs to be published 1990.
      B.C.U. Yorkshire & Humberside region)

Sea Canoeing

John Lilley & Gillie Ltd on the fish quay at North Shields will cater for the most adventurous sea canoeist with charts and pilots for the most exotic places from the Galapagos islands to the Persian Gulf.

Admiralty Charts

These are basically the O.S. maps of the sea with information about depths, lighthouses and other navigational information.

Chart No	160	Farne Islands to St Abbs	1:75,000
Chart No	111	Farne Islands to Berwick	1:35,000
Chart No	156	Tyne to Seahouses	1:75,000
Chart No	1934	Entrance of Tyne to Dunston	1:75,000
Chart No	152	Tyne to Tees	1:75,000
Chart No	134	Hartlepool to Whitby	1:75,000

Books

H.M.S.O. publish a series of Admiralty Pilots which contain much detailed coastal, navigational, and tidal information. They cover a large area with the North Sea (West) pilot covering the whole of the North-East coast. Priced at over £20 they are for the more enthusiastic sea canoeists who enjoys a little light bedtime reading.

(i)   *The Divers Guide to the North East* by P. Collins.
      Collings & Brodie 1986
(ii) *N.P.54 North Sea (West) Pilot.* 1st Edition. 1973.
      H.M.S.O.
(iii) *Sea Canoeing* by Derek Hutchinson. 2nd Edition.
      Adam & Charles Black.

CICERONE PRESS BOOKS

Cicerone publish a range of guides to walking and climbing in Britain and other general interest books

LAKE DISTRICT
LAKELAND VILLAGES
WORDSWORTH'S DUDDON REVISITED
REFLECTIONS ON THE LAKES
THE WESTMORLAND HERITAGE WALK
THE HIGH FELLS OF LAKELAND
IN SEARCH OF WESTMORLAND
CONISTON COPPER MINES - A Field Guide
CONISTER COPPER - A History
SCRAMBLES IN THE LAKE DISTRICT
MORE SCRAMBLES IN THE LAKE DISTRICT
WINTER CLIMBS IN THE LAKE DISTRICT
THE REGATTA MEN
LAKELAND - A Taste to Remember. (Recipes)
THE CHRONICLES OF MILNTHORPE
WALKS IN SILVERDALE/ARNSIDE - Area of
Outstanding Natural Beauty
BIRDS OF MORECAMBE BAY
THE EDEN WAY
OUR CUMBRIA
PETTIE (Memories of a Victorian Nursery)

NORTHERN ENGLAND
THE YORKSHIRE DALES
WALKS IN THE YORKSHIRE DALES
LAUGHS ALONG THE PENNINE WAY
(Cartoons)
THE RIBBLE WAY
NORTH YORK MOORS
WALKING THE CLEVELAND WAY AND
MISSING LINK
WALKS ON THE WEST PENNINE MOORS
WALKING NORTHERN RAILWAYS -
Vol.1. East Vol.2. West
BIRDS OF MERSEYSIDE
ROCK CLIMBS IN LANCASHIRE AND THE
NORTH WEST
THE ISLE OF MAN COASTAL PATH
HERITAGE TRAILS IN N.W. ENGLAND
THE LANCASTER CANAL

DERBYSHIRE PEAK DISTRICT
WHITE PEAK WALKS Vol. 1 & 2
HIGH PEAK WALKS
WHITE PEAK WAY
KINDER LOG

WALES
THE RIDGES OF SNOWDONIA
HILL WALKING IN SNOWDONIA
ASCENT OF SNOWDON
WELSH WINTER CLIMBS
MOUNTAIN SUMMITS OF WALES
SNOWDONIA , WHITE WATER, SEA & SURF

WELSH BORDER
ROCK CLIMBS IN THE WEST MIDLANDS

SOUTH & WEST ENGLAND
WALKS IN KENT
THE WEALDWAY & VANGUARD WAY
THE SOUTH DOWNS WAY & DOWNS LINK
WALKING ON DARTMOOR
SOUTH WEST WAY - Vol. 1 & 2
THE COTSWOLD WAY

SCOTLAND
SCRAMBLES IN LOCHABER
SCRAMBLES IN SKYE
THE ISLAND OF RHUM
CAIRNGORMS, WINTER CLIMBS
WINTER CLIMBS BEN NEVIS & GLENCOE
SCOTTISH RAILWAY WALKS
TORRIDON

**CICERONE
PRESS**

Also a full range of guide-books to walking, scrambling, ice-climbing, rock climbing, and other adventurous pursuits in Britain and abroad.

Available from bookshops, outdoor equipment shops or direct (send for price list) from: CICERONE PRESS, 2 POLICE SQUARE, MILNTHORPE, CUMBRIA LA7 7PY